Praise for *PT 109*

"Impressive. . . . Enlightening. . . . Doyle makes a compelling case for why PT 109 should be remembered. . . . [An] engrossing combination of adventure and analysis. . . . Doyle's work has all the makings of a definitive account—the last word on the story. And as such it's a tale few are likely to forget."
                                                                —*USA Today*

"You-are-there history as crisp as a 1940s newsreel. . . . The story of JFK's bravery, leadership, and stamina isn't well-known. It should be, and now a cinematic new book brings this remarkable saga back to life. . . . Doyle expertly re-creates a crucial moment in shark-infested waters, the stunning aftermath, and the life of a future president."
                                                   —*Christian Science Monitor*

"A revealing and breathtaking account about what happened to John F. Kennedy's Patrol Torpedo boat 109, and the famous war story's engrossing aftermath."   —James Patterson

"Drawing on a firsthand account by Kennedy, documents from the John F. Kennedy Presidential Library and Museum, Japanese wartime archives, and fresh interviews with the remaining living links to the events, Doyle, formerly director of original programming at HBO, tells a cinematic story of survival that involves an SOS note carved into a coconut and a spy network of Solomon Island natives." —*Boston Globe*

"Fast-paced, gripping, and superbly researched, William Doyle's *PT 109* conveys the dramatic story of JFK's wartime service and its surprising aftereffects with a refreshing, brisk authority. Doyle's gift for details and vivid descriptions put the reader squarely in the middle of this epic tale."   —Dan Hampton (USAF, Ret.), *New York Times*
                                       bestselling author of *The Hunter Killers*

"I have to say, William Doyle's *PT 109* is the finest book I've ever read on the subject: the best written, the most well-researched and accurate. It covers every aspect and brings many new things to light. Doyle has done a wonderful job."
    —William Liebenow, Lt. Commander, USNR (Ret.), skipper of PT 157,
John F. Kennedy's tentmate, battle colleague and boat commander of the
        mission that rescued Kennedy behind enemy lines in August 1943

"Compelling. . . . Explosive."   —*Daily Mail* (UK)

PT 109

AN AMERICAN
EPIC OF WAR, SURVIVAL,
AND THE DESTINY OF
JOHN F. KENNEDY

★

WILLIAM DOYLE

wm

WILLIAM MORROW
An Imprint of HarperCollinsPublishers

HarperCollins books may be purchased for educational, business, or sales
promotional use. For information please e-mail the Special Markets
Department at SPsales@harpercollins.com.

A hardcover edition of this book was published in 2015 by
William Morrow, an imprint of HarperCollins Publishers.

FIRST WILLIAM MORROW PAPERBACK EDITION PUBLISHED 2016.

Designed by Jo Anne Metsch
Maps designed by Nick Springer, copyright © 2015 Springer Cartographics LLC

Library of Congress Cataloging-in-Publication Data has been applied for.

ISBN 978-0-06-234659-9

17 18 19 20   OV/RRD   10 9 8 7 6 5 4 3 2

To Naomi and Brendan,
and to my American and Japanese families.
And to my friend John K. Castle.

CONTENTS

★

INTRODUCTION

★

"Without PT 109, there never would have been a President John F. Kennedy."

—DAVID POWERS, White House official,
Kennedy Administration

"Jack's life had more to do with myth, magic, legend, saga, and story than with political theory or political science."

—JACQUELINE KENNEDY

In the early morning darkness of August 2, 1943, during a chaotic nighttime skirmish in the South Pacific, a Japanese destroyer struck the U.S. Navy's motor torpedo boat PT 109, killing two American sailors instantly. Eleven others were shipwrecked in enemy waters. As the survivors clung to the sinking wreckage, the sea around them burned; 1,200 feet of ink-black, shark-infested water loomed beneath.

Written off for dead by their superior officers, the Americans emerged from a harrowing ordeal of survival seven days later, rescued by the combined efforts of a heroic group of Solomon Island natives, an intrepid Australian Coastwatcher, and a courageous American naval officer, Lieutenant William "Bud" Liebenow, captain of PT 157.

The incident received brief national publicity during the war, but it forever transformed the PT 109's young commander, John F. Kennedy, the son of the former U.S. ambassador to England. Despite long-simmering controversy among some veterans and military historians over whether he was negligent in the sinking of his boat, Kennedy came home from the Pacific a decorated hero, receiving a medal for "his courage, endurance, and excellent leadership [which] contributed to the saving of several lives." After the war, when Kennedy's ambitions turned to politics, the event played a role in molding his public image from "child of privilege" to "battle-tested combat veteran" and helped propel him into the House of Representatives in 1947, into the U.S. Senate in 1953, and into the White House in 1961.

The ordeal shaped Kennedy's view of the world and of himself, and established a touchstone by which his character would be defined for the rest of his life. "Everything" about JFK, wrote journalist Robert T. Hartmann in 1960 of Kennedy's PT 109 experience, "dates from that adventure," "the only time Kennedy ever was wholly on his own, where the $1 million his father gave him wouldn't buy one cup of water." Kennedy's mettle and leadership had been proven, and yet his brush with death marked him. The tragic episode haunted Kennedy, and triggered the little-known story of his 1951 journey to American-occupied Tokyo to try to find the Japanese man who had nearly killed him, and who did take the lives of two men in his command. But when he got to Japan, disaster stalked Kennedy, and he was once again thrown upon the gates of death.

In short, the PT 109 incident made John F. Kennedy—both the man and the myth. It is therefore, a critical "ripple point" in our national story. Without the PT 109 episode, there might not have been a President John F. Kennedy, and in turn, the contours of modern American history that Kennedy helped shape during his brief but consequential presidency—including civil rights, the Vietnam War, space travel, the Cold War, and the nuclear confrontation with the Soviet Union—might have turned out quite differently.

Kennedy himself considered his command of the PT 109, and his experiences in combat during World War II, to be central to his own destiny. "I firmly believe," he wrote, "that as much as I was shaped by anything, so I was shaped by the hand of fate moving in World War II. Of course, the same can be said of almost any American or British or Australian man of my generation. The war made us. It was and is our single greatest moment. The memory of the war is a key to our characters. It serves as a break wall between the indolence of our youths and the earnestness of our manhoods. No school or parent could have shaped us the way that fight shaped us. No other experience could have brought forth in us the same fortitude and resilience. We were much shrewder and sadder when that long battle finally finished. The war made us get serious for the first time in our lives. We've been serious ever since, and we show no signs of stopping."

Before he died, JFK hoped, as veterans sometimes do, to seek out and reconcile with his former enemy. So he sent his younger brother Robert to Tokyo in 1962 to begin preliminary planning for what would be the first-ever U.S. presidential state visit to Japan, a journey that would culminate in an emotional reunion in Japan of JFK and the surviving members of Kennedy's PT 109 with the veterans of the Japanese warship that destroyed her. But as the Japanese nation watched on live TV, a riot brewed when Attorney General Robert F. Kennedy took the stage at a tumultuous gathering of thousands of students at Tokyo's elite Waseda University. In the chaos, Robert Kennedy delivered an impassioned, impromptu speech that amazed the people of Japan and strengthened the two former enemies' historic postwar embrace, a relationship that was vividly renewed with the arrival of John F. Kennedy's daughter Caroline as the U.S. ambassador to Japan in 2013.

I grew up in the America that was shaped by John F. Kennedy. I also was raised in JFK's New York City, the place where the Kennedy family based much of its operations from the 1920s through the 1960s. For years, patriarch Joseph P. Kennedy ran his financial, motion picture, real estate, and investment empire from offices in Manhattan, commuting by limousine and train from Grand Central Terminal to family estates in Riverdale and Westchester. John Kennedy grew up as a seasoned part-time New Yorker, spending boyhood years in Bronxville and Riverdale, briefly attending Riverdale Country Day School in the Bronx and frolicking in Manhattan hotspots as a young man. Indeed three of the pivotal scenes of the PT 109 story took place in Manhattan—at the Plaza hotel, the Stork Club, and the offices of the *New Yorker* magazine on West Forty-Third Street.

Like John Kennedy, my father (also named William Doyle) was an Irish Catholic and a veteran of military service in the South Pacific combat zone during World War II. As an Army military police and intelligence officer on the island of New Guinea, he became friendly with U.S. Navy PT boat crews stationed nearby. While posted in Port Moresby on April 7, 1943, my father was subjected to the dual-pronged Japanese mass aerial attack that JFK simultaneously endured near Guadalcanal, the biggest such Japanese air raid since Pearl Harbor. He became a devoted admirer of Kennedy in the 1950s, and he cheered on each JFK campaign victory like a football fan. My mother Marie Louise Doyle served as a volunteer at John F. Kennedy's presidential campaign office in New York City, and today she still vividly recalls the day in 1960 when

Robert F. Kennedy came through the door. The office was packed, and RFK was short, so he stood on a chair to give the workers a pep talk. "Thanks to you," he said, "my brother *will* be president."

Soon after, my family was attending Mass at St. Patrick's Cathedral on Fifth Avenue, as we did every Sunday. I was three years old. On that day, I experienced one of the first clear memories of my life, a recollection no doubt sharpened by years of family retelling. My father suddenly realized that a few feet away from us, John F. Kennedy, then a forty-three-year-old U.S. senator and presidential candidate, had slipped into a nearby pew. Kennedy was already rocketing to stardom, but in this age before presidential candidates became surrounded by large security retinues, he had only a single aide with him. My father elbowed my mother. She then leaned down and whispered to me, "*This is very, very important. I want you to remember this.* Do you see that man right there? He is going to be the next president of the United States." At Communion, she made a special point of taking me with her, and slowly walking right past the man, now kneeling in the pew with his head bent. I remember two things about John F. Kennedy that bounced around my toddler brain. Like my father, he looked like a nice guy. And he had a deep, golden suntan.

In the years that followed, I stood a few feet away from a diminutive U.S. Senate candidate Robert F. Kennedy and an elephantine President Lyndon Johnson as they held a joint 1964 campaign speech on the corner of Fourteenth Street and First Avenue in our neighborhood of Stuyvesant Town; watched Robert F. Kennedy march up Fifth Avenue in the St. Patrick's Day Parade; saw Jackie Kennedy strolling near her Upper East Side home; and saw John F. Kennedy Jr. running or Rollerblading around the Central Park Loop and walking through Midtown in a business suit as starstruck pedestrians pirouetted and murmured in his wake. One morning a few years ago I rode a nearly empty downtown No. 6 local subway train as Caroline Kennedy sat across from me pleasantly looking at subway ads, unnoticed and unbothered. To me and many New Yorkers, the Kennedys were not only an American political dynasty; they were kind of like neighbors.

John F. Kennedy has been portrayed by some as a great man, and by others as a sex-crazed scoundrel. I see him as a fascinating character, a bridge across twentieth-century American history, someone who chatted with Herbert Hoover on the Oval Office phone and greeted Bill Clinton in the Rose Garden. He catalyzed the television news age, pioneered modern political campaigning, grappled with civil rights, made catastrophic mistakes in Vietnam and Cuba, launched mankind toward the moon, navigated through a potentially apocalyptic nuclear showdown with the Soviet Union, and projected an inspiring vision of the United States and its ideals to the world. Without the PT 109 incident he may have still become president, or instead he might have wound up a failed congressional candidate, an obscure New York writer or Ivy League history professor, or just another handsome, forgotten son of a rich man with a Park Avenue penthouse and a desk in the family investment office. As Kennedy's longtime aide David Powers once said, "Without PT 109, there never would have been a President John F. Kennedy." Looking back in 2015, former JFK aide Richard Donahue agreed, saying the PT 109 episode "was the entire basis of his political life." That makes Kennedy's lost, grueling seven days in the South Pacific, and the events that flowed from the ordeal, both consequential and fascinating.

This book is based on an examination of a wide range of archival material in the John F. Kennedy Presidential Library and the national archives of the United States, Australia, the Solomon Islands, and Japan, much of it not available to authors of previous accounts of the incident, including a long-lost account written by JFK himself in 1946. Of invaluable importance was a series of extensive interviews with a critical living link to the event, William Liebenow, the PT boat commander who served in combat with John F. Kennedy and led the hazardous mission that set out to rescue Kennedy and his crew in enemy waters. The project was further aided by interviews with sixteen surviving contemporaries of John F. Kennedy in the PT boat service, interviews with political aides to JFK, and interviews with two family members with intimate connections to events in this book: John Kennedy's sister-in-law Ethel Kennedy, and his nephew Maxwell Kennedy, the son of Robert and Ethel Kennedy.

This is a true tale of war, survival, the randomness of fate, the fog of battle, the vagaries of memory, and the power of myth.

It is an account of how thirteen American sailors went into battle on the night of August 1, 1943, and how eleven of them wound up stranded and shipwrecked deep in enemy waters, alone and forgotten, stalked by injuries and starvation.

It is the creation story of a young naval officer who became America's most admired modern president.

W.D.

New York City, 2015

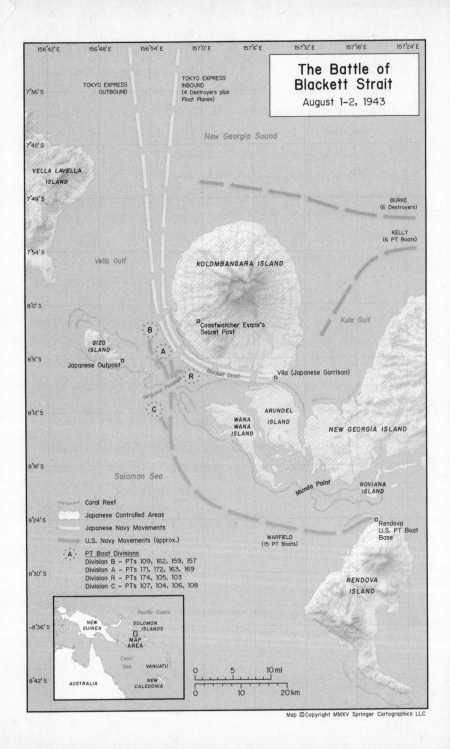

The Battle of Blackett Strait

August 1–2, 1943

TOKYO EXPRESS OUTBOUND

TOKYO EXPRESS INBOUND (4 Destroyers plus Float Planes)

New Georgia Sound

VELLA LAVELLA ISLAND

BURKE (6 Destroyers)

KELLY (6 PT Boats)

Vella Gulf

KOLOMBANGARA ISLAND

Kula Gulf

Coastwatcher Evans's Secret Post

GIZO ISLAND

Japanese Outpost

B

A

R

Blackett Strait

Vila (Japanese Garrison)

Ferguson Passage

C

WANA WANA ISLAND

ARUNDEL ISLAND

NEW GEORGIA ISLAND

Solomon Sea

Munda Point

ROVIANA ISLAND

Rendova U.S. PT Boat Base

WARFIELD (15 PT Boats)

RENDOVA ISLAND

Coral Reef
Japanese Controlled Areas
Japanese Navy Movements
U.S. Navy Movements (approx.)
A — PT Boat Divisions
Division B – PTs 109, 162, 159, 157
Division A – PTs 171, 172, 163, 169
Division R – PTs 174, 105, 103
Division C – PTs 107, 104, 106, 108

Pacific Ocean

NEW GUINEA

SOLOMON ISLANDS

MAP AREA

Coral Sea

VANUATU

AUSTRALIA

NEW CALEDONIA

0   5   10 mi

0   10   20 km

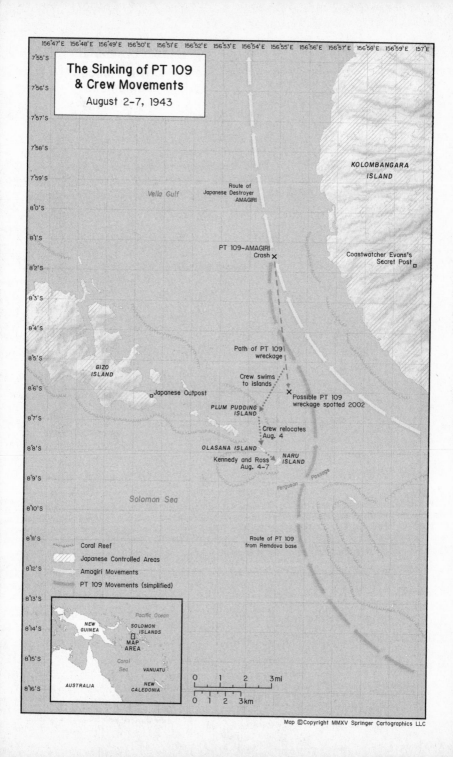

The Sinking of PT 109
& Crew Movements
August 2-7, 1943

KOLOMBANGARA
ISLAND

Vella Gulf

Route of
Japanese Destroyer
AMAGIRI

PT 109–AMAGIRI
Crash ✕

Coastwatcher Evans's
Secret Post ▫

Path of PT 109
wreckage

GIZO
ISLAND

Crew swims
to islands

✕ Possible PT 109
wreckage spotted 2002

▫ Japanese Outpost

PLUM PUDDING
ISLAND

Crew relocates
Aug. 4

OLASANA ISLAND

NARU
ISLAND

Kennedy and Ross
Aug. 4-7

Ferguson Passage

Solomon Sea

Route of PT 109
from Remdova base

Coral Reef

Japanese Controlled Areas

Amagiri Movements

PT 109 Movements (simplified)

Pacific Ocean

NEW
GUINEA

SOLOMON
ISLANDS

MAP
AREA

Coral
Sea

VANUATU

AUSTRALIA

NEW
CALEDONIA

0   1   2   3mi

0 1 2 3km

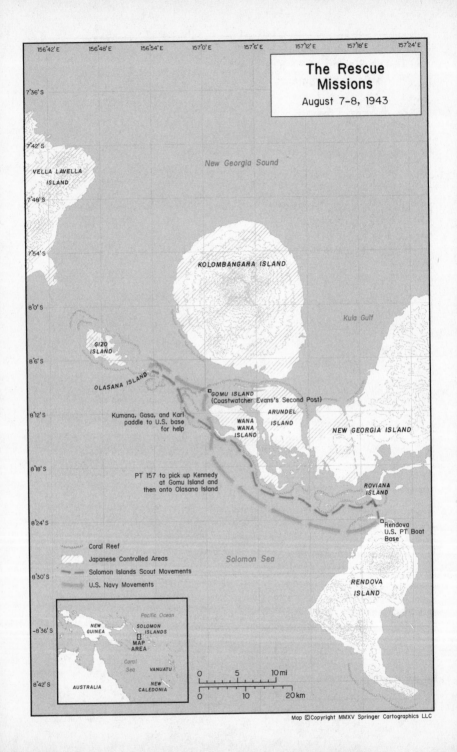

PROLOGUE: SAMURAI IN THE MIST

★

He thought of the River Styx, the boundary between Earth and the Underworld.

Lieutenant Commander Kohei Hanami stood at the helm of the 2,000-ton Imperial Japanese Navy destroyer *Amagiri,* or "Heavenly Mist," as it sped through the darkness at 34 knots.

He saw nothing ahead but the black of a moonless night cloaked by low cloud cover and rainsqualls. Patches of haze hung over the water.

"I stood on the bridge, straining to see as we moved northward up Blackett Strait," Hanami later remembered, referring to a reef-choked channel in the central Solomon Islands. "I had ordered 'battle alert,' since we were under constant harassment by U.S. planes in the daytime and by night raiders and torpedo boats at night."

Hanami, the thirty-four-year-old grandson of a feudal samurai warrior, graduated from the Japanese Naval Academy in 1929, and joined a Japanese Navy goodwill training cruise to the United States. As he journeyed to Hawaii, the West Coast ports, through the Panama Canal, and up to New York City, Hanami grew fond of America and was impressed by the friendliness and exuberance of Americans. He recalled that on the eve of America's entry into World War II, "All of us felt a terrible thing was about to happen. Most naval officers were opposed to a war with the United States. We realized Japan had virtually no chance of victory. But if it had to be war, we resolved to do our best."

On this night, Hanami's destroyer was acting as a scout ahead of three other destroyers—*Arashi* ("Storm"), *Shigure* ("Drizzle"), and *Hagikaze* ("Clover Wind")—on an operation launched from the Japanese regional superbase at Rabaul on the island of New Britain. Their mission was to ferry fresh combat troops, as well as food, ammunition, and other supplies, to the advance Japanese garrison at Kolombangara island in the middle of the Solomon Island chain, then the front line of the Empire of Japan's twenty-one-month-long war with the United States and its allies. The almost perfectly round jungle island was an imposing redoubt, nine miles across and capped by a massive volcano whose peak loomed 5,800 feet above the base's docks.

In the summer of 1943 the Pacific War was roughly stalemated. The Japanese still possessed substantial fighting strength and controlled vast territories from the Indian border to Manchuria, Indonesia, and the Aleutian Islands, but over the past fifteen months the Allies had blunted Japanese momentum with victories at the battles of the Coral Sea, Midway, and Guadalcanal. Here in the Solomon Islands, on the southeasternmost perimeter of Japanese expansion, a fierce war of attrition was under way; Japanese shipping losses were heavy, and their aircraft and pilot casualties had reached alarming levels.

As the three ships quickly and efficiently unloaded their men and cargo on Kolombangara, the *Amagiri* screened them by running a wide rectangular patrol pattern south of the island, in Blackett Strait, at the brisk speed of 21 knots. Now all four ships were heading northwest back toward their base and picking up speed. After briefly losing track of the other boats, Hanami found his ship was 2,000 meters west of the pack, and he maneuvered to regain the lead position.

Some Japanese destroyer officers hated these supply runs, which made them feel more like mail carriers than gallant warriors. Captain Yasumi Toyama, chief of staff to the Destroyer Squadron 2 commander, griped in a diary entry, "We are more a freighter convoy than a fighting squadron these days—the damned Yankees have dubbed us the Tokyo Express—we transport cargo to that cursed island—what a stupid thing! Our decks are stacked high with supplies and our ammunition supply must be cut in half. Our cargo is loaded in drums which are roped together. We approach the island, throw them overboard, and run away—it is a strenuous and unsatisfying routine."

The warships were surrounded by Japanese-held islands, but American air superiority forced them to travel at night with their light sources blacked out, except for colored signal-blinker lights. The darkness held the threat of hidden underwater reefs and torpedo attacks by much smaller, nimble American PT (patrol torpedo) boats. Lieutenant Commander Hanami had ordered his 245-man crew and thirteen officers to be extra alert: they had lost ten men to enemy shellfire in nearby waters several weeks before, and only a few hours earlier on their inbound journey to Kolombangara their four-boat convoy was the target of a ragged, futile torpedo

The *Amagiri*, or "Heavenly Mist," destroyer of the Japanese Imperial Navy. (Japanese Government Photo)

attack by a small picket line of PT boats—an attack the Japanese easily brushed aside with a few shots from their guns and over-flights by Japanese floatplanes zeroing in on the PT boats' telltale phosphorescent wakes.

Captain Tameichi Hara, the skipper of the nearby destroyer *Shigure*, braced himself throughout the journey as he considered these reef-infested waters a "weird and treacherous" zone. "The enemy, with his tight scout networks in this area, must have de-tected our activities," he recalled, "and might spring out from any of the myriad shoals that lined the mazelike strait." The convoy accelerated to 30 knots to make its getaway: "This was a truly breakneck speed for such a hazardous waterway. In peacetime no ship would have ventured here at night in excess of 12 knots, even with all lights burning. We, of course, were running fully blacked out. The night was sultry, but cold sweat stood out on every brow." The convoy drew into a tight column formation with only 500 meters between ships.

On board the *Amagiri*, skipper Hanami had posted ten lookouts at spots around the bow and bridge, and they now were sweeping the horizon with binoculars. Standing nearby on the bridge was Hanami's superior officer, Captain Katsumori Yamashiro, commander of the 11th Destroyer Flotilla. Yamashiro was the senior ranking officer on the multi-ship operation, and Hanami was the ship's skipper, having taken command of the *Amagiri* several weeks earlier.

Hanami took note of his speed, which now approached 34 knots. In shakedown trials, the 382-foot-long *Amagiri* registered up to 39 knots, and Hanami had every reason to feel confident in the capabilities of his ship. The destroyer boasted powerful engines, a highly maneuverable design, nine torpedo tubes equipped with accurate and lethal Type Eight "Long Lance" torpedoes, ten guns, mine-laying equipment, and twelve depth charges. The *Amagiri* was a member of the innovative *Fubuki* ("Snowstorm") class of Japanese destroyers, which the U.S. Navy's own analysts acknowledged "led contemporary destroyer design the world over, introducing enclosed twin-gun mounts, shielded torpedo tubes, and high, all-steel bridges."

"Ship ahead!" a lookout called out suddenly.

"Look again!" Hanami ordered.

"Torpedo boats to the forward port!" declared the lookout.

Hanami leaned over the rail at the extreme starboard side of the bridge, straining to see forward. There he spotted a small dark object churning up white waves in the water some 800 to 1,000 meters distant, just slightly to the right by 10 degrees—almost dead ahead.

Immediately, he recognized it as an American torpedo boat. He figured they would collide with the craft in less than twenty seconds. Hanami raced through his options: "I had come to the conclusion that it was too difficult to shoot and hit a target as small and fast as a torpedo boat, and that ramming was the best method of dealing with them. Such an opportunity had never arisen in my many previous encounters with torpedo boats, but this was a favorable situation for ramming and I decided to try it." He added, "To veer away would have meant exposing our flank to torpedo attack at point blank range. My decision was to ram, and I gave the order."

"Ten degrees turn," Hanami ordered the helmsman, "full speed ahead!"

"Ram into them!"

In a *Rashomon*-style clash of conflicting memories, Hanami's superior officer, Captain Yamashiro, recalled giving an order that was the exact opposite of Hanami's command: to *avoid* hitting the smaller boat.

"For just an instant I thought it was one of our inter-island steamboats [small transport barges], and then I knew it was an enemy torpedo boat," Yamashiro remembered years later. "It did not change its heading in the slightest, but continued steadily to approach. The bow of the boat seemed to be pointing to starboard [due east] of *Amagiri*. In the event of a collision we would be damaged too, and if a torpedo should be detonated, it would be much worse. Instantly, in an attempt to pass astern of the boat, I extended my left arm and shouted 'Hard aport!'" Adding to the confusion, on another occasion, Yamashiro recollected giving the order in the opposite direction, or "Hard astern!" Hanami had no memory of an order from Yamashiro, and years later, the man then at the wheel of the *Amagiri*, Coxswain Kazuto Doi, said diplomatically that "Captain Yamashiro does not remain much in my memory."

No one disputes what happened next: the enemy vessel disappeared as if the *Amagiri* had swallowed it up; there was an instantaneous dull thud, followed by a brilliant flash of light and the smell of smoldering cotton.

"We crashed right into it," remembered Hanami. "I saw the enemy ship break in two with a tremendous roar. White gasoline flames shot out. The torpedo boat disappeared in the dark. I knew that at least one half and probably both halves sank."

Lookouts on the Japanese destroyer scanned the dark waters, but they saw nothing except bits of wreckage. According to Hanami, the *Amagiri*'s rear gunners fired a few salvos back in the direction of the wreckage as the destroyer headed onward at 28 knots. He noted, "The thing for us was to get out of the enemy's theater of air superiority as quickly as we could."

On board the nearby destroyer *Shigure*, skipper Captain Tameichi Hara was flashed a message from the *Amagiri:* "Enemy torpedo boats encountered! One rammed and sunk!" At this, he remembered, cheers of joy and laughter erupted on each destroyer as they continued running at top speed. "I understood the elation at our good fortune," he added, "but could not join in the merrymaking. My spine was still creeping at the thought of the close shave we had had, as I recalled the loss of *Terutsuki* ['Pale Moon'], in December 1942, to torpedo boats." He realized the same fate could have just as well befallen them on this night if the Americans had spotted them a few minutes earlier.

When the convoy safely returned to Rabaul a few hours later, Lieutenant Commander Hanami and Captain Yamashiro were

greeted on the flagship cruiser *Sendai* by the towering figure of
Rear Admiral Matsuji Ijuin, who laughed triumphantly and play-
fully chided them, "Why didn't your radio report say that the torpedo boat had been crushed underfoot?"

The Imperial Japanese Navy saw a rare, morale-boosting publicity opportunity in the dramatic incident, and within forty-
eight hours, the Tokyo newspapers were ablaze with jubilant
headlines and bulletins celebrating the highly unusual events,
some comparing the *Amagiri*'s feat to that of a master samurai
swordsman: "Enemy Torpedo Boat Run Through," "Enemy Torpedo Boat Rammed Through in the Dark of the Night!" "Super-
human display of courage," "Going full force at high speed, it
rode straight through one of them sending it instantly to its
watery grave. This is the very first instance where one of our destroyers has sailed into an enemy ship since the beginning of the
Greater East Asia War and it well illustrates the dauntless spirit of
the Japanese destroyer fighting units," "Enemy Torpedo Boat
Sliced in Two: Our Destroyer Saves Companion Ships by Crashing Bodily into Enemy Craft," "This heretofore unheard of feat
which transcends all common naval fighting practices is an event
for rejoicing that has no precedence in the history of naval affairs.
Because of this unusual action, enemy morale has been dealt a
heavy blow while the encouragement it gives to our allies is im-
measurable."

After the flurry of attention from the crash soon evaporated,
Kohei Hanami returned to his duties as a Japanese naval commander. "I thought probably no one aboard the small boat survived," recalled Hanami.

But he was wrong. As the *Amagiri* sped away from the crash in
the early hours of August 2, it left eleven American men widely

scattered across the surface of the ocean, several of them wounded, struggling in pools of burning gasoline and choking from the fumes amid the wreckage of their boat.

For these eleven men lost in enemy waters, their ordeal was just beginning.

1

GIVE ME A FAST SHIP

★

I wish to have no connection with any ship that does not
sail fast for I intend to go in harm's way.

—COMMANDER JOHN PAUL JONES, 1780

John F. Kennedy loved the sea as "a child, boy, and man," observed
his widow Jacqueline.

"I have been interested in the sea from my earliest boyhood,"
Kennedy himself once wrote. "My earliest recollections of the
United States Navy go back to the days when as a small boy, I used
to be taken to the USS *Constitution* in Charlestown, Massachusetts. The sight of that historic frigate, with its tall spars and black
guns, stirred my imagination and made American history come
alive for me."

Growing up as one of nine children of the fabulously wealthy
financier Joseph P. Kennedy, young "Jack" Kennedy learned to
pilot small sailboats with the help of a family sailing instructor at
their oceanside vacation estate in Hyannis Port, Massachusetts,
and later at their winter mansion in semitropical Palm Beach,
Florida.

In his teens, Kennedy became a keen swimmer and a highly skilled, competitive sailboat racer. He preferred to command a boat rather than serve in the crew, and he took racing very seriously, firmly chastising crew members who didn't measure up. In 1936, at the age of twenty, Kennedy won the Nantucket Sound championship in the Star boat category and represented the sound in the Atlantic Coast championships. As a student at Harvard University, he was on the crew that won the McMillan Cup in the annual collegiate competition at Annapolis, Maryland. When he was fifteen, Kennedy's parents gave him his own wooden 26-foot Wianno Senior sailboat, called the *Victura,* which he would enjoy as a young man, congressman, senator, and as president.

While he occupied the White House, Kennedy speculated that humanity was drawn to the ocean because it was our primordial home. "I really don't know why it is that all of us are so committed to the sea, except I think it's because in addition to the fact that the sea changes, and the light changes, and ships change, it's because we all came from the sea," he told an audience gathered in Newport, Rhode Island, for the 1962 America's Cup race. "And it is an interesting biological fact that all of us have, in our veins the exact same percentage of salt in our blood that exists in the ocean, and, therefore, we have salt in our blood, in our sweat, in our tears. We are tied to the ocean. And when we go back to the sea—whether it is to sail or to watch it—we are going back from whence we came."

For himself, Kennedy may also have seen the open water as an escape from a life of frequent physical agony inflicted by a progression of illnesses that plagued him from birth. The precise origins and nature of his lifelong back pains still are uncertain based on the available medical records, but Kennedy appears to have been born with a slightly malformed and unstable back, which, according to private conversations Kennedy had with his Navy doctors,

ABOVE Family patriarch and financial mogul Joseph P. Kennedy (center) had a master plan to engineer his eldest sons Joseph Jr. (top right) and John (top left) into national politics. (John F. Kennedy Presidential Library)

BELOW From boyhood, John F. Kennedy had a passion for the sea—seen here aboard the *Victura*. (John F. Kennedy Presidential Library)

was strained by a 1938 car trip through rough roads in Europe and a 1940 tennis injury. These conditions periodically required him to wear back braces and crutches and eventually necessitated two spinal surgeries.

Although he once recalled his childhood as "an easy, prosperous life, supervised by maids and nurses, with more and more younger sisters to boss and play with," Kennedy's frequent illnesses as a child and adolescent included chicken pox, ear infections, appendicitis, fatigue, mumps, a near-fatal case of scarlet fever at the age of two and a half, whooping cough, bronchitis, and German measles. Late in his twenties he was diagnosed with Addison's disease, a deterioration of the adrenal glands that can trigger symptoms including fatigue, dizziness, muscle weakness, weight loss, difficulty standing up, nausea, sweating, and changes in personality and mood. He remained underweight well into adulthood. Navy doctor Lee Mandel, who examined Kennedy's medical records years after Kennedy's death, speculated that Kennedy's Addison's disease was probably caused by a rare condition, called autoimmune polyendocrine syndrome type 2, or APS 2, which also likely caused Kennedy's hypothyroidism, diagnosed in 1955, according to Mandel's report, published in the *Annals of Internal Medicine* in 2009.

Kennedy also often fell victim to abuse from his older brother Joseph Kennedy Jr., a relentless bully. Younger brother Bobby Kennedy recalled lying in bed at night as a boy and hearing "the sound of Joe banging Jack's head against the wall."

"It is said that famous men are usually the product of unhappy childhood," wrote Winston Churchill in his biography of John Churchill, *Marlborough,* one of Kennedy's favorite books. "The stern compression of circumstances, the twinges of adversity, the spur of slights and taunts in the early years, are needed to evoke that ruthless fixity of purpose and tenacious mother-wit without which great actions are seldom accomplished." John Kennedy's boyhood suffering was cushioned somewhat by his father's increasingly spectacular wealth, which funded large family homes, chauffeur-driven Rolls-Royces, and trips in private railway cars. But amid the privilege, Kennedy also seemed to have felt a lack of maternal warmth. "My mother never hugged me, not once," he once recalled. A family friend explained of the Kennedy children, "They really didn't have a real home with their own rooms where they had pictures on the walls or memorabilia on the shelves but would rather come home for holidays from their boarding schools and find whatever room was available." A youthful John Kennedy would ask his mother, Rose, "Which room do I have this time?"

While immobilized for endless days in hospitals and sick beds for tests, treatment, and recuperation, the young Kennedy escaped his physical torments by reading multitudes of books, through which he conjured up dreamscapes of adventure, heroism, history, and fantasy. As a boy he read tales of King Arthur and the Knights of the Round Table, the stories of Sir Walter Scott, the Billy Whiskers children's book series about a globe-trotting goat, *Kidnapped* and *Treasure Island* by Robert Louis Stevenson, *Lays of Ancient Rome*, *Ivanhoe*, James Fenimore Cooper's stories of the American frontier, Rudyard Kipling's *The Jungle Book*, *Peter Pan*, *Black Beauty*, *Pilgrim's Progress*, *Arabian Nights*, and *Wonder Tales from East and West*.

Family friend Kay Halle had a vivid memory of seeing a "very pale" fifteen-year-old Kennedy lying in a Palm Beach hospital bed "so surrounded by books I could hardly see him. I was very impressed because at this point this very young child was reading *The World Crisis* by Winston Churchill." Kennedy's wife, Jacqueline, recalled, "History made him what he was. You must think of this little boy, sick so much of the time, reading history, reading the

Knights of the Round Table, reading *Marlborough*. For Jack, history was full of heroes." She described JFK's adult reading habits vividly: "He'd read in the strangest way. He'd read walking, he'd read at the table, at meals, he'd read after dinner; he's read in the bathtub . . . he'd really read all times you don't think you have time to read. He was always reading—practically while driving a car." Jim Reed, a wartime buddy of Kennedy in the South Pacific, recalled, "He had read almost every book on the American presidents. He had read every word that Winston Churchill had ever published. He'd read T. E. Lawrence and was a devotee of Lord David Cecil's racy account of Lord Byron and Lady Caroline Lamb in *The Young Melbourne*." JFK biographer Nigel Hamilton speculated that Kennedy was attracted to combat on the eve of World War II by "the wayward urge to cut a figure—and be seen to do so—that would bind him to his latest hero, Lord Byron, the roguish star of David Cecil's *The Young Melbourne*."

In a passage from Kennedy's favorite book as an adult, *Pilgrim's Way* (1940), the aristocratic British politician and adventure novelist John Buchan wrote that the sea "was a wholesome emancipation" that "seemed to slacken the bonds of destiny and enlarge the horizon." Describing the "debonair and brilliant and brave" English noble Raymond Asquith, who died in World War I, Buchan wrote a passage John F. Kennedy recited from memory for the rest of his life, perhaps because it reminded him of himself on the eve of World War II: "The War which found the measure of so many never got to the bottom of him. . . . He went to his fate cool, poised, resolute, matter-of-fact, debonair." One of Kennedy's best British friends, David Ormsby-Gore, who served as ambassador to the United States during Kennedy's presidential years, theorized, "Whether Jack realized it or not, I think he paralleled himself after Asquith all the way, I really do."

On the pages of his personal copy of *Pilgrim's Way*, Kennedy marked up passages describing the famed British Arabist, narcissist, and World War I guerrilla chief T.E. Lawrence, a figure who clearly fascinated him: "His character has been a quarry for the analysts, and I would not add to their number. It is simplest to say that he was a mixture of contradictories which never were—perhaps could never have been—harmonized. His qualities lacked integration. He had moods of vanity and moods of abasement; immense self-confidence and immense diffidence. He had a fastidious taste which was often faulty. The gentlest and most lovable of beings with his chivalry and considerateness, he could also be ruthless." In Lawrence, Kennedy might have seen reflections of his own self-image: the refined rebel, the charismatic loner, the sensitive young officer ready for battle.

Before the war, as well as after, Kennedy's dreams of adventure and conquest found an outlet in sex, a sport he appeared to pursue with obsessive devotion. In the spring of 1943 Kennedy was only twenty-five years old, but he had already conducted affairs with a seeming multitude of women—so far their numbers included a fashion model, an actress, an heiress, students, and members of the European aristocracy. His adventures have variously been interpreted as evidence of compulsive risk taking and an obsessive search for the maternal intimacy that was withheld from him as a boy, or they may have simply been routine male promiscuity sharply magnified by near-unlimited wealth and mobility, and striking personal seductiveness. Kennedy's physical magnetism was so powerful it led one female reporter to remember that Kennedy "didn't have to lift a finger to attract women; they were drawn to him in battalions."

Kennedy's own father, whose influence on his life was near supreme, likely also inspired and encouraged his promiscuity. JFK once explained to Clare Boothe Luce, "Dad told all the boys to get laid as often as possible." And he asserted, "I can't get to sleep unless I've had a lay."

Among Kennedy's conquests before he went overseas on his first combat assignment was the twice-married, Danish-born journalist Inga Arvad, who shared a VIP spectator box with Adolf Hitler at the 1936 Olympics in Berlin, befriended other top Nazis like Hermann Goering and Joseph Goebbels, and was suspected of being a Nazi sympathizer by FBI director J. Edgar Hoover, who put her under surveillance and authorized the bugging of her apartment and tapping of her telephone line. In early 1942, in the course of electronically surveilling Arvad, the FBI reportedly generated audiotapes of her lovemaking with John F. Kennedy, then a junior U.S. Navy officer.

While briefly attending Stanford University in 1940, Kennedy, who had previously attended mostly all-male classes at private eastern boarding schools and Harvard, wrote to a friend, "Still can't get use to the co-eds but am taking them in my stride. Expect to cut one out of the herd and brand her shortly, but am taking it very slow as do not want to be known as the beast of the East." The actor Robert Stack, later star of *The Untouchables* TV series, witnessed Kennedy in action on the Stanford campus, and recalled, "I've known many of the great Hollywood stars, and only a few of them seemed to hold the attraction for women that JFK did, even before he entered the political arena. He'd just look at them and they'd tumble." Kennedy himself wasn't quite sure why this happened. He once wrote to a college friend, "I can't help it. It can't be my good looks because I'm not much handsomer than anybody else. It must be my personality."

That personality was highlighted by a relaxed, powerful charm, a genuine curiosity in other people and their opinions, a sharp, sardonic of humor, and a striking sense of confidence and optimism, all of which inspired powerful bonds of affection and loyalty with many of the people he met, female and male alike.

By his early-twenties, John F. Kennedy was living one of the most extraordinary young American lives of the twentieth century. He traveled in an orbit of unprecedented wealth, influence, global mobility, and power. As a student and as diplomatic assistant to his father, who served as U.S. ambassador to the United Kingdom from 1938 to 1940, Kennedy journeyed to England, Ireland, France, Moscow, Berlin, Beirut, Damascus, Athens, and Turkey, pausing briefly from a vacation on the French Riviera to sleep with the actress Marlene Dietrich. He met with top White House officials and traveled to Cuba, Rio de Janeiro, Buenos Aires, Santiago, Peru, and Ecuador. He gambled in a casino in Monte Carlo; visited Naples, Capri, Milan, Florence, Venice, and Rome; rode a camel at the Great Pyramid at Giza; attended the coronation of Pope Pius XII; and witnessed a rally for Italian dictator Benito Mussolini. He recalled of these momentous years, "It was a great opportunity to see a period of history which was one of the most significant." In a visit to British-occupied Palestine, Kennedy recalled, "I saw the rock where our Lord ascended into heaven in a cloud, and [in] the same area, I saw the place where Mohammed was carried up to heaven on a white horse."

In 1939, in an encounter that could have been written into a Merchant Ivory script, Kennedy, dressed in silk knee breeches, met the king and queen of England at a court levee. Spotting their dark-haired, thirteen-year-old daughter, Princess Elizabeth, Kennedy was soon chatting up the future queen over tea. "She is still pretty young but starting to look like a looker nonetheless," he wrote to a friend. "I think she rather liked me and now I wouldn't be surprised if she has a thing for me. The knee breeches are cut tight to show off my crotch at its best, and the uniform—worn by everyone but Dad at these court functions—seems to have caught the polite eye of the young heir."

That summer, Kennedy attended a grand coming-out ball for seventeen-year-old Lady Sarah Spencer-Churchill at the mammoth Blenheim Palace, which he told a friend was "nearly as big as Versailles." British politician Sir Henry Channon described the dazzling scene: "I have seen much, traveled far and am accustomed to splendor, but there has never been anything like tonight. The palace was floodlit, and its grand baroque beauty could be seen for miles. The lakes were floodlit too and, better still, the famous terraces, they were blue and green and Tyroleans walked about singing." He added, "it was gay, young, brilliant, in short, perfection," with "literally rivers of champagne" flowing. On one of the grand terraces, John Kennedy could see Anthony Eden smoking cigars and gossiping with the great man himself, Winston Churchill. It was the culmination of what many remembered as a fairy-tale summer of 1939 in England, a spell that was shattered on September 1, when Germany invaded Poland and World War II descended upon Europe.

Kennedy even hit the bestseller lists in 1940 with *Why England Slept,* an analysis of the British appeasement at Munich and the path to World War II. Adapted from his senior thesis at Harvard, Kennedy's book relied on his insider's perspective of events in England to take the contrarian view that the chief culprit in failing to block Hitler's expansion was not Prime Minister Neville Chamberlain, but rather the system of British democracy itself, which was too slow to respond to the Nazi threat.

With American involvement in the conflicts in Europe and Asia growing increasingly inevitable, Kennedy enlisted in the military in 1941, along with millions of young men of his era. "I am rapidly reaching a point where every one of my peers will be in uniform," he wrote to a friend, "and I do not intend to be the only one among them wearing coward's tweeds. I am sure there is somewhere where I can make a contribution in all this, despite whatever glaring physical deficiencies might be in evidence on my illustrious person." Given his lifelong connection to the sea, it was natural for Kennedy to be drawn to the Navy, and in September 1941, with the help of behind-the-scenes string-pulling by his father, he was appointed as an ensign in the U.S. Naval Reserve and put on the staff of the Office of Naval Intelligence at the Pentagon in October.

Weeks before, in the summer of 1941, as he sailed his personal sloop *Victura* from Hyannis Port to Martha's Vineyard, Kennedy was struck by the sight of a strange-looking vessel at the Edgartown dock. It was a "motor torpedo boat," or PT (patrol torpedo) boat, that the U.S. Navy had put on exhibition. PT boats were new fast-attack and patrol craft, sometimes called "mosquito boats," that typically carried four torpedoes, two depth charges, a smoke screen generator, mounted machine guns, and a small crew of a dozen or more men. They were inspired by similar models already being used by Britain and Germany. President Franklin Delano Roosevelt and General Douglas MacArthur championed their development for use in defending the Philippines, where their speed and maneuverability made them ideal for patrolling labyrinthine coastal waters. Journalist Robert Donovan, who interviewed Kennedy about the Edgartown encounter, reported that "the trim lines and scrappy look" of the boat fascinated Kennedy: "when he inspected her he had an urge to climb behind the wheel and open the throttles wide." Soon Kennedy learned the tiny new PT fleet offered naval officers the opportunity of being able to command their own boat very early in their career—an attractive draw for JFK and many other sailors, especially those such as himself with experience in handling small craft.

Kennedy later described the versatile capabilities of PT boats, which eventually saw wartime action across the Pacific, the Mediterranean, and the English Channel: "Small though they were, the PT boats played a key role. Like most naval ships, they could carry out numerous tasks with dispatch and versatility. In narrow waters or in fighting close to land they could deliver a powerful punch with torpedo or gun. On occasion they could lay mines or drop depth charges. They could speed through reefs and shark infested waters to rescue downed pilots or secretly close to the shore to make contacts with coast watchers and guerilla forces." Kennedy added, "PT boats filled an important need in World War II in shallow waters, complementing the achievements of greater ships in greater seas."

During the Japanese attack on Pearl Harbor on December 7, 1941, PT boat personnel were among the very first Americans to draw blood during World War II when Motor Torpedo Boat Squadron 1 Gunner's Mate Joy van Zyll de Jong and Torpedoman's Mate George B. Huffman, aboard the PT 23, opened fire with .50-caliber machine guns and shot down two Japanese Nakajima "Kate" torpedo bombers.

With United States' formal entry into the war in the days that followed, Ensign John F. Kennedy yearned for an overseas combat assignment, but to his extreme frustration, he was condemned to eight months of dreary paper-pushing and office work stateside. At the end of July 1942, after passing two physical fitness tests, Kennedy finally maneuvered himself into the naval officer training course at Northwestern University, outside Chicago. If he passed the course, he hoped to be sent overseas on assignment to a combat zone.

The battlefield was where Kennedy's heroes King Arthur, Winston Churchill, and T. E. Lawrence proved themselves, where they forged their reputations and tested their manhood. Now Kennedy was poised to join them.

2

SUMMIT MEETING ON FIFTH AVENUE

★

Joseph P. Kennedy had a favor to ask.

The Kennedy patriarch decided his twenty-five-year-old, second-born son, John, had a chance of becoming president of the United States someday, and he had a long-range plan to make it happen. He was already maneuvering his eldest son, Joseph, Jr., toward national politics and a path into the White House, but Kennedy knew that having two strong cards in play would increase his odds of winning the ultimate prize in America.

Kennedy's New York City operations usually revolved around his business headquarters at 30 Rockefeller Center, lunch spots like the Oyster Bar in Grand Central Station, and suites at the exclusive Carlyle hotel. But for a critical occasion like this, he chose the opulence of the centrally located Plaza hotel, an imposing French Renaissance–style "château" which boasted idyllic views of Central Park. It was the perfect setting to stage a seduction. He had a proposition to make, and he was not a man who took no for an answer.

On this day, Kennedy thought he could change history by launching an American political dynasty.

The target of his scheme was the most popular American fighting man of the day, Lieutenant Commander John D. Bulkeley, the compact, blunt-talking, New York–born commander of Motor Torpedo Boat Squadron 3. Earlier that year, Bulkeley had staged a series of daring operations in the Philippines and helped orchestrate the escape by PT boat of General Douglas MacArthur and his family from capture by Japanese forces converging on the doomed American garrison at Corregidor. "Bulkeley, you've taken me out of the jaws of death," a deeply grateful MacArthur told Bulkeley, "and I won't forget it." True to his word, MacArthur recommended him for the Silver Star and sent him back to the United States to publicize the morale-boosting exploits of PT boats, as well as to lobby for a fleet of two hundred of the vessels that could be dispatched to the Pacific Theater as fast as possible.

Bloodied by defeats at Pearl Harbor and the Philippines, America yearned for heroes at this early stage of the war, and Bulkeley, a modest, dark-haired thirty-one-year-old boat captain with an exotically beautiful wife and a young baby, fit the bill perfectly. He was showered with adoring publicity when he returned to the United States, and New York City rewarded Bulkeley with two rapturous celebrations, starting with a ticker-tape parade down Seventh Avenue on May 13, 1942, that drew some 250,000 spectators. Four days later, 1,250,000 people turned out to salute Bulkeley in and around Central Park. City officials estimated it was the biggest crowd ever gathered in American history. On August 4, 1942, Bulkeley had the nation's highest military citation, the Medal of Honor, placed around his neck by President Roosevelt in the Oval Office.

Joseph Kennedy had never met Bulkeley, but he sent a telegram

PT boat recruiting poster featuring Lt. John Bulkeley. (USN)

to the officer summoning him to a lunch meeting at his Plaza hotel suite. Bulkeley accepted, no doubt intrigued at the prospect of meeting one of the most wealthy and powerful men in America. The intensely charming, sandy-haired Joe Kennedy was, in the words of writer Jacob Heilbrunn, a "ruthless businessman and investor" who "capitalized on his wealth to become perhaps America's premier social climber, an Irish-Catholic outsider who stormed the bastions of the WASP aristocracy." The son of a solidly middle-class Boston tavern owner and Democratic Party activist and ward boss, Kennedy attended Harvard and became a banker and financier, propelled by a hunger for family prestige, wealth, financial manipulation, deal making, and social and political power.

In a brilliantly prescient financial maneuver, Kennedy cashed out most of his stock market holdings shortly before the Crash of

1929, protecting his family's wealth through the Great Depression. "From the beginning, Joe knew what he wanted—money and status for his family," said a close friend. "He had the progenitor's sense; to him, his children were an extension of himself. Therefore, what he did, he did with them always in mind. He played the game differently than if he had been after something entirely for himself." The elder Kennedy was capable of tremendous charm, with a confident, quick smile, a firm handshake, and a meticulous personal presentation, which featured a wardrobe that was hand-tailored (down to his underwear) in London and Paris.

In the 1920s and 1930s, Kennedy was well on his way toward amassing a personal fortune that the *New York Times* valued at $500 million at the time of his death in 1969. He earned his money through banking, real estate, corporate takeovers and consulting, liquor importing, and movie production, displaying a Machiavellian flair that left a trail of broken companies and smashed careers in his wake. Movie superstar Gloria Swanson, who was Kennedy's mistress and management client before he double-crossed and abandoned her, recalled that Kennedy "operated just like Joe Stalin"; "their system was to write a letter to the files and then order the exact reverse on the phone." When she met Kennedy, Frances Marion, America's highest-paid screenwriter at the time, thought, "He's a charmer. A typical Irish charmer. But he's a rascal." In a stunning four-year raid on Hollywood, Kennedy took over three movie studios and ran them each simultaneously, launched the talking-picture revolution, established the prototype of the modern motion-picture conglomerate, and cashed out with millions of dollars in his pocket. Betty Lasky, daughter of Paramount founder Jesse Lasky, observed, "Kennedy was the first and only outsider to fleece Hollywood."

Joe Kennedy was, in short, a master manipulator of money and people. In the words of a January 1963 profile in *Fortune* magazine, he was "a smart, rough competitor who excelled in games without rules. A handsome six-footer exuding vitality and Irish charm, he also had a tight, dry mind that kept a running balance of hazards and advantages. Quick-tempered and mercurial, he could move from warmth to malice in the moment it took his blue eyes to turn the color of an icy lake. Friendships shattered under the sudden impact of brutal words and ruthless deeds, yet those who remained close to him were drawn into a fraternal bond." Kennedy had, in the opinion of one colleague, a gift for speculation, based on "a passion for facts, a complete lack of sentiment, a marvelous sense of timing." Another colleague attested to his magnetic personality, which pulled people into his orbit: "Joe led people into camp. It was the showman in him. You were riding with human destiny when this glamorous personality beckoned you to his side." Biographer David Nasaw has written, "Those who had worked with him in the past marveled at the energy he expended, the impossibly long hours he kept, his ability to concentrate on several matters at once, and his capacity for juggling numbers, accounts, personalities, staffs, employees, and contracts as he flitted back and forth from office to office, city to city, coast to coast."

Joe Kennedy did have one personality defect: he had a big mouth, a flaw which eventually sank his own political career. In two bursts of devilish humor, his friend Franklin D. Roosevelt appointed Kennedy to jobs for which he appeared grossly unsuited. First, in 1934, he tapped notorious inside trader and stock manipulator Kennedy to be the first chairman of the Securities and Exchange Commission, making him in effect the top cop of Wall Street. In private, FDR wisecracked, "It takes a thief to catch a thief!" Then, in 1938, Roosevelt appointed the highly opinionated, often blunt-talking and undiplomatic Irish-American Kennedy to the top diplomatic post in the U.S. foreign service: ambassador to the United Kingdom. Less than three years into the job, after being largely ignored and bypassed by both FDR and the British Foreign Office, and with the Nazis advancing virtually unopposed across Europe, a dispirited and increasingly isolationist Kennedy blurted to a reporter, "Democracy is finished in England." With that remark and the firestorm of bad press it triggered, Kennedy's career in public service was over by the end of November 1940. He resigned under pressure from FDR's State Department and transferred his ambitions for political power to his male children Joseph Jr. and John, both of whom he could envision capturing the White House someday—with his help. In September 1942, securing Lieutenant Commander John Bulkeley's help in placing John into the PT boat service was a key step in his plan.

At the appointed hour of 1 P.M., Bulkeley arrived at Joe Kennedy's Plaza suite, accompanied by his wife, Alice. It would be a marathon meeting, stretching from lunch into the dinner hour, finally ending at 8 P.M. Fifty years later, Bulkeley described the Plaza summit: "Joe Kennedy had been fired as ambassador to England by his old friend Roosevelt, and he had a lot of bitter things to say about the president. Kennedy said that his son was a midshipman at Northwestern [University], and that he thought Jack had the potential to be the president of the United States. Joe said he wanted Jack to get into PT boats for the publicity and so forth, to get the veteran's vote after the war."

This impulse for shaping his family's outward image through public relations was typical of Joe Kennedy, a shrewd student of the emerging business arts of advertising and media promotion. Among the mantras he ingrained in his children were "It's not who you are that counts, it's who they *think* you are," and "Things don't happen, they are *made* to happen in the public-relations field."

According to Bulkeley, Joe Kennedy wanted to know if Bulkeley had "the clout to get Jack into PT boats." Bulkeley assured Kennedy he did, and, if the son measured up, he said he would recommend his acceptance into the service. Kennedy was delighted, though asked that his son not be sent someplace "too deadly."

Bulkeley would soon deliver the first part of the arrangement, by admitting John Kennedy into the PT boat service. He did not however, fulfill Joe Kennedy's request to protect his son by stationing him out of harm's way. JFK himself would soon sabotage that idea.

A few weeks after the meeting at the Plaza, John Bulkeley and his deputy Lieutenant John Harllee were at Northwestern University, looking for PT officer candidates. Bulkeley was at the zenith of his popularity—a bestselling book had been written about him, *They Were Expendable*. Bulkeley dazzled Ensign John Kennedy and hundreds of his classmates with a rip-roaring speech about the PT boat's alleged exploits. "The PT boat is a great weapon," declared Bulkeley. "The enemy has not yet won a brush with one. Our little half squadron sank one Jap cruiser, one plane tender and one loaded transport, badly damaged another cruiser, set a tanker on fire and shot down four planes." After the war, when Japanese naval loss records were examined by U.S. Naval Intelligence experts, it was learned that these claims were inaccurate and exaggerated.

"Those of you who want to come back after the war and raise families need not apply," Bulkeley declared. "PT boat skippers are not coming back!" The audience loved it. Alvin Cluster, who later became Kennedy's squadron commander, remembered, "America desperately needed heroes after Pearl Harbor, and they would seize on any exploit or any battle to show how great we were. The only reason PT boats ever got the attention they did was that we had nothing else! They really didn't do a lot of damage. But Roosevelt had to point to somebody, and that's why Bulkeley and PT boats got all that attention." With his superstardom and barnstorming tour of parades and motivational speeches, John Bulkeley was, claimed Cluster, "a joke to a lot of officers."

Years later, Bulkeley's assistant Lieutenant Harllee recalled encountering the young John F. Kennedy on their visit to Northwestern: "He was selling himself hard and expressed a great desire to get in close combat with the enemy as soon as possible. This was one of the main reasons why both John Bulkeley and I voted to select him. The other reasons were that he was an intercollegiate sailing champion, had graduated from Harvard *cum laude* and made a favorable impression with relation to his appearance and personality. He did not have to take a physical for PTs." Also in Kennedy's favor were the stellar marks he had earned at naval officer-training school.

Even if he hadn't been the son of powerful man, Kennedy appeared to be an excellent candidate to command a PT boat, given his intellect and experience piloting small craft. What almost no one else knew was that by now Kennedy's back troubles were so severe he had spent almost two months earlier that year in hospitals. His doctors recommended corrective surgery. He was sleeping on top of a hard plywood board to try to relieve the pain. Bulkeley later said he had "no idea Kennedy had any trouble with his back. And if I had known, it wouldn't probably have made a blind bit of difference, 'cause I had no idea what a dislocation of the spine was. I was looking for men who would fight!"

In keeping with his promise to Joe Kennedy, an impressed Bulkeley endorsed John F. Kennedy's application to be a PT boat officer, and recommended him for the eight-week PT training

A rare photo of John F. Kennedy (center) at the U.S. Navy PT boat training facility at Mellville, Rhode Island. (Frank J. Andruss Sr.)

JFK's Navy ID card, c. 1943.
(Frank J. Andruss Sr.)

course at the Motor Torpedo Boat Squadron Training Center (MTBSTC) at Melville, Rhode Island, which was close to the Kennedy family summer home at Hyannis Port. On entering the school, JFK was promoted from ensign to lieutenant, junior grade, or "jg." He performed well at Melville in subjects like boat handling and maintenance, communications, attack tactics, and torpedo firing—so well that when the course ended in November 1942, Lieutenant Harllee, who was the senior instructor at the facility, assigned Kennedy to stay on as a training instructor, rather than immediately ship out for an overseas post. On December 7, 1942, Kennedy earned his first assignment to command a boat of his own, the PT 101, a 78-foot training boat built by the Huckins Yacht Corporation.

Once more, Kennedy was thwarted in his quest to enter combat. Weeks later he was bitterly disappointed to learn he was going to be sent with PT Squadron 14 to Jacksonville, Florida, and then on to Central America to help guard the Panama Canal. He complained "I got shafted!" so often to his colleagues that they took to calling him "Shafty."

Then abruptly, on February 20, 1943, Lieutenant Kennedy's formal change-of-assignment request seeking to be "reassigned to a Motor Torpedo Squadron now operating in the South Pacific" was approved by the Navy's Bureau of Personnel in Washington.

Lieutenant Harllee was surprised to hear Kennedy was being sent to the combat zone, and assumed powerful strings had been pulled. "This suspicion was later confirmed when I had occasion to review his record in the Bureau of Naval Personnel in 1947," remembered Harllee years later. He uncovered a paper trail revealing that "tremendous effort had been brought to get him into the combat zone." Spotting a "smoking gun" letter signed by Kennedy family crony and U.S. senator from Massachusetts David I. Walsh, chairman of the Senate Naval Affairs Committee and the most powerful member of Congress on naval affairs, Harllee realized an invisible hand had indeed been at work.

In fact, John F. Kennedy had bypassed his own father and instead contacted Walsh through his maternal grandfather, John "Honey Fitz" Fitzgerald, former mayor of Boston. Having later learned of Kennedy's debilitating health problems, Harllee remembered, "Jack Kennedy's pulling strings to get into combat, was, of course, one of the most vivid examples of his stubborn, indomitable courage. But the military's standards of physical fitness for men going into combat are set not so much for the sake of the man himself as for others who might depend on his physical capabilities in a tight situation. It could be said, then, that he was also reckless and irresponsible and somewhat selfish in this act. It must also be said that he was not alone in taking such an action, and that that sort of action was generally admired in that war."

On March 15, 1943, Kennedy shipped off from San Francisco aboard the transport ship USS *Rochambeau* bound for the South Pacific, to take up assignment as a replacement officer for Motor Torpedo Boat Squadron 2, based in the Solomon Islands.

3

INTO THE LABYRINTH

★

Lieutenant John F. Kennedy looked to the sky from the deck of the American landing ship *LST 449*, and watched the terrifying spectacle of the largest Japanese air attack since Pearl Harbor.

More than 250 Japanese and Allied aircraft were pitted in aerial combat, with sixty-seven Aichi D3A2 "Val" dive bombers screened by 110 Zero fighters pitted against a pack of seventy-six American fighter planes, including P-38s, Corsairs, Wildcats, P-40 Warhawks, and P-39 Airacobras.

Nine Japanese planes were focused keenly on Kennedy's ship, the 4,000-ton "Landing Ship, Tank, 449," gliding and diving toward it and the nearby destroyer USS *Aaron Ward* (DD-483), which was trying to protect the LST as it zigzagged frantically to evade Japanese bombing runs. One 500-pound bomb exploded close enough to the *LST 449* that it threw the ship's captain across the bridge, fracturing his neck. Two more bombs detonated near the starboard bow, soaking the deck with geysers of salt water. One

massive blast pushed the ship's stern out of the ocean and forced it
into a 20-degree list. These were Kennedy's first moments in
combat: "a hell of an attack," he later remembered.

"I happened to be looking back at Kennedy's ship while four
dive bombers were attacking it," recalled a sailor on a nearby American ship. "There were so many exploding bombs along with the
resulting water spouts that I could not see the LST." The ship was
loaded with fuel oil and ammunition, and a direct hit would have
almost certainly destroyed the vessel in an immense fireball.

The twenty-five-year-old Kennedy was at the end of a month-
long sea journey from the United States to Guadalcanal to take
up his first command in the southern Pacific Theater, as skipper
of an as-yet-to-be-assigned PT boat. Kennedy was transfixed by
the spectacle of scores of warplanes locked in dogfights overhead,
and although he was only a passenger aboard the LST, along with
nearly two hundred other servicemen, he scrambled to join the
fight.

The battle was unfolding over "Ironbottom Sound," the name
given by Allied sailors to the Savo Sound because of the many ships
and aircraft sunk there during the long Battle of Guadalcanal,
before the Allies fully captured the island in January 1943. While
Japanese forces still occupied many South Pacific islands to the
north and west, the Savo Sound—off the Solomon Islands of Guadalcanal, Savo Island, and Florida Island—was now dominated by
ships of the U.S. fleet. "A gallant sight at that hour," wrote historian
Samuel Eliot Morison of the American combat squadron steaming
into Savo Sound that summer, "the cruisers so proud and handsome with their curling bow waves and frothy wakes, the destroyers
thrusting and turning, now golden with the sun, now dark shad-
ows against the sea; and this is a gorgeous afternoon, with bright

cumulus clouds under a thin layer of cirrus and Ironbottom Sound blue as the Gulf of Maine."

Earlier that day, April 7, 650 miles northwest of Kennedy's ship, at the Lakunai airdrome at the huge Japanese naval and air base at Rabaul, Admiral of the Fleet Isoroku Yamamoto stood in his gold-braided, snow-white dress uniform and waved at his warplanes taking off for battle, into a sunrise so beautiful it seemed an omen of victory. The diminutive sixty-year-old Yamamoto was the visionary and charismatic star admiral of the Japanese fleet, architect of the stunning Pearl Harbor attack; he was among the first naval strategists to realize how the new age of airpower was eclipsing the role of battleships.

Although he was suffering from fatigue and beriberi exacerbated by jungle heat, on this day he insisted on personally meeting and saluting his pilots. Yamamoto was directly overseeing the multipronged series of air attacks on Kennedy's vessel and other American targets around Guadalcanal, the Solomon Islands, and New Guinea in a counteroffensive dubbed *I-Go Sakusen,* or Operation A, which lasted from April 1 to April 16, 1943. The attacks were a desperate attempt to blunt Allied forces from island-hopping north and west from Guadalcanal to capture Japanese-held territory in the Solomon Islands and beyond and extending the reach of Allied airpower. Days earlier, Yamamoto stood atop a platform, bowed to a portrait of Japanese emperor Hirohito, and spoke to his fliers. "Now we are approaching the difficult battle," he announced. "However difficult a time we are having, the enemy also has to be suffering. Now we must attack his precious carriers with Rabaul's great air strength, and cut them down so they cannot escape. Our hopes go with you. Do your best."

As the *LST 449* was being strafed and bombarded by Yamamoto's planes, Kennedy pitched into the fight by passing shells to the ship's 40 mm antiaircraft gun station. "I was only sixteen years old and scared to death," recalled a nearby sailor from the hills of South Carolina named Ted Guthrie; "our ship had just been strad-dled by bombs and our gun tub [antiaircraft station] was knee deep in water. I wanted to run, but gained strength from the courage shown by Mr. Kennedy." Earlier on the voyage of the LST, Guthrie had heard Kennedy was "a rich man's son," and dismissed him as "a sissy." But as Guthrie later wrote to Kennedy, "When you stood there and helped pass those shells to our tub, I gained a new per-spective in life."

In a letter to a friend in the United States, Kennedy described how a Japanese pilot parachuted into the water and the *LST 449* went to rescue him as he bobbed in the water. At first, Kennedy was struck by how young the pilot looked, with his powerful build and close-cropped, jet-black hair. But Kennedy was stunned by what happened next. When the LST got to within twenty yards, the pilot abruptly pulled out a revolver and opened fire at the bridge of the American craft. "I had been praising the Lord and passing the ammunition right alongside," Kennedy later explained, "but that slowed me a bit, the thought of him sitting in the water bat-tling an entire ship." The Americans replied with so much gunfire it seemed to Kennedy the water was boiling with bullets, but every-one was too surprised to shoot straight. "Finally an old soldier standing next to me picked up his rifle, fired once, and blew the top of his head off," recalled Kennedy. "He threw his arms up, plunged forward and sank, and we hauled our ass out of there."

As the attack ended, Kennedy was hit with a powerful realiza-tion: *it was going to take a very long time to finish the war.* Fearing further attacks from Japanese aircraft over Guadalcanal, Kennedy's ship retreated three hundred miles southeast back to its port of embarkation, the island of Espiritu Santo.

A United States Marine Corps map of the Solomon Islands theater as it stood when Kennedy arrived.

Admiral Yamamoto was delighted to hear his returning pilots' reports of overwhelming successes, claims that were so exaggerated they led him to end the air assault operation on April 18 believing he'd achieved victory. Emperor Hirohito cabled his congratulations. But in fact, Allied losses were relatively light. In the April 7 attack, twenty Allied personnel were killed, seven more listed as missing, and three ships were sunk: the destroyer USS *Aaron Ward,* the oil tanker USS *Kanawha,* and the Royal New Zealand Navy minesweeper corvette HMNZS *Moa.* More than twenty Japanese planes were shot down, while the Allies lost only seven. As tragic as the losses were, Operation A had little effect on Allied strength.

Eleven days after Kennedy's first combat experience aboard the *LST 449,* on April 18, 1943, American P-38 Lightning aircraft,

acting on intelligence gained by decoded Japanese military transmissions, ambushed and shot down a transport plane carrying Admiral Yamamoto over the island of Bougainville. He had been on
his way to congratulate aircrews who took part in Operation A.

One of the pilots who was credited with firing into Yamamoto's
plane, Captain Thomas G. Lanphier, did a victory roll as he returned to Henderson Airfield on Guadalcanal. Among the Americans who witnessed the P-38's salute was John F. Kennedy, who on
April 13 had joined his assigned PT boat unit, Squadron 2, at its
base on the tiny island of Tulagi, the U.S. Navy's regional PT boat
headquarters located on the north end of Iron Bottom Sound, directly across from Guadalcanal. He had arrived at the front lines of
the Solomon Islands campaign, a turning point in the greatest
armed conflict the world had ever seen. Not for the last time, Kennedy's life and world events seemed to turn on the same axis.

Later that month, on April 25, 1943, Kennedy took command
of Motor Torpedo Boat 109, or "PT 109."

THE FRONT LINE

★

U.S. NAVY PT BOAT BASE
TULAGI, THE SOLOMON ISLANDS
APRIL 25, 1943

I wish I could tell you about the South Pacific. The way it actually was. The endless ocean. The infinite specks of coral we called islands. Coconut palms nodding gracefully toward the ocean. Reefs upon which waves broke into spray, and inner lagoons, lovely beyond description. I wish I could tell you about the sweating jungle, the full moon rising behind the volcanoes, and the waiting. The waiting. The timeless, repetitive waiting.

JAMES MICHENER, *Tales of the South Pacific*

John F. Kennedy's boat, the PT 109, was an 80-foot long, 56-ton, giant weaponized speedboat that was built by the Electric Boat Company (or "Elco") factory in Bayonne, New Jersey, in June 1942. It was sturdy and maneuverable, constructed on a framework of one-inch planks of mahogany. Its three 12-cylinder Packard 4M-2500 engines guzzled 3,000 gallons of aviation gasoline and could generate 1,350 horsepower each, achieving a top speed of more than 40 knots.

The PT 109 was designed for a crew of nine or ten enlisted crewmen and two or three officers. PT boats typically included a radio operator, quartermaster, torpedoman's mates, gunner's mates, motor machinist's mates (or "motormacs," also called engineers), and a cook. Each man on a PT boat was cross-trained for many of these duties, in order to pitch in when injury or crisis struck a specialist.

The PT 109 carried a 20 mm Oerlikon antiaircraft gun mounted on the rear of the boat, two twin .50-caliber machine gun turrets, four 21-inch torpedo tubes, an assortment of small arms, a voice radio with a maximum 75-mile range, a blinker light for communication, and a smoke generator at the rear of the boat. Under two previous skippers, as part of Motor Torpedo Boat Squadron 2, the PT 109 had conducted twenty-two combat patrols in and around Ironbottom Sound between November 1942 and February 1943, clashing with Japanese forces on six occasions.

"We learned that a PT boat had three engines, each operating its own screw," explained Kennedy's friend Dick Keresey Jr., then the skipper of the PT 105. "This was most important in maneuverability. It meant that we could have one or two engines going forward and one going astern or vice-versa, giving the ability to turn on a dime." Keresey recalled being intrigued by the craft's "graceful, almost delicate profile" as it skimmed across the top of the water at speeds over 40 knots under ideal conditions. "Dead in the water, a PT is squat and beamy," wrote Navy Captain Robert J. Bulkley. "It was designed for speed, and in speed lies its beauty. As a PT gains momentum, its bow lifts clear of the water and it planes gracefully over the surface, throwing out a great wave from the chine on either side and a rooster tail of white water astern. The men who rode PTs cursed them for their pounding and discomfort, but loved them for the beauty that is born of their speed."

John Kennedy soon discovered for himself that life aboard a PT boat in the combat zone of the South Pacific could be a wretched existence. The mountainous Solomon Islands, while scenically beautiful, were rich with cockroaches, rats, lizards, sand crabs, black flies, mosquitos, malaria, dengue, dysentery, trench foot, tropical fever, elephantiasis, and periods of unrelenting rainfall. Crews often slept aboard the boats, where clothes and mattresses were drenched in sweat and stink from the stifling tropical heat and humidity. As naval historian Charles W. Koburger wrote, "Even before one ripe corpse rotted in the jungle, the Solomons stank. The miasma they gave off was a queasy mixture of too lush vegetation, swift to rot, growing on a bed of primeval slime humming with malarial mosquitos, black with flies, and breeding nameless bacteria. They were hot. They were rich only in mud and coconuts. They were wet from May to October, rainy from November to April, and humid all the time." Amid the misery, PT boat crews occasionally savored flashes of tropical beauty: a sandy cove flanked by lush vegetation, a sun-drenched vision of deep, crystal-clear water, a passing breeze with a honeysuckle scent.

The monotonous food largely came out of cans containing Spam, Vienna sausage, powdered eggs, and baked beans. In a letter to his family, William Barrett Jr., skipper of the PT 107, described the "quite poor" food situation: "We eat entirely out of cans, mostly corned willie [beef], cheese and stew. We also eat Aircraft Emergency rations in between times. They are rich, but quite good. Coffee and cigarettes are the main staples (and our only luxuries). Aspirin gets quite a play, and we take vitamin A pills all the time, as they are supposed to improve our night vision, which latter is extremely important, in fact is almost everything."

On the PT 109, seaman Edman Edgar Mauer was deputized by Kennedy to act as the cook, though he had little culinary experience; his repertoire revolved largely around variations on Spam. Whenever he could, Lieutenant Kennedy scrounged, begged, and traded with cargo boats or Army PX stations in the region for delicacies like Oh Henry! candy bars, real eggs, powdered ice cream that could be reconstituted with ice in the boat's small refrigerator, and bread and cheese for his treasured cheese sandwiches.

If life aboard a PT boat could be miserable, conditions at the PT bases onshore were equally squalid. Fresh water to drink and bathe in was scarce, and insomnia, bad nutrition, and weight loss sapped the health of many sailors. At least one sailor resorted to stripping naked and soaping up at the first drop of rain, hoping the shower would last long enough for him to rinse off. "PT sailors thought of themselves as having rugged duty," wrote Robert Bulkley. "And so they had. When patrols were not dangerous, they were tedious. Officers and men alike had few comforts, and besides the obvious enemy, they had to contend with such hazards and discomforts as heat, rains, uncharted reefs, dysentery, malaria, and a variety of tropical skin diseases known collectively as 'the crud.'"

As for the strategic outlook for Allied forces in the region, victory was far from preordained. At this point in the conflict, U.S. war planners had every reason to expect that pushing Japanese forces out of the Solomons and back toward the Japanese home islands would be a long, intensely bloody business, costing tens or even hundreds of thousands of American lives. The Guadalcanal campaign alone took longer than six months to complete, and sacrificed more than seven thousand American lives by the time it was over in February 1943. Torpedo boats like Kennedy's PT 109 were intended to supplement Allied air and naval power by harassing Japanese

PT boats docked at Tulagi. (PT Boats, Inc.)

supply ships, serving as patrol and rescue boats, and, it was hoped, sinking Japanese capital ships including destroyers.

In the spring of 1943, Japanese aircraft flying out of Rabaul, Vila, and Bougainville were attacking Allied targets on a regular basis, probing for fuel depots and engineering shacks, the loss of which could then shut down a base. After a week of such terrifying bombing, one PT boat crewman was shipped off in what his skipper called a "catatonic trance."

In the Solomons, Lieutenant Kennedy and his comrades were subjected to frequent sudden air attacks by Japanese planes. One day, at a temporary posting at M'Banika Island, Kennedy and several colleagues were lounging in their quarters, a tin-roofed plantation house. The skipper of the PT 47, George S. Wright, recalled that Kennedy was in his bunk, reading, his favorite pastime, surrounded by mosquito netting. "A Jap plane came out of nowhere," remembered Wright, "and started dropping bombs near us. Suddenly there was a terrifying rain of shrapnel on that tin roof." While his colleagues dived into a slit trench outside, Kennedy, in haste to escape his bunk, got snared in netting. "He had a hell of a time," according to Wright, "then he finally broke loose and dived in with us."

In the unlikely event that any of the Americans stationed at Tulagi managed to forget why they were there, a large sign posted on the hillside gave them a stark reminder. Placed there on the order of Admiral William E. "Bull" Halsey, the notice declared, "KILL JAPS. KILL JAPS. KILL MORE JAPS. You will help to kill the yellow bastards if you do your job well." Years later, Kennedy described the visceral impact of seeing the sign: "it went right through you."

In the weeks between April 25 and July 20, 1943, the final crew of the PT 109 took shape. Kennedy's executive officer and second-in-command aboard the PT 109 was a former football star from Sandusky, Ohio, named Ensign Leonard Jay Thom, a strapping blond who resembled a Viking. In a letter to his parents, Kennedy quipped, "Have my own boat now, and have an executive officer, a 220-pound tackle from Ohio State—so when the next big drive comes—will be protected." Thom was a holdover from the previous skipper and had been a former student of Kennedy at the Motor Torpedo Boat Squadron Training Center in the Melville, Rhode Island, training facility. "Lennie wrote me that he really liked Jack the minute they met," recalled his wife. "Their personalities meshed immediately. He would write me jokes about Jack's money. Jack never had any cash, it seemed. He was always borrowing money from Lennie at the PX." Kennedy, in turn, was highly impressed by Thom and quickly formed a close working partnership with him.

On April 25, the day Kennedy became commander of the PT 109, Gunner's Mate Second Class Charles Albert "Bucky" Harris also reported for duty. He was twenty years old and a former tire factory worker from Watertown, Massachusetts. On May 1, a quiet, friendly twenty-five-year-old from Georgia named Andrew Jackson Kirksey joined the crew as torpedoman second class. He was married, with a three-year-old son named Jack and a five-year-old stepson named Hoyt. "He was a very strong and nice guy," recalled Hoyt in an interview more than seventy years later. "I used to go down to the ice plant and watch him make ice. Even though I was his stepson, he took great pride in introducing me to his coworkers as his son." Early on, Kennedy grew fond of Kirksey, and enjoyed looking at his family pictures as Kirksey told him stories about his sons.

On May 5, John Edward Maguire, twenty-six, joined the PT 109 crew as radioman second class. A native of Dobbs Ferry, New York, he grew up skinny-dipping in the waters of the Hudson River along the New York Central railroad tracks; he quit his factory job to follow his brother into the South Pacific PT service. When he first met a khaki-clad Kennedy on the dock at Tulagi, Maguire confided to a friend, "Geez, I don't know if I want to go out with this guy. He looks fifteen."

In the following weeks, other crewmen arrived, including twenty-year-old Seaman First Class Raymond Albert of Akron, Ohio, and four motor machinist's mates: six-year Navy veteran Gerard Emil Zinser from Illinois; Patrick H. McMahon; Harold William Marney, nineteen, from Massachusetts; and thirty-three year-old former truck driver and Scottish-born William Johnston, also from Massachusetts. As "motormacs," these four had the tough job of working down in the hot engine room, tending to the PT 109's loud, temperamental engines. Edman Edgar Mauer, of St. Louis, served as boat's quartermaster and cook.

Motormac "Pappy" or "Pop" McMahon, the PT 109's oldest crew member and an Illinois native, enlisted in the Navy because his stepson was serving on a submarine. Kennedy developed a special affection for McMahon, about whom he wrote at length in an unpublished 1946 narrative: "He was forty-one [actually thirty-seven] years old with a wife and son and before the war he taught at a small public school near Pasadena. At the time of Pearl Harbor his son joined the Navy and volunteered for submarine service. McMahon continued to teach for a few restless months and then one day told his wife that he was going to join the Navy, too. He enlisted in the Navy, was assigned to boot camp, and in one of those queer inexplicable acts, the United States Navy assigned him to the motor torpedo boat school at Melville, Rhode Island, for PT boat duty, although he was well over the age limit for these hard-riding boats. After completing his course, he was assigned to an engineering staff for shore duty and some months later proceeded to the Solomon Islands to work around the base. His age prevented him, it was thought, from sea duty." But, Kennedy explained, as the casualties mounted during the long Solomon Islands campaign, the need for trained engineers increased, and so McMahon was assigned to PT 109.

Torpedoman Second Class Raymond L. Starkey of Garden Grove, California, was a stocky twenty-nine-year-old with a wife and child. He transferred to the PT 109 because he was fed up with his previous skipper, who was, in his words, an "Ivy League snob." Kennedy, despite his Harvard pedigree, struck Starkey as "all business, but with a sense of humor and modest and considerate of enlisted men." Other crewmen would rotate in and out due to injuries and routine manpower shuffles. But these twelve members of the PT 109 crew—Kennedy, Thom, McMahon, Starkey, Albert, Johnston, Zinser, Kirksey, Maguire, Mauer, Harris, and Marney—formed its core. They would soon be forever bonded together.

———

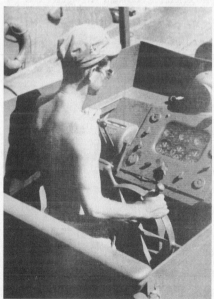

Kennedy in the armor-plated cockpit of the PT 109. When he first met Kennedy, one crewman said to a friend, "Geez, I don't know if I want to go out with this guy. He looks fifteen." (John F. Kennedy Presidential Library)

From their first days together, many of the PT 109's crewmen felt a strong affection for their skipper, who impressed them as fair, humble, approachable, and relaxed, yet also confident, highly capable, and willing to dirty his hands and pitch in when the boat needed painting or other manual labor. "The name Kennedy didn't mean anything to me," recalled Pat McMahon. "He didn't throw his weight around. He was always hungry. He never carried any money on him. I remember one night Kennedy said he didn't know why the enlisted men didn't have beer like the officers. That kind of made me feel good for Kennedy. That he'd stick up for his men." One PT 109 crewman, Maurice Kowal, who transferred off the boat due to injury, recalled, "He was terrific, he was a good man. He took care of us all the time. He would go over to Guadalcanal and bum supplies, particularly ice cream. He was crazy for ice cream."

A few of his fellow naval officers later claimed they sensed even during the war that a great political career awaited Kennedy. "He was amiable, always the first to laugh at someone else's joke, and a pleasure to be around," recalled Dick Keresey, skipper of the PT 105. "He was a man of courage, the kind of captain I wanted to see off my side on patrol. He'd stick with you all the way down to death." Kennedy's tent mate Johnny Iles recalled to naval historians Joan and Clay Blair, "His boat was shipshape and his crew was well organized, orderly. He was twenty-five—he was an old man—the rest of us were a bunch of kids." He added, "It was written all over the sky that he was going to be something big. He just had that charisma. You could tell just by his nature, by the way people would stop by and visit with him, and the fact that he was writing to important people, he was writing to very powerful people. It was obvious that politics was in his blood."

William C. Battle was commanding officer of another PT boat, a tent mate of Kennedy, and later became the U.S. ambassador to Australia. He recalled, "Jack Kennedy impressed me as almost being right out of central casting for a job as skipper of a PT boat. He was exciting. He was smart, quick, great sense of humor. He could laugh at himself. Just a wonderful companion." Battle added, "He was a young, lanky officer, bright, active, highly idealist, obviously intent on making the greatest possible contribution that he could. Always concerned about the welfare of his crew, this was one of his outstanding traits."

When Kennedy entered the combat zone, as author of a bestselling book and the son of the superwealthy former ambassador to England, he was already a minor celebrity, at least among some in the officer corps, though many enlisted men either didn't know of Kennedy's prior notoriety or, with a war going on around them, couldn't have cared less. The previous skipper of the PT 109, Bryant L. Larson, who handed the boat off to Kennedy in a brief transition period, recalled, "He was not the average guy. He was the millionaire son of Ambassador Kennedy, most of us knew that, and for that reason he had a mark on his forehead. It was a handicap, I thought. It meant he would be subjected to the most critical kind of review. But he bore the handicap well. I found him to be not only personable, a really fine man, but thoroughly competent and sincere in what he was doing."

From May through July 1943, Kennedy wrote a series of upbeat letters to his friends and family, revealing flashes of wry humor and island color as he painted a vivid picture of his life at the front lines. To his parents, he wrote, "Going out every other night for patrol. On good nights it's beautiful, the water is amazingly phosphorescent, flying fishes which shine like lights are zooming around and you usually get two or three porpoises who lodge right under the bow and no matter how fast the boat goes keep just about six inches ahead of the boat." To a friend, he wrote of an officers' club on the base that served a makeshift concoction of alcohol: "Every night about 7:30 the tent bulges, about five men come crashing out, blow their lunch and stagger off to bed."

Like many American servicemen, Kennedy was equally fascinated and wary of the local residents of the Solomon Islands, around whom titillating rumors swirled regarding their sexual freedom and alleged cannibalism: "Have a lot of natives around and am getting hold of some grass skirts, war clubs, etc. We had one in today who told us about the last man he ate. 'Him Jap him are good.' All they seem to want is a pipe and will give you canes, pineapples, anything, including a wife." To his sister, he wrote of the stark reality of island life: "That bubble I had about lying on a cool Pacific island with a warm Pacific maiden hunting bananas for me is definitely a bubble that has burst. You can't even swim, there's some sort of fungus in the water that grows out of your ears, which will be all I need, with pimples on my back, hair on my chest and fungus in my ears I ought to be a natural for the old sailors home in Chelsea, Mass."

In May 1943, Kennedy's squadron commander gave him a perfect 4.0 fitness report rating in ship handling, and a 3.9 in "ability to command," writing that Kennedy "met all situations with proficiency and daring that make him a credit to the naval service." In his spare time, Kennedy managed to continue his intellectual passions, by devouring as many books and periodicals he could lay hands on, and by holding informal discussion groups on politics and current affairs in his tent. He also had a portable Victrola record player, on which he spun his favorite pop and show tunes, like "That Old Black Magic," "Blue Skies," and Frank Sinatra's "All or Nothing at All." The song he played over and over was "My Ship," from the 1941 Kurt Weill Broadway show *Lady in the Dark*. The lyrics, penned by Ira Gershwin, seemed written for a daydreaming sailor:

"My ship has sails that are made of silk, / The decks are trimmed with gold, / And of jam and spice, / There's a paradise in the hold. / My ship's aglow with a million pearls, / And rubies fill each bin, / The sun sits high in a sapphire sky, / When my ship comes in."

Despite the exotic locale, Kennedy continued attending Sunday mass in the Russell Islands, recalled Joseph Brannan, a crewman then stationed on the PT 59. "There was an old Catholic missionary church a few miles down a jungle road from the base," remembered Brannan in a 2014 interview. "Every Sunday, we Catholics would pile into a jeep and head over. When Kennedy was at the wheel, you knew your life was in danger. He drove as fast as all hell, making hairpin twists and turns that scared the pants off me. He was a nice guy but a wild driver."

One day, while racing the PT 109 back to base after a mission, Kennedy crashed into the dock and shattered a tool shed, knocking men off the dock and throwing some of his men on the deck of the boat. The botched stunt enraged the men ashore, who screamed and cursed at Kennedy. The PT 109 slipped away and the incident blew over, but the boat's skipper had earned a new nickname: "Crash Kennedy."

On May 30, one day after his twenty-sixth birthday, Kennedy's craft and others were sent north to the Russell Islands to replace PT boats that were moving out to support a bloody new stage of the Solomon Islands campaign, the American assault on New Georgia.

As Allied forces prepared to take the offensive in the region, PT boats were used on coastal patrols aimed at harassing the Japanese efforts to resupply their outposts in the Solomons. The boats also would be used as search-and-rescue craft to assist downed Allied pilots or survivors of sunken ships. PT skipper William Liebenow explained: "PT boats were night operators; it was rare that they moved in daylight anywhere near enemy areas. The blacker the night the better! You quickly learned to love the blanket of blackness that hid you from enemy planes and made it possible for you to slip in close to the enemy ships. There was the disadvantage of not being able to see your own forces, however."

The most lethal enemy for the PT boats were Japanese floatplanes. At night, they hunted for the boats' phosphorescent wakes. PT boat officer Al Cluster stressed the danger the PT crews faced from these wakes, whose bright glow resulted from microscopic marine life being churned up and excited as their boats raced through the water. Japanese floatplanes would spot the long V-shaped wake of the PT boats in the phosphorescent waters, follow the tip of the V and bomb the boat, which alerted other Japanese air and surface craft to attack the Americans. In a letter to his parents, Kennedy explained how a typical floatplane attack unfolded: "They usually drop a flare of terrific brilliance, everything stands out for what seems like miles around, you wait then as you can't see a thing up in the air, the next minute there's a hell of a craaack, they have dropped one or two [bombs]." Another skipper described the PT boat's bright phosphorescent wake as "a long, shining arrow pointed right up our ass."

At some point soon after his first exposure to combat in the South Pacific, Kennedy experienced a spiritual crisis, and he bluntly confessed to a friend that he had "lost his religion." Through his life, Kennedy seemed to be a fairly perfunctory churchgoer who adhered to the family traditions and Irish rituals of Roman Catholicism. He periodically discussed spiritual themes, especially as they related to the ideals of the American republic and its founding, but he did not appear to spend much time grappling with spirituality and the finer points of theology. Until now, outside of his troubled health history, Kennedy had led a charmed life. But here, in the war zone, with the threat of violent death all around him, and with friends and acquaintances suddenly vanishing into the abyss, his faith evidently had been badly shaken.

In Kennedy's first months in the combat zone, the American PT boats in the Solomon Islands operated under a hidden curse.

Their torpedoes didn't work.

Incredibly, almost no one, except perhaps the Japanese, fully absorbed how bad the American World War I–vintage Mark VIII torpedoes were, but their stunning ineffectiveness meant that the PT boats fired many hundreds of the underwater missiles at Japanese targets and only very rarely hit anything.

At 27 knots, the 3,150-pound Mark VIIIs were so slow it took great luck or skill to have a chance of hitting a Japanese destroyer barreling along at 30-plus knots. In later Navy experiments, more than 50 percent of the warheads failed to detonate. If the torpedo wasn't launched "on an even keel" relative to the surface, the guidance gyroscope would tumble and fail. They were not very accurate at long ranges of a few thousand yards, and the weapons had a habit of either running deeper than set, or higher, when they would "porpoise," or break the water's surface.

Sometimes, on firing, the torpedoes' black powder charge would ignite the launch tube's interior lubrication coating of oil and grease, triggering a bright "flare-up" in the nighttime darkness that alerted the enemy to the boat's position. On other occasions, the torpedo would fail to launch and its motor would keep running inside the tube until it burned out and exploded, blowing potentially lethal fragments around the PT's deck unless the crew could shut it down first. The firing mechanism was so unreliable that, as one highly experienced PT boat skipper, William Liebenow, explained in 2015, "Nine times out of ten, when we pushed the button in the cockpit to fire the torpedoes, nothing happened. The torpedoman had to hit the firing pins with a hammer." Saddled with such inaccurate and unreliable torpedoes, the lightly armored PT boats had to sneak dangerously close to a target before attacking, to a range of two miles or less. This placed them directly in the kill zone of the enemy destroyer's large-caliber guns. After firing their torpedoes, the PT crew had to race away under cover of a smoke screen expelled by a smoke generator mounted on the back of the boat, in a desperate effort to escape before enemy gunfire detonated the 100-octane aviation-grade gasoline in the boat's fuel tank.

For many tragic months, Navy bureaucrats back in the United States stubbornly believed that the fault with the Mark VIII torpedoes wasn't their design or manufacturing but the ineptness of the firing crews. The Japanese, on the other hand, fielded the behemoth Type 93 destroyer torpedo, later dubbed the "Long Lance," which cruised up to 45 knots at a range of over 20,000 yards, and boasted more than 1,000 pounds of high explosive. It was significantly faster, more powerful, and more accurate than the U.S. Navy's Mark VIII, and unlike those on the Mark VIII, the detonators on the Type 93s usually worked.

As bad as the Mark VIII torpedoes turned out to be, equally baffling in John Kennedy's mind was the Navy's reluctance to train PT crews sufficiently in torpedo warfare, a problem that evidenced, in Kennedy's words, the "super-human ability of the navy to screw up everything they touch." Another liability was the fact that Kennedy's boat was not equipped with radar in mid-1943. Before JFK took command, the PT 109 had been outfitted with an experimental radar set as part of tests by the Navy, but the equipment proved unreliable and the sets were removed.

The PT boats were fighting an exceedingly frustrating form of combat in the Solomons, where the Japanese were moving troops and supplies around on small armored personnel barges they called *Daihatsus,* or cargo trucks. As barge hunters, the PT boats were mostly a failure. The nimble Japanese barges had shallow drafts that made it nearly impossible to hit them with a torpedo shot, and they rode so low in the water they were hard to spot in the first place. The PT's .50-caliber gunfire ricocheted helplessly off the barges' steel hulls.

One PT boat squadron commander recommended that bigger U.S. ships take over barge-hunting duties from the PTs. Admiral William Halsey agreed, concluding, "The use of PT boats as barge destroyers leaves much to be desired." In fact, PT boats carried a stigma described by Kennedy's squadron commander, Al Cluster: "The old hide-bound battleship navy had no use for PT boats at all. We were thrown loosely into that term the 'hooligan navy.'" In an interview thirty years after the war, former PT boat skipper Leonard Nikoloric explained: "Let me be honest. Motor torpedo boats were no good. You couldn't get close to anything without being spotted. I suppose we attacked capital ships maybe forty times. I think we hit a bunch of them, but whether we sank anything is questionable. I got credit for sinking a destroyer, but I don't think she sank. The PT brass were the greatest con artists of all times. They got everything they wanted, the cream of everything, especially personnel. But the only thing PT's were really effective at was raising War Bonds."

For Japanese military forces in the Solomons, the greatest danger came not from the threat of motor torpedo boats like Kennedy's PT 109, but instead from the air, as American air superiority was forcing upon the Japanese an "inflection point" from which they would never recover. U.S. fighter aircraft roamed through the region, sinking Japanese troop and supply ships and shredding

Japanese airfields, ships, and planes. The number of Japanese air-craft in the region plunged from a peak of over 200 serviceable planes in mid-1943 to only ten by the end of the year. Because of these high losses, the lack of a pilot rotation system, and the Japa-nese abandonment of Guadalcanal, the morale of the Japanese pilots plummeted rapidly after February 1943, according to records in the National Archives of Japan and military archives.

Captain Takashi Miyazaki, commanding officer of the Impe-rial Japanese Navy's Fourth Air Squadron at Rabaul from Septem-ber 1942 to April 1943, recalled the impact of American air attacks in a postwar interview with American military interrogators: "The loss of shipping was the most serious loss in our operations. We were dependent upon shipping for all of our supplies, except air-craft. Without fuel, ammunition and replacement of technical per-sonnel our aircraft were useless." He added, "We also lost most of our best naval pilots in this period. Beginning in 1943 we were unable to replace these losses with equally trained pilots. This loss became most serious in our later naval operations. During the cam-paign our aircraft and pilot losses became too great to make it prac-tical to continue to hold the Solomons."

According to the postwar interrogation report of Imperial Japa-nese Navy Commander Ryosuke Nomura, who was posted at the 11th Air Fleet at Rabaul from November 1942 to July 1943, "The naval land-based aircraft losses in the Rabaul–Solomons–New Guinea areas were extremely high and finally resulted in the de-struction of the cream of the Naval air forces. The high losses are attributed to the superiority of American fighter aircraft; break-down of Japanese aircraft supply system, [and the] inability of the Japanese to replace experienced pilots and maintenance personnel." In Nomura's words, Japanese pilots "had a horror of American fighters." They thought their workhorse fighter plane, the Zero, was the equal of the American P-40 and F4F, but understood it was no match for the F4U and the F6F, which they especially feared.

The Japanese supply situation was so bad that Shuichi Miyazaki, no less than a lieutenant general and the chief of staff of the 17th Army, stationed in Solomons, spent two months in a field hospital in summer of 1943 for malnutrition. After the war was lost, he summed up the Japanese predicament in the Solomons: "The biggest problem of all was destruction of our supply lines as a result of air attack upon shipping."

In late June 1943, a major Allied offensive signaled a new phase of the Solomon Island Campaign. Admiral William Halsey unleashed two aircraft carriers, six battleships, nine cruisers, and more than sixteen destroyers upon Japanese-held islands in the New Georgia group. The campaign ground north and west through 1943, making slow, bloody progress against entrenched Japanese opposition. One by one, islands fell into the hands of the Americans, and PT boats advanced to new bases. To support the campaign, the PT 109 was ordered on July 15 to move from its post at the Russell Islands and proceed to a base on the exact front line of combat, at the island of Rendova.

By mid-July 1943, about twenty-five PT boats, mostly from Squadrons 10, 9, and 5, were stationed at the newly captured outpost at Rendova, including the PT 109, which was now attached from Squadron 2. From their station at tiny Lumbari Island, just off Rendova, the PT boats had three main missions: to intercept Japanese barge traffic between enemy-held islands, to harass the "Tokyo Express" Japanese supply convoys, and to block Japanese attacks in the area. By now, many in the Navy were beginning to realize the PT boats on their own did not have the strength, range, or accuracy to directly face off against large enemy surface craft like destroyers.

The new base commander at Rendova (and therefore Kennedy's temporary commanding officer) was Lieutenant Commander Thomas G. Warfield, a former gunnery instructor at the U.S. Naval Academy. Warfield was a short-tempered, by-the-book officer who already was disliked by several of the base officers. "He was a first-class SOB, a Captain Queeg," said Kennedy's squadron commander, Al Cluster, recalling the day Warfield took command. Warfield immediately demanded that a brig be built at the end of the dock, to house two men he had detained at sea for an unknown infraction. According to Cluster, Warfield declared the men would stay in the brig, even if there was an air raid.

When PT boat skipper Paul "Red" Fay accidentally got his boat stuck on a sand spit, he too felt the lash of Warfield's temper. "We got it off without damage," Fay remembered, but when Warfield learned of the incident, he relieved Fay of command on the spot. Years after the episode, Fay recalled bitterly of Warfield, "He was a shit." In Warfield's defense, however, yet another PT boat commander in Warfield's Squadron 10, Philip Potter, recalled, "Warfield was a good man. A lot of the guys in the squadron didn't like him because he was all business." As for Red Fay, Potter reported, "He was considered a joke. The squadron clown. Warfield was out there to fight a war. I'm sure he never even considered giving him [Fay] command of a boat in combat." Years later, Potter was stunned to learn John F. Kennedy, as president, had appointed his avuncular World War II chum Red Fay to be undersecretary of the Navy.

One PT boat crewman, Glen Christiansen, remembered Warfield with unrestrained bitterness. "You couldn't find anything good to say about that son of a bitch, I swear!" he explained. "He was pitiful to work for, just a bad fellow all the way around. They even had fellows that pushed him off the dock, knocked him into the water a couple of times, they disliked him so much, they'd run

In July 1943, Rendova Island was the site of an American PT boat base that was on the very front line of a turning point in the Pacific War. (National Archives)

like hell so he couldn't find out who they were. Things like that start happening when you're a bad officer."

As the new commander of a blended force of PT boats abruptly mixed together from several different boat squadrons, Thomas Warfield rarely rode on the boats himself, preferring to run operations from behind the front lines in his command tent at the Rendova base. "Warfield obstinately vested his trust in the powerful new radio aerial [antenna]," wrote naval historians Clay and Joan Blair, "and a belief in attack by numbers." John Meade, then a PT boat officer based at Tulagi, later called Warfield "the biggest shit in the Pacific. He simply never learned the tactical lessons of the year before that PT boats were ineffective in groups larger than two. Because they [multiple-boat formations] were ordered by

Warfield to keep strict radio silence save in emergency, the lead boat could not signal the trailing boats that he was about to move out. The second boat would react to the movements of the first boat, but at a delay. The delay was magnified with each boat. So, often, the fourth boat would get detached." For the crew of the PT 109, this command flaw would soon have dire consequences.

In a series of major naval clashes between July 5 and July 13 around the Solomon Islands, the Americans and Japanese each lost two destroyers and one cruiser. While technically a draw, the actions, later dubbed the Battle of Kula Gulf and Battle of Kolombangara, succeeded in slowing the Tokyo Express. Soon after, between July 15 and July 31, Kennedy's PT 109 completed seven combat patrols, during three of which the 109's group of boats were chased and attacked by Japanese floatplanes.

Amid crippling darkness and plagued by bad communications, the PT boats were entangled in a series of friendly-fire incidents, though none involved Kennedy. After U.S. forces captured Rendova on June 30, PT boats led by Lieutenant Commander Robert Kelly launched torpedoes at the 10,000-ton transport USS *McCawley,* the flagship of Admiral Richmond Kelly Turner, believing it was a Japanese ship. The boat was already damaged by Japanese fire, and empty, being towed out of the battle zone. The episode was one of only three confirmed sinkings of major vessels by PT boats in World War II—unfortunately it was an American ship.

On the night of July 17–18, Commander Warfield ordered a large formation of twelve PT boats out into the darkness to ambush the Tokyo Express in Blackett Strait, a roughly seven-mile-long passage of water that lay to the south of the island of Kolombangara. A daisy chain of confusion ensued. Spotting what he thought

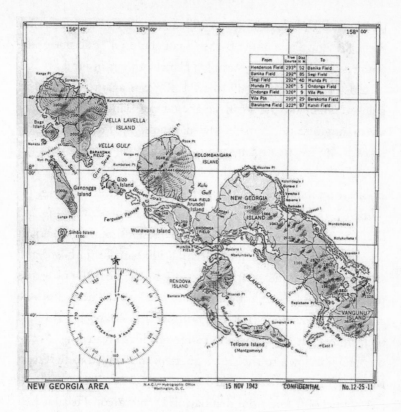

From	True Course	Dist N M	To
Henderson Field	293°	52	Banika Field
Banika Field	292°	85	Segi Field
Segi Field	292°	40	Munda Pt
Munda Pt	326°	5	Ondonga Field
Ondonga Field	326°	9	Vila Ptn
Vila Ptn	295°	29	Barakoma Field
Barakoma Field	322°	87	Kahili Field

NEW GEORGIA AREA   N.A.C.J/mi Hydrographic Office Washington, D.C.   15 NOV 1943   CONFIDENTIAL   No.12-25-11

were six Japanese destroyers speeding along at nearly 40 knots, PT 159 skipper Oliver Hayes led an attack that launched ten torpedoes toward the ships. The PT boat crews thought they scored hits on two of the targets, but luckily, they were wrong. The vessels turned out to be American destroyers. They, in turn, had been alerted to attack the PT boats, which had been mistaken as Japanese vessels by a Navy patrol plane. The pattern of friendly fire incidents finally turned tragic on July 20, when a formation of Army B-25 bombers and three PT boats from Squadron 10 mistakenly attacked each other in broad daylight. Eleven PT sailors were wounded by strafing, and three American airmen died when PT boat antiaircraft guns shot down one of the B-25s. "I got confused," said one of the gunners, "and thought it was a Jap plane with our insignia."

On the night of July 19, the PT 109 was again patrolling in Blackett Strait off the small Japanese-held island of Gizo. After several uneventful hours in the darkness, then-crewman Leon Drawdy spotted an airplane approaching at an altitude of less than a hundred feet, close enough for him to see the red Rising Sun emblems on the plane's wings.

Before the crew could react to Drawdy's shouts of warning, the boat was rocked by two close bomb explosions marked by bright orange bursts, which slammed the PT 109 hard to starboard and sent fragments of hot metal shrapnel into the boat. Drawdy was propelled out of a hatch, knocking his head on the deck. Both he and fellow crewman Maurice Kowal suffered shrapnel wounds to their limbs that drew blood but were not life-threatening. Kowal was brought down to the crew's quarters and tended to by Edgar Mauer. "My shoes were soaked with blood," recalled Kowal. "It just poured out. And from that day on I was scared." He added, "I was terrified. First time away from home, first time I got shot at, so I was terrified from that day on, until I got home."

Kennedy tried to engage the idling engine, but it stalled. Engineer McMahon, despairing that they were now sitting ducks for a second attack, managed to reengage all three engines, enabling Kennedy to circle out of the plane's path. Kowal and Drawdy, both lightly wounded, left the PT 109 for treatment, never to return. Another one of the PT 109 crewmen, Andrew Jackson Kirksey, was so upset by the attack that he had a premonition of his own imminent death.

"I won't be around much longer," Kirksey darkly mused.

Kennedy later explained: "He never really got over it; he always seemed to have the feeling that something was going to happen to him. He never said anything about being put ashore—he didn't want to go—but the next time we came down the line I was going to let him work on the base force. When a fellow gets the feeling that he's in for it, the only thing to do is to let him off the boat. Because strangely enough they always seem to be the ones that do get it. I don't know whether it's just coincidence or what." While Kirksey did not shirk his duties or request a transfer, Kennedy decided to replace him the next time they went back to Tulagi.

That day would never come.

5

THE RAID

★

On the afternoon of August 1, John F. Kennedy and his crew were focused on figuring out how to attach an old 37 mm U.S. Army antitank gun to the foredeck of the PT 109, in an experiment to beef up the boat's firepower. The idea for the extra armament was the brainchild of South Pacific area commander Admiral William "Bull" Halsey, who thought that if the wooden PT boats were equipped with high-caliber guns, they might be effective against agile, fast-moving Japanese transport barges made of steel. So far, of course, the PTs had mostly been a bust as barge hunters.

Kennedy was enthusiastic about the idea, but he was having problems fastening the gun onto his torpedo boat. It was an unwieldy, breech-loading antitank weapon that was mounted atop a two-wheeled carriage with bracing posts. Since it had no protective armor or turret, the gunner would be exposed to enemy fire, and its manual operation meant new shells had to be loaded by hand, one at a time. Kennedy was looking for a carpenter to construct wooden supports for the improvised gun mount, and since he and his crew hadn't figured out how to firmly fasten the gun onto the vessel by themselves, they opted to use rope to temporarily lash it and some large wooden support planks onto the deck until a carpenter could be found.

To make room for the gun, they removed the PT 109's life raft.

The crew of the PT 109 was operating on the very edge of the front line of the Pacific War. From atop nearby Rendova Peak, one could easily see the series of Japanese-controlled or contested islands of the New Georgia group of the Solomon Islands, some of which held thousands of enemy troops. To the north and west was a fifty-mile network of Japanese-occupied jungle islands including the imposing Kolombangara, home to its 6,000-foot-high volcano and a Japanese garrison of thousands of soldiers.

Just five and a half miles north across a narrow channel from Rendova was Munda Point, where a Japanese airfield was under constant American bombardment from U.S. air and naval forces, and from Rendova's long-range heavy 155 mm artillery guns. On Munda Island, the U.S. 43rd Infantry Division and 9th Marine Battalion were locked in a fierce stalemate with Japanese forces.

The PT base at Rendova was described by one sailor as a "lousy place" composed of "tents with water-filled slit trenches just outside the door." It also was well inside the range of Japanese warplanes. Some twenty PT boats based at Rendova Island were moored close to shore in groups of two or three, ready to scatter in case of Japanese attack from the air.

PT boats docked at Rendova. (navsource.org)

In the midafternoon of August 1, as Kennedy and his crew pondered the problem of the antitank gun and waited for the carpenters, a Rendova radio operator decoded an urgent message from Admiral Theodore Wilkinson, the amphibious commander in the region, and rushed it to PT base commander Thomas Warfield in his tent. What Warfield couldn't have known was that the message was the product of one of the war's most closely held secrets: in mid-1942, Allied cryptologists had cracked a series of key Japanese naval codes, giving them advance warning of major enemy ship movements. By the time he finished the note, Warfield realized he was being ordered to orchestrate one of the largest mass PT boat attacks of World War II.

"Most secret indications," the message read, were that the Tokyo Express Japanese naval supply convoy would run that evening, the night of August 1–2, evidently in a large operation to support the garrison on Kolombangara. The message ordered: "Warfield operate maximum number [of] Peter Tares [PT boats] in Area Baker," which meant Blackett Strait, the stretch of water immediately west and south of Kolombangara. Additionally, it continued, Lieutenant Commander Robert Kelly, now stationed at the smaller Rice Station–Lever Harbor PT base on New Georgia, was to scramble all his available PT boats to Kula Gulf, as Admiral Arleigh Burke prepared to station no less than six of his destroyers north of Kolombangara by 12:30 A.M. on August 2 to strike the Express. The Express would hopefully be trapped at any one of three possible approach points.

Commander Warfield immediately grasped that a defining moment in his career was at hand. Even though his PT boats were a fallback force in case Admiral Burke's destroyers and Lieutenant Commander Kelly's PT boats missed the Express on the northern approaches to Kolombangara, Warfield knew that if his torpedo boats could stop or sink the ships of the Tokyo Express south of the island, the victory would be a major feather in his cap. He quickly formulated a plan to attack the Express, which he would unveil at his late afternoon planning briefing with his boat commanders.

Inside his command tent, Warfield read aloud the message's ominous warning, "Jap air[craft] out to get Peter Tares [PTs]."

The radioman assured him, "We're on Condition Red, sir." This increased level of alert meant the enemy was in the vicinity or imminently expected, and boat crews were positioned on or near their vessels, prepared to scatter. "When they declared Condition Red," according to PT skipper William Liebenow, "we hit the boats and got ready to go."

Soon after, as if on cue, air raid sirens blared, and a voice cried, "Dive bombers!"

At least eighteen Japanese fighter planes suddenly appeared over the base from behind the protective cover of Rendova Peak, their machine guns blazing, swooping so low one American sailor remembered seeing an enemy pilot's "droopy Charlie Chan mustache."

Officers and enlisted men scrambled out of tents and dove into foxholes for cover as antiaircraft blasts peppered the sky, along with machine-gun fire from the berthed PT boats. John Kennedy, who was visiting one of the officer's tents, jumped into a foxhole, and then rushed off to be with the PT 109, which was moored nearby.

On the PT 109, crewman Pappy McMahon froze at the sight of one Japanese plane bearing directly toward him, its bomb clearly visible under its wing. A thought gripped his mind: "If I don't keep watching it, I'll be hit." With the help of Andrew Kirksey, Charles Harris pushed an ammunition drum into the PT 109's 20 mm antiaircraft gun and fired upon an enemy plane, while Harold Marney jumped into one of the boat's twin .50-caliber machine gun turrets and opened fire. Geysers of water erupted in the harbor as Japanese bombs and torpedoes fell.

"Cast off!" shouted Kennedy from the PT 109's cockpit. He steered the craft through a scene of pandemonium. The other undamaged PT boats dashed out of the harbor while firing at the enemy planes, while overboard crewmen splashed in the water amid floating debris and drifting columns of smoke. A Japanese dive bomber crashed and exploded in a PT boat nest, detonating the PT 164 and killing two of its crewmen. The impact blew two torpedoes off the 164, which careened around the harbor before beaching themselves without exploding. The PT 117 was also destroyed, though its crew survived.

Minutes later the all-clear siren sounded. It was a "one-pass" raid—a Japanese tactic that reduced their exposure to antiaircraft fire but also minimized the damage they themselves could inflict. Warfield correctly figured the raid was an attempt to weaken the American PT force in advance of the Express convoy predicted for that evening. He also accurately estimated the convoy's destination to be the Japanese outpost at Vila Plantation, on southern Kolombangara.

"It looks as if the Japs mean business this time," declared Commander Warfield as he listened to battle damage reports from his skippers, who were crowded around chairs and on the floor in Warfield's command tent.

Among the PT boat commanders gathered into the meeting along with Kennedy was Lieutenant (jg) William F. "Bud" Liebenow Jr., the youngest of the group at twenty-three years old. He was an athletic and highly respected Virginia-born skipper who had proved himself to be an aggressive, skilled commander in operations with Kelly's Squadron 9 the previous month. For the past five days he had been John Kennedy's bunkmate, along with Ensign William Battle, in the field tent they shared while their crews slept on the torpedo boats. Liebenow was pleased to see Kennedy at the base, as he remembered him fondly from the PT training facilities at Melville, Rhode Island. "He was a friendly, capable PT boat officer," recalled Liebenow more than seventy years later. "I didn't even know he was an ambassador's son, that just didn't register with me at the time." Like Kennedy, he was attracted to the PT boat service because it gave him a chance at commanding his own boat much earlier than would be the case in the regular Navy.

"This is going to be a real big night," announced Warfield, who then read Admiral Wilkinson's message. Warfield stressed that the Japanese convoy would come down through Vella Gulf and then go back up, offering the PT boats two chances to attack it. It would soon become an especially dark, moonless night with heavy cloud

JFK's tent mate William "Bud" Liebenow (center) with PT boat colleagues, 1943. (William F. Liebenow)

On August 1, 1943, Lt. Commander Thomas Warfield (pictured here with his officers in 1944) was given three hours to plan one of the biggest mass-torpedo-boat attacks of World War II. The resulting Battle of Blackett Straight was, according to one participant, "the most fouled-up PT operation in history." (National Archives)

cover, which would increase the difficulty of spotting the fast-moving Japanese warships hugging the blacked-out silhouettes of the Solomon Islands.

"We've got to use everything we have," announced Warfield to the skippers. "How many boats are in condition?" Fifteen vessels were seaworthy, came the answer. Only four of them had primitive radar equipment. Warfield then announced a rudimentary plan of action, which assigned the boats into four groups that would lie in ambush along a southeast line through Blackett Strait, poised to strike the destroyers of Tokyo Express in the event Admiral Arleigh Burke's destroyers failed to stop the convoy.

Warfield assigned Kennedy's PT 109 and Liebenow's PT 157 to a four-boat group, or "division," led by PT 159's combat-seasoned, twenty-six-year-old Lieutenant Henry "Hank" Brantingham, who also was deputized field commander of the entire operation. Brantingham was a U.S. Naval Academy graduate and former executive officer of Lieutenant Commander Kelly's Squadron 9; he had served with Commander John Bulkeley in the Philippines and joined in the famous operation to smuggle General Douglas MacArthur and his family to safety. The fourth boat in Kennedy's assigned group was the PT 162, commanded by Lieutenant (jg) John Lowrey, who, like Kennedy and several other skippers going out that night, did not have much combat experience.

These four PT boats—109, 157, 159, and 162—formed "Division B" of Warfield's plan. They would occupy the northwesternmost patrol region, in Vella Gulf off a point on the west coast of Kolombangara called Vanga Vanga.

Next in the southeast-running line, was Division A, was led by Warfield's executive officer at the Rendova base, Lieutenant Arthur Henry Berndtson. It was assigned to patrol in Blackett Strait off the

southwest coast of Kolombangara across from a village named
Gatere. Berndtson, another Naval Academy graduate, would be
stationed in the PT 171. His formation included Lieutenant (jg)
Stuart Hamilton's PT 172, Ensign Edward H. Kruse's PT 163, and
Lieutenant (jg) Philip A. Potter's PT 169. Potter was another "green"
skipper with little combat experience in the PT boats.

To the southeast of Berndtson's group was Division R, a three-
boat formation led by Lieutenant Russell Rome in PT 174, assigned
to patrol east of Makuti Island in Blackett Strait. The final of the
four units, designated Division C, was led by Lieutenant George E.
Cookman of PT 107 and was assigned to patrol Ferguson Passage
as a reserve formation to back up the first three divisions—and to
protect Rendova in case the Tokyo Express was not a resupply
convoy, but rather an assault force.

Commander Warfield revealed his plan to his officers. When a
target appeared on radar, the division leader would attack, launch
his torpedoes, and then get out of the way so the other boats in the
formation could fire their torpedoes. Those boats were supposed to
stay in close visual contact with the leader, and follow his movements.

"When the leading boat saw something and attacked, the other
boats were to follow right along without further ado and no further
conversation," Brantingham later said. "That was the practice of
our squadron." After the leaders transmitted initial contact reports,
radio communications between the boats and with Warfield's command tent at Rendova would be held to an absolute minimum to
avoid tipping off the Japanese to the size and position of the PT
boat formations. The Japanese ships had radio direction equipment
that could pinpoint the location of the PT boats.

According to witness Lieutenant William Liebenow, there was

no discussion of contingency plans should a boat got lost, damaged, or sunk. Nor were they provided search-and-rescue procedures in case men were lost at sea. "We always got the feeling that PT boat crews were expendable," recalled Liebenow in 2015. "If you got in trouble and could get yourself out of it, well, fine, but you were on your own." Warfield's brusque manner discouraged any discussion or input from his officers. They were expected to follow orders, period.

In theory, Warfield's plan appeared logical, but in practice, it was a recipe for mass confusion. Beyond the stunning ineffectiveness of the Mark VIII torpedoes, the operation would be plagued by a series of problems and contradictions that essentially doomed it from the start. On a battle map, it may have looked to Warfield as if he was setting up a solid picket line of mutually reinforcing attack craft that would be well positioned to ambush the Tokyo Express. But in reality, with fifteen boats scattered in the ocean in the black of night, enjoined to maximum radio silence, most of them operating without radar, they would be acting largely independently as if in their own worlds, and from a very weak position given the disparity in firepower between them and a Japanese destroyer.

Further, neither Kennedy nor any of the other PT boat skippers had successfully performed such a complex, multi-boat torpedo attack before. And while many were by now experienced combat veterans, a number of the newer PT boat commanders, Kennedy included, were relatively untested in combat. Kennedy had never directly engaged a Japanese surface vessel before, other than firing at an apparently unmanned Japanese barge a few weeks earlier. Warfield himself was fairly "green" and had yet to distinguish himself in commanding PT boat attacks.

Additionally, for a combat force to function effectively in battle, unit commanders in the field need to operate from a common set of procedures. However, many of the fifteen boat commanders headed for Blackett Strait that night were recently mixed in from different squadrons, and were therefore not familiar with each other's operational practices and habits when under fire. At least two skippers at Warfield's briefing, William Liebenow of PT 157 and Richard Keresey of PT 105, did not clearly understand that Warfield's "hit and run" plan apparently meant the four radar-equipped lead boats, after firing their torpedoes, would withdraw not only from the skirmish line but in fact all the way back to the Rendova base, inexplicably leaving their formations without radar coverage.

On top of this, after weeks of constant operations in much smaller groups, many of the PT boat crews were exhausted. Keresey, the PT 105's experienced commander, recalled the crews being especially tired on this evening. "Most of us had been out almost every night for two weeks," he explained. "On the majority of those nights we'd been in gun battles with enemy barges, bombed by enemy floatplanes, or had a couple of mix-ups with our own forces. Sleep came in two-hour stretches. During the day there were things to get done. Refueling from fifty-gallon drums was a long process when a good two thousand gallons were needed. We also had to work on the engines, torpedoes, guns, and radio, all of which needed cleaning and adjustments after a night of bouncing around."

But the biggest problem by far was Warfield's stubborn refusal to go out on patrol with his own boats, which meant he failed to grasp the simple fact that when it was pitch dark, the blacked-out PT boats could often not see each other. On this evening, his order that the boats stay in close visual contact with each other was unrealistic: without effective radio coordination, it would condemn the PT boats to a state of near-total confusion in enemy waters. Warfield had banned the use of radio unless it was a dire emergency. To make matters even worse, the ship-to-ship radios most of the boats used for interboat transmissions were often unreliable, as they frequently hit dead spots and drifted off signal.

With no debate, no clarifying questions, and no input from his skippers, Warfield ended the briefing. "Those of you who weren't supposed to be going out tonight will have to get ready in a hurry," he announced. "Better get to it."

It was now late afternoon. As John Kennedy headed to the PT 109 to break the news of the operation to his crew, he had a chance encounter with Ensign George "Barney" Ross, another acquaintance of his from the PT training base at Melville, Rhode Island. Ross was a "man without a boat," as he had been executive officer of the PT 166, which was accidentally sunk by friendly fire by American B-25s ten days earlier. Seeing Kennedy, Ross had an idea.

"Do you mind if I come along, Jack?" he asked.

"No, come on," said Kennedy. "I'm short of men anyway."

When they reached the PT 109, Kennedy, referring to the weapon lashed to the foredeck, asked, "Do you know anything about these 37 millimeters?"

"No, I'm afraid I don't," said Ross.

"Well, I don't think any of us are too well informed on it, either," Kennedy responded. The two officers fiddled with the 37 mm gun and eventually managed to figure out how it worked.

In this way, Ross joined the crew of the PT 109 that evening as a guest passenger, to act as a forward lookout on the vessel, and as the gunner on a weapon he never fired before. The addition of Ross brought the total number of crew to an unlucky thirteen. At least one man on the PT 109 crew thought such an arrangement, and the unusual addition of a "visitor" on an operation, were bad omens.

"We're going out tonight," announced Kennedy to his crew. "Let's get ready." This provoked scattered groans, as the PT 109 had been scheduled to take the night off.

In the boat's galley after dinner, Andrew Jackson Kirksey's hands trembled so badly he had to place his coffee cup on the table to sip from it. The persistent premonition of death he had felt for days was intensifying. He had as much courage and skill as any other sailor, but he could not shake the feeling of imminent doom.

"Will you take care of my things?" Kirksey asked fellow crewman Charles Harris.

"You're nuts," retorted Harris.

"I won't be going home," declared Kirksey.

Laughing, Harris repeated, "You're *nuts*."

Kennedy and several of the crewmen tried to talk Kirksey into not taking part in that night's operation, assuring him no one would think differently about him. There would be no repercussions, they said.

Edman Mauer told Kirksey, "I think you ought to stay ashore tonight. No one will make anything of it. You'll be okay in the morning."

But Kirksey insisted on going on the mission. "They'd say I'm yellow," he said, apparently fearing dishonor even more than death.

Kirksey and the rest of the crew donned their life jackets, checked their gear and equipment, and prepared to cast off.

"Wind her up," ordered Kennedy. "Cast off." In his boat's small cockpit, or "conn," Kennedy pushed the three throttle handles, and in response, motormac Gerard Zinser down in the engine room activated the engines.

Andrew Jackson Kirksey, a quiet, friendly twenty-five-year-old from Georgia. Kennedy was fond of Kirksey, but in the days before August 2, 1943, he grew alarmed that Kirksey was having frequent premonitions of death. (Jack Kirksey & Frank J. Andruss Sr.)

As dusk fell and overcast skies enveloped the region, a procession of fifteen torpedo boats moved out of Rendova Harbor through Ferguson Passage toward Blackett Strait, journeying northwest nearly forty miles into enemy waters.

By 9:30 P.M. all the boats were holding at their patrol stations. To increase their coverage, Lieutenant Brantingham divided his division into two separate sections: his own boat paired with Bud Liebenow's PT 157, and John Lowrey's PT 162 was coupled with the PT 109.

At about 11 P.M., while drifting close to the beach of Kolombangara, the PT 109 was suddenly illuminated by a powerful searchlight from the island, followed by artillery fire. Ensign George Ross recalled, "Some kind of heavy gun was firing at us, fairly close, and so Jack took what they call evasive action. The whole idea of PT boats is of course to surprise the enemy, and when they surprise you with a searchlight the idea is to get out of the path of the searchlight. We'd been just cruising with one engine as quietly as possible so we wouldn't be discovered, and so we gunned the motors and Jack zigzagged around and pretty soon the light went out."

Kennedy put the crew at "general quarters," and the PT 109's sailors went to their battle stations.

In the cockpit of the PT 109, radioman John Maguire clutched a string of beads and silently prayed the rosary: "Glory be to the Father, and to the Son, and to the Holy Spirit. As it was in the beginning, is now, and ever shall be, world without end, Amen."

Beside him, John F. Kennedy gripped the wheel, watched, and waited.

tion we went." Eventually Liebenow linked up with Brantingham's boat near Gizo Island.

John F. Kennedy was expected to stay close to Brantingham in keeping with basic PT boat training and practice, but the PT 109 was nowhere to be seen. At some point in the patrol, probably before midnight when it dodged an enemy searchlight, Kennedy apparently became separated from his formation.

In the first of many communications fiascoes of the evening, two of the boats in Brantingham's division, Kennedy's PT 109 and John Lowrey's PT 162, had no details of Brantingham and Liebenow's first engagement with the enemy, because Brantingham did not radio a contact report to them. The PT 109's temporary crewman Ensign Ross later said simply, "We didn't know what the score was." By now, the 109 and 162 were separated from the two lead boats and well out of visual range with them.

Over the next two and a half hours, the men on board the PT 109 did hear garbled bursts of chatter on the radio: "I am being chased through Ferguson Passage. . . . Have fired fish . . . Well, get the hell out of there!" But without a visual picture of events (by neither sight nor radar) and no radio contact reports being relayed, Kennedy couldn't clearly understand what was going on.

Even if there had been effective communication between boats, PT skipper William Liebenow observed that "in the middle of combat, with all three engines running wide open with the mufflers off, you couldn't hear the radio at all." Further, "the radio man was often away from the radio, to help wherever else he was needed," said Liebenow, who like John F. Kennedy operated an 80-foot "Elco" PT boat.

Liebenow described how he believed Kennedy got separated from him during the attack: "The simplest explanation of all is probably the true one: the PT 162 and PT 109 just lost contact with the rest of section 'B'—that is, the PT 159 and PT 157. In other words, they got lost. This undoubtedly happened sometime before we made contact with the enemy and made the initial attack. It is doubtful Kennedy or Lowrey knew that the 159 and 157 had made an attack. Of course they had seen and heard the firing of the Jap destroyer, but had assumed it to be from shore batteries on Kolombangara." Liebenow's theory that Kennedy mistook the initial engagement with enemy destroyers for shore batteries from Kolombangara seems sound: the PT 109 already had evaded enemy fire from the island that evening, and besides, the Tokyo Express was not due for at least another half hour, after having run through a gauntlet of American destroyers whose encounter would surely have been relayed through the American radio channels. "Certainly if it had been shore batteries the best tactic was to lay low unless you're discovered," Liebenow continued. "The 162 and 109 boats were probably at a distance of five to ten miles from us."

After Brantingham fired all his torpedoes, and missed, Commander Thomas Warfield then made a fateful decision from the comfort of his command tent at Rendova. By radio, he ordered the PT 159, the only boat in Division B with radar, to return directly to base. This left the other three boats of the division, including Kennedy's PT 109, "blind" and without radar coverage for the rest of the night. Perhaps Warfield was already having trouble managing the mental calculus of tracking the many moving pieces of the chaotically unfolding engagement. Or he may have felt confident in his ability to assert control over the operation from his radio-equipped command tent. But as it would happen, the order to bring PT 159 back to base, compounded by Brantingham's failure to radio his movements to the other boats in his formation, set off a chain reaction that would soon have tragic results.

———

PT 109 seemed to be drafting in its own universe. It was separated from the other boats by a thousand yards or more, visibility was nonexistent in the black, moonless night, and most of the boats were trying to observe radio silence, as ordered.

Incredibly, at least two of the PT 109's crewmen recalled operating in a state of near-complete ignorance of the mission's objectives. Further, as Liebenow later suspected, much of the crew failed to grasp the significance of the thirty-minute-plus barrage of explosions, spotlights, frantic bursts of emergency radio traffic, shelling, and bombing that had erupted through Blackett Strait. Radio operator John Maguire recalled: "We never got any word that there were destroyers in our area. There were no instructions at all. Once we got out there we never heard from anybody. I remember hearing that somebody was shooting or firing, and somebody said [on the radio], 'Let's get the hell out of here.' I assumed it was one of our other patrols."

It was not unusual for Navy enlisted men to know much less about an operation than their officers, but Maguire's fellow PT 109 crewman Charles Harris also recalled a stunning lack of information on the scene: "We had no idea there were ships [Japanese destroyers] out there that night. We didn't know the Express had gone down to Vila. We thought it was shore batteries firing. Our lead boat, the radar boat, picked something up, but they didn't tell us anything about it. They took off after it and left us sitting there. We laid smoke once because the shells were landing pretty close. When we got back we were really going to look up that skipper [Brantingham] and give him the business for leaving us high and dry like that. We were kind of mad. He had the eyes [radar] and we didn't." The PT 109 and PT 162, now separated from the PT 157, moved away from Kolombangara and the inbound path of the Tokyo Express, toward the island of Gizo.

Although PT 109 crew members Harris and Maguire did not recall any warning of destroyers, one man on the boat clearly did: their skipper, Lieutenant Kennedy. In a never-before-published passage from a 1946 narrative of the incident written by Kennedy himself, a document discovered in 2014 in the archives of the John F. Kennedy Presidential Library during the research for this book, Kennedy confirmed that at "about midnight a report was picked up that Japanese destroyers were in the area." Why Maguire, the PT 109's radioman, would not remember this is a mystery.

What's certain is that the ships of the Tokyo Express, unscathed by the first assault by Kennedy's boat formation, continued barreling toward their destination, the Japanese military outpost at Vila Plantation on Kolombangara.

At 12:04 A.M. on August 2, four blips traveling as fast as 30 knots appeared on the radar screen of the PT 171, the lead boat of the second American picket line, Division A, commanded by Arthur Berndtson, who also did not have details of the earlier action of Division B. Berndtson correctly figured they were destroyers hugging close to the shore of Kolombangara. Spotting the big phosphorescent bow wakes of the destroyers, he swung forward to launch an attack. At a distance of 1,500 yards, the Japanese destroyer opened fire on the PT 171.

As enemy shells landed around him spraying water onto his boat's deck, Berndtson radioed the three other vessels in his group, but got no reply. He tried reaching them with his blinker tube, to no avail. Berndtson explained: "We lined up on the second ship and let fly four torpedoes at about fifteen to eighteen hundred yards. Our tubes flashed and we had a nice bright fire. That alerted them. One of the destroyers turned toward us to comb our torpedoes [present a narrower target area]. They turned on searchlights and started firing big guns at us. Well, we put on power, zigzagged, and laid smoke. There was shrapnel raining on deck. It looked like a junkyard." All four of the PT 171's torpedoes missed their target. Berndston tried to radio a warning to Bill Rome, the next group leader in the picket line, but couldn't establish radio contact with him either.

In a replay of the earlier retreat by his fellow division leader, Berndston withdrew the radar-equipped PT 171 from the area, heading first toward Gizo Strait and then home for the Rendova base, without giving a contact report to the other three boats in his Division A, PTs 163, 169, and 172. Now those boats were without leadership or radar coverage, just like John Kennedy's PT 109. Lieutenant Phil Potter in the PT 169, one of the skippers in Berndt-son's division, tried to maneuver his craft away from Japanese five-inch shells that were bursting overhead, but all three of his engines went dead. It took his motor machinists ten minutes to restart the engines, whereupon he fled the scene.

Still unmolested by the American attacks, the Tokyo Express quickly entered the sights of the boats in the third picket line, Division C. Two blips appeared on the radar screen of the PT 107, skippered by George Cookman, who was leading the four PT boats of Division C south of Ferguson Passage. Cookman's group had no details of the two previous failed attacks, though Warfield's after-action report would note that "a searchlight and gunfire had been seen to the north." In a farcical reprise of the first two failed ambushes, division leader Cookman charged his boat forward to launch all four of his torpedoes, each of which missed its target, and he headed back toward Rendova without leaving a contact report or instructions with the other boats in his formation. Seventy-two years after the battle, in an interview for this book, PT 107 gunner's mate John Sullivan explained why he thought the

PT 107 beat such a hasty retreat: "I think our skipper was afraid of getting hurt."

The three boats abandoned by the PT 107—PTs 104, 106, and 108—now without radar coverage, patrolled aimlessly through Blackett Strait, dodged an attack by an enemy floatplane, and then headed back toward Rendova. In a 2015 interview for this book, Chester Williams, then quartermaster on the PT 106, stressed the chaotic reality of the experience aboard the American vessels: "That battle was very, very confused. The PT boats were all separated. We did not fire any torpedoes that night because we were out of position. We were all positioned in the wrong places. It was a black night. We never saw anything; it was too dark."

Back at the Rendova PT boat base, Commander Thomas Warfield whipsawed between following a hesitant, hands-off approach and a sporadic urge to exert direct control over events by radioing orders. Years after the skirmish, he described the night as "pandemonium," and tried to deflect blame onto his boat captains in the field, claiming: "There wasn't much discipline in those boats. There really wasn't any way to control them very well. I just had to leave them pretty much up to their own judgment. Some of them stayed in position. Some of them got bugged and didn't fire when they should have." Warfield continued, "A lot of these skippers were pretty green, hell yes, we could hear them hollering, they were all excited and all hell broke loose and they fired their torpedoes, you'd think the damn war was starting all over again."

At one point that evening, an enraged Warfield called into his microphone, "What the hell is the matter with you fellows? Get in there and fight!" This infuriated several of the PT boat skippers, one of whom later compared Warfield to a quarterback directing his team from the sidelines.

Finally, the Japanese destroyers, now moving at high speed,

came into range of the Americans' fourth picket line—the three PT boats of Division R commanded by PT 174's Russell Rome, who was alerted to the approach of the incoming Tokyo Express by directly observing flashes, searchlights, and gunfire to the west. Rome spotted the outlines of a destroyer that seemed to be guarding the entrance to Blackett Strait from Ferguson Passage, not far off the coast of Kolombangara; and at 12:25 A.M., Rome's PT 174 fired its spread of four "fish" (torpedoes) from a range of 1,000 yards. All missed their targets. Pursued by a Japanese floatplane attempting to strafe the PT 174, Rome then decided to withdraw toward Rendova, which would leave behind the two other boats in his division—the PT 103, which fired four torpedoes from an impossibly long range of 4,000 yards, and PT 105, skippered by Lieutenant Richard Keresey.

Keresey experienced a scene of total confusion in Blackett Strait. He sensed Rome was panicking, which "scared the hell" out of him. In what Keresey remembered as "the shrill voice of a man gripped by fear," Rome shouted over the radio: "I have fired torpedoes! I am under heavy fire from Jap destroyers! I am under heavy fire! Shells all around me!" Keresey realized Rome was not being shelled by a destroyer but rather was being bombed by Japanese planes drawn to his high-speed wake.

"What the hell is he talking about?" Keresey mused aloud. He radioed Rome to ask, "Where is the target, over?"

"Get out of there, you're in a trap, you're in a trap!" came the screaming response from Rome. "Get out!"

"That son of a bitch fired his torpedoes and ran," Keresey growled to one of his crewmen.

Then Keresey was stunned to get an angry radio message directly from Commander Warfield at Rendova: "Get out of there!"

Keresey recalled bitterly, "I was getting a direct order from base command to carry out the orders of a dingbat [Lieutenant Rome] who'd done a complete funk, had fired torpedoes from out of range, and then had run away, leaving me without radar guidance." Keresey remembered, "There was more confusion in that battle than at any time in the history of PT boats. We had fifteen boats. Everybody attacked on their own. Nobody communicated anything of any value. Shouts and screams on the radio were all I heard."

Keresey decided to ignore Warfield's order to retreat. "Don't do it," he thought to himself. "What the hell does he know sitting in a dugout fifty miles away? There are enemy ships to the north of the 105. If I carry out his order, I'll miss the chance to do what we came all the way out here to do. But if I don't turn around, I may find myself court-martialed."

Just then Warfield radioed an order to all the vessels: "Boats that have fired torpedoes return to base. All others return to station."

Kennedy condemned Warfield's instructions as "the dumbest order in the entire dumb-ass operation." He added, "This rattled me no end. If you think these things are conducted with great skill and aplomb, forget it."

In the forward gun turret of the PT 105, Keresey's gunner's mate spotted an enemy destroyer. Keresey ordered two torpedoes to be fired, which sailed off target. Their position exposed, a Japanese floatplane swooped down and dropped bombs toward the PT 105, which also missed.

Keresey chose to stay out on patrol by himself and try to attack the Tokyo Express on its return voyage. He decided he'd rather face the possibility of a court-martial than turn tail and run away from the enemy.

———

So far that night, fifteen American PT boats had fired twenty-four torpedoes, every one of which had missed the Japanese convoy. Unscathed and undeterred, the ships of the Tokyo Express arrived at the Vila Plantation garrison on the island of Kolombangara at 12:30 A.M. and began efficiently offloading their supplies and cargo. Nine hundred Japanese soldiers streamed off the ships to reinforce the outpost. Their mission complete, the *Amagiri, Shigure, Arashi,* and *Hagikaze* headed back on their return voyage to Rabaul at around 2 A.M.

Kennedy's PT 109 and four other PT boats remained in Blackett Strait, while five more waited outside the strait. The first American craft to encounter the homebound Tokyo Express was Richard Keresey's PT 105, which was stationed just inside Blackett Strait near Ferguson Passage. Gunfire around the Kolombangara coast, possibly from Japanese shore batteries on the island, illuminated the outline of a destroyer some 2,000 yards away to the east of Keresey's position, traveling slowly to the north at a speed of about 10 knots. Keresey fired his two remaining torpedoes at the enemy ship. They missed.

By now, Kennedy's and Lowrey's boats had moved north of Kolombangara, in the direction of the island of Vella Lavella, groping for direction. By chance at 2 A.M. they linked up with another "lost boat," Lieutenant (jg) Philip Potter's PT 169 from the now-scattered Division A. The three American vessels drifted in the darkness, but soon they had trouble staying together. Kennedy suggested to Lowrey and Potter by VHF radio that they should try to link up with other remaining PT boats. They agreed, and began motoring to the southeast, each carrying their full load of four torpedoes.

When the three PT boats arrived at their new patrol area, they drifted apart again in the darkness, and soon were separated by wide gaps of several thousand yards or more. They did not realize that William Liebenow's PT 157 had also wound up in the same general area, still observing radio silence and himself unaware of where any other PT boats were. "We didn't know what the score was," recalled the PT 109's Barney Ross, "so we resumed our patrolling back and forth with the other boat," Lowrey's PT 162.

Richard Keresey, commanding the PT 105 several miles east, issued an open broadcast warning by radio shortly after 2 A.M.: "Destroyers coming up through the passage. Have fired fish [his two remaining torpedoes] and am withdrawing through Ferguson Passage." It is not known if Kennedy heard this on the often unreliable ship-to-ship radio. No one was issuing clear details of what was going on, either from Blackett Strait or from Commander Warfield's command tent at Rendova. Warfield himself was making no coherent effort to coordinate the overall action. With radio communications so fragmentary and visibility so limited, Kennedy, Potter, and Lowrey apparently still had little concrete information on either the earlier skirmishing in Blackett Strait or the exact trajectory of the Tokyo Express. The PT 109 was now separated in the darkness from the nearest PT boat, the 162, by a distance of several thousand feet—at, or beyond, the limits of visual contact.

As the clock passed 2:15 A.M., Kennedy was at the wheel in the cockpit of the PT 109, with radioman John Maguire standing next to him. Harold Marney manned the forward gun turret. Barney Ross was acting as lookout on the forward deck near the 37 mm gun. Pappy McMahon was on watch at his post down in the engine room. Raymond Albert stood watch near the machine gun on the port side of the boat, gunner Raymond Starkey was acting as lookout in the rear gun turret, and Gerard Zinser was on the deck, having just come off watch. Four men were not up and alert: Ensign Lenny Thom was reclined on the port, or left, side of the deck, while Charles Harris, William Johnston, and Andrew Kirksey were off duty, relaxing or dozing on the deck.

The boat was caressed by a gentle ocean breeze and the sound of water lapping at its sides. Only one of the PT 109's three 1,500-horsepower engines were engaged; the rest were idling to cut down the boat's telltale wake, which also allowed the crew to better hear the approach of the PT's nemesis, Japanese float-planes. According to Kennedy, visibility "was poor—the sky was cloudy—and there was a heavy mist over the water."

Suddenly, Ensign Ross, the night-blind night lookout on the bow of PT 109, sensed an immense shape less than 1,000 yards away, and closing rapidly.

"Ship at two o'clock!"

When Lieutenant Kennedy heard the warning shouted by Harold Marney from the forward .50-caliber machine-gun turret, he had less than twenty seconds to react.

At first Kennedy thought it was another PT boat, but he quickly sensed the massive hull of a Japanese warship looming like a wall speeding for the right side of his boat, which at 80 feet long was less than a third of the size and height of the Japanese vessel. According to Kohei Hanami, the Japanese commander of the approaching destroyer *Amagiri,* its speed was 34 knots.

"Lenny, look at this," Kennedy said matter-of-factly. Ensign Thom, who had been lying on the deck outside the cockpit, stood up to behold the awesome sight of a Japanese warship bearing down on them on a collision course.

"As soon as I decided it was a destroyer," Kennedy recalled of seeing the phosphorescent wake of the *Amagiri*'s bow barreling toward him, "I turned to make a torpedo run."

Kennedy thought, impossibly, of firing one of his notoriously unreliable and inaccurate Mark VIII torpedoes straight at the target like a Wild West gunslinger, evidently hoping a lucky hit would detonate near the enemy vessel's bow, somehow deflect it off its path, and save the thirteen souls he had aboard his boat, including his own.

To achieve this, Kennedy would need to engage his two idling engines, rotate his 56-ton PT 109 to starboard by 30 degrees and into a firing position, and simultaneously command his crew to line up a deck-launched torpedo shot at a target that was speeding north toward them at the point-blank range of a thousand yards. Kennedy apparently did not seriously consider the option of trying to move out of the way of the oncoming vessel—there was no time. Instead, he chose to confront it in the seconds that remained.

"Sound general quarters!" Kennedy told his radioman John Maguire, who was standing beside him.

Maguire relayed the order with a shout, "General quarters!" and turned the keys to prepare to fire the boat's torpedoes. Within a few seconds, the enemy destroyer was so close Maguire heard excited Japanese voices coming from its deck. The Japanese ship was "hauling ass" for a direct collision. Maguire grasped the Miraculous Medal hanging around his neck and began to pray. "Mary, conceived without sin, pray for us. . . ."

On the foredeck, Barney Ross moved to jam a shell into the 37 mm antitank gun that had been lashed on to the deck the previous afternoon. But the breech was closed—dooming his slim chances of getting off a shot in time. Out of the darkness, the *Amagiri* rose before him, its size multiplying with each quickened heartbeat.

"It was the first time I'd ever seen an enemy ship," Ross later recalled. "The next thing I knew he was turning into us. We all shouted at once. Kennedy started turning the boat. It happened fast, very fast." Like a predator closing on its prey, the Japanese destroyer strained toward the PT 109. From Ross's perspective, the *Amagiri* was making such a hard, sharp turn that its mast was at a 45-degree angle to the water.

"He turned into us, going like hell," Kennedy recalled.

Their fate now inescapably upon them, several members of the crew were too stunned and helpless to move. Some felt their feet were gripped by a strange paralysis.

"This is how it feels to be killed," thought the PT 109's skipper.

At 2:27 A.M. the night air was shattered by the sound of the steel bow of the *Amagiri* cracking into the wooden hull and steel sections of the PT 109. The Japanese destroyer "broke out of the mist on top of the PT 109," Kennedy later recounted, "and smashed into it." The sharp bow of the *Amagiri* pierced the PT 109 near its front starboard torpedo tube, close to the cockpit where Kennedy was stationed. In the cockpit, Lieutenant Kennedy was knocked down from the impact and crashed hard against a steel bulkhead, which may have injured one of his spinal disks. Now on his back, Kennedy looked up and saw the Japanese destroyer plowing through the gun turret of his boat just a few feet away. A flash of bright light exploded and illuminated the destroyer.

The *Amagiri* proceeded to cut through the PT 109 diagonally, crunching open the boat's unarmored mahogany hull like a wooden toy, and shearing off a large piece of the starboard stern, or right rear, portion of the vessel.

Much of the boat's stern quickly sank below the surface of the water.

Kennedy recalled, "I can best compare it to the onrushing trains in the old-time movies. They seemed to come right over you. Well, the feeling was the same, only the destroyer didn't come over us, it went right through us."

Two sailors, nineteen-year-old Harold William Marney and twenty-five-year-old father of two Andrew Jackson Kirksey, vanished in the collision, never to be seen again. Marney had been stationed in the starboard (right-hand side) gun turret, directly in the path of the *Amagiri*'s bow, and he had shouted out the first warning as the enemy ship charged toward the PT 109. Kirksey was lying down on the aft (rear) starboard side of the boat, also squarely in the impact area. Both men were incapacitated by the impact of the crash and explosion, if not killed instantly; their bodies likely descended underwater with the wood and metal wreckage of the boat's aft section. No trace of them was ever found. Kirksey's eerie premonitions had been realized: he and Marney joined the estimated 331 PT men who were killed in action during the war.

A hundred-foot-high fireball rose from the crash site, fed by thousands of gallons of fuel that spilled into the water from the crippled boat. Despite the night's poor visibility, the inferno was visible for miles.

The crash propelled seven of the thirteen men into the blazing ocean, most of them wearing life jackets and helmets: Ray Starkey, Raymond Albert, Gerard Zinser, William Johnston, Charles Harris, George Ross, and John Maguire. They fell into a world of horror—a black, shark-infested ocean punctuated by pockets of flaming gasoline, lethal fumes, and muffled shouts and screams, with their boat nowhere to be seen. As they struggled in the water and gulped salt water and gasoline, they had every reason to believe they could very soon be drowned, consumed by fire, or eaten alive from beneath.

At first, only Kennedy and Edman Mauer remained on the wreckage of the boat—a piece of the craft's bow that stayed afloat because of its sealed watertight compartments. Mauer had been knocked onto the deck, sustaining a bruise to his right shoulder.

Radioman John Maguire was thrown out of the cockpit onto the canopy atop the dayroom, then tumbled into the ocean. He glimpsed that a part of the Japanese ship was aflame, probably from burning gasoline from the PT 109 splashing onto the vessel, and he recalled hearing two "cannon" shots coming from the ship, which corresponds with Lieutenant Commander Hanami's report of his rear gunners firing back at the wreckage. Maguire quickly climbed onto the boat's wreckage, joining Kennedy and Mauer.

The only sailor belowdecks at the time of the collision was Motor Machinist's Mate "Pappy" McMahon, who was down in the engine room, in the boat's rear. The *Amagiri* sliced straight through McMahon's position, thrusting him painfully against the boat's auxiliary generator. He wondered if the boat had hit an underwater obstacle: "I felt a hell of a jar," he recalled. "I thought we had hit a rock." Gathering himself, he looked up through an open hatch in the forward of the engine room and screamed, "Oh my God! There's fire!" Then he clinched his lips. In training he had been told not to breathe in case of fire, because the boat's aviation fuel would roast a man's lungs on contact.

A blast of fire hit McMahon, followed by a curtain of water as the sea rushed in. The stern of the boat began sinking, pulling the PT 109's motormac down with it. Kennedy described the scene: "McMahon was thrown against the starboard bulkhead. A tremendous burst of flame from the exploding gas tanks covered him. He pulled his knees up close to his chest and waited to die." According to Kennedy, McMahon was dragged underwater by the momentum of the *Amagiri*'s churning propellers, pulled directly underneath them, and was pounded, twisted, and turned below the surface until, incredibly, he popped up nearly five hundred yards from the wreckage of the PT boat.

Unfortunately, McMahon came to the surface inside a large

Harold Marney (left in right photo), the nineteen-year-old gunner's mate who shouted the first warning of danger as a Japanese destroyer was about to hit the PT 109. He was never seen again. Pictured in photo at right with his brother Roland Marney, home on leave in Springfield, Mass. (Dennis Harkins & Frank J. Andruss Sr.)

gasoline fire. "I hit the surface, right in flames," McMahon remembered. "How I ever got out of there I don't know." His face, chest, and limbs were seared by fire, and his whole body was consumed in pain. He frantically beat his hands in the ocean, trying to clear a safe patch of water.

George "Barney" Ross mistook the first burst of flames from the collision for a searchlight, and was afraid that Japanese troops above were about to open fire. He was also scared of getting snagged in the ropes that held the 37 mm gun to the deck, so he lowered himself into the water and took shelter behind the boat's hull. There he witnessed the gasoline ignite, which he described as "not an explosion but a terrific roar."

Once in the water, Ross choked and passed out amid the gasoline fumes.

Motor Machinist's Mate Second Class William Johnston was asleep on the deck when the collision flipped him overboard. He glimpsed fire and the shape of the Japanese destroyer and its sailors scampering around the deck. Like McMahon, Johnston then was pulled underwater by the force of the ship's pounding propeller, where he was spun around, shaken, and pummeled by the thrust of the churning water. Johnston's lungs exploded with the pain of drowning; he realized he was being pushed to the ocean floor. He was tempted to surrender to the water, but then he thought of his wife, Nathalie. Fighting his way up toward a bright glow, he surfaced, battered but alive, in a pool of burning gasoline, frantically trying to push it away. He inhaled gas fumes and began to faint.

Gunner's Mate Charles A. "Bucky" Harris also was asleep on the deck, using his life jacket as a pillow, when a shout awoke him to the terrifying sight of the charging *Amagiri*, now just a few yards away. He jumped up and dove over a torpedo tube, out toward the water. As he was in midair, the Japanese destroyer hit the PT 109.

A flying object struck Harris, propelling him sideways in the air and injuring his leg. Once in the water, he somersaulted upright into a floating seated position, grateful that somehow his life jacket wound up around his neck, untied. Soon his leg went completely numb.

When the Japanese destroyer struck, Motor Machinist's Mate First Class Gerard Zinser had just come off deck watch. "Before I knew what had hit," he recalled, "I was flying head over heels." The impact thrust him into the ocean, where he burned his arm and chest in the flaming water. He remembered, "I was hurled into the air. I was unconscious ten to fifteen minutes. When I woke up there was a lot of small fires. I heard other voices."

Crewman Raymond Starkey was slammed down on the deck by the collision and also tumbled into the water. Seeing flames everywhere, he wondered, as he began to pass out, if this was what Hell looked like.

Meanwhile, the *Amagiri,* raced away into the void, leaving a trail of fire in its wake.

Minutes earlier, aboard the *Amagiri,* nineteen-year-old Gunner's Mate Third-Class Haruyoshi Kimmatsu was standing at his post at the forward Number One gun turret, staring into the blackness ahead and thinking of his home in city of Nagoya.

"Ship ahead off port bow!" called out the Japanese destroyer's lookout.

"Look again!" shouted Commander Kohei Hanami from the bridge, "report instantly!"

Kimmatsu spotted a moving object in the water ahead, shooting toward the *Amagiri* at incredible speed. At first, he could make no sense of what he was seeing—"a sleek, black whale!" he thought. Then he realized it was an American PT boat. Stabbed with fear, he

The *Amagiri*. (John F. Kennedy Library)

felt his guts knot in his torso and he could not breathe. He had never seen the enemy so near.

"Fire! Fire!" yelled Petty Officer Mitsuaki Sawada from the gunnery command. But the target was coming in so low and close that the forward auxiliary gun crew could not fire their weapon in time.

Holding a shell in his hands, Kimmatsu stood motionless at his loading station in the gun turret, his body paralyzed with terror. He knew the two craft were about to collide. Seconds passed, but time felt suspended.

The port torpedo crew was poised at the ready, waiting for the order to fire. But torpedo officer Lieutenant Hiroshi Hosaka realized it was too late, the target was so close the torpedoes would travel right under it.

At nearly the same instant that Commander Hanami snapped an order to Kazuto Doi, the experienced coxswain at the wheel, the piercing klaxon horn of the ship's collision alarm went off, warning of an impending impact.

"Then, at the very last moment the PT answered its helm and seemed about to glide away," remembered Kimmatsu, "the full-throated roar of her mighty motors piercing through the night as if it responded to full throttle." He felt the *Amagiri* throb heavily beneath his feet as the engines strained and accelerated into a hard turn more of more than 23 degrees to starboard. *We're going to run it down,* he felt, *we're going to deliberately ram it lest it escape to strike at us again.*

The night air erupted with the sounds of the crashing impact.

Kimmatsu braced himself for a detonation he felt was sure to follow. "Hard on the heels of the collision, a billowing cloud of flaming gasoline exploded with a loud swoosh against the side of our ship . . . as she rode over the little craft."

Kimmatsu watched in horror as waves of flaming fuel and oil splashed up on to the ship's bridge and washed down onto the pitching main deck, creating pools of crackling, blazing liquid that threatened to engulf men and equipment. Hanami issued orders frantically into the intercom, summoning fire-control teams who attacked the blazes with fire extinguishers. The ship was a bedlam of confusion.

Kimmatsu now was gripped by a frightening realization: "We were sitting ducks in this brightly lighted stage of macabre loneliness, waiting to be torpedoed or shelled in the middle of the sea." Initiating evasive action, the *Amagiri* lurched violently into a turn, tossing Kimmatsu against the gun turret so hard the shell he had been holding flew out of his hands and tumbled toward a group of his friends who were stamping flames. The shell bounced to a stop next to one sailor "whose arm almost instantly shot out in an unbelievable exhibition of adrenalized strength, flicked up the weighty shell and flung it into the sea as it were only a toy."

Kimmatsu fell onto the deck. "Terrified that I would be roasted alive, I tried desperately to cry out, but no sound came from my rasping throat," he remembered. He prepared to die. Looking up, he saw his fellow gunner's mate stagger out of the flaming turret, fall from the ladder and disappear directly into the powder magazine.

Just as a pool of flaming oil was about to wash over him, Kimmatsu was dragged to safety by a team of medical corpsmen, who eventually carried him down to the sick bay. There, he joined several other casualties of burns and smoke inhalation, including the friend he saw fall from the ladder.

"You all right, Haru?" the friend asked, his ankle badly sprained and his face and hair singed by fire. Kimmatsu nodded.

"I fell through the hatch and landed hard on the needles [shells] below," explained his friend.

Meanwhile the ship seemed to be slowing to a dead stop. Commander Hanami had decelerated the *Amagiri* both to diagnose the ship's severe vibrations and to minimize the ship's drafts in an attempt to help the fire-control teams put out the fires. "Following the standard battle practice, we had instantly separated from the other ships and severed all communications so as to not silhouette them for the enemy," Kimmatsu explained years later. "This greatly increased our own danger, since, every moment, the chance of attracting further enemy patrols increased." Kimmatsu also braced himself for the possibility that Japanese shore batteries would mistakenly open up on the *Amagiri*, as it was drifting off its planned course.

Fortunately for the Japanese, the *Amagiri's* fires were quickly extinguished, and the engines were re-engaged to a slower speed to minimize the hammering produced by the damaged propeller. The other ships soon rejoined the *Amagiri* to form a protective escort to safety. Kimmatsu's despair gave way to feelings of relief and confidence that they had met the enemy, defended themselves, and triumphed.

The "Battle of Blackett Strait" ended as the Tokyo Express vanished in the western darkness. On their return journey, the Japanese warships just narrowly missed the six American destroyers of Admiral Arleigh Burke's attack force positioned north of Kolombangara, which had withdrawn around 3:00 a.m. to escape the danger of Japanese air attack at daylight.

PT 105 skipper Richard Keresey summarized the dismal results of the skirmish: "Fifteen PT boats ventured out into Blackett Strait to attack four Japanese destroyers, the best odds PT boats ever had. We fired thirty-two torpedoes, including four from my 105. We hit nothing! The destroyers kept right on going straight down Blackett Strait and then straight back a couple of hours later." He added, "when the 109 got in the way, they ran over it." Similarly, naval historian Commander Robert J. Bulkley, Jr. noted: "This was perhaps the most confused and least effectively executed action the PTs had been in." Years later, John F. Kennedy dismissed the night's events as a "fucked up" series of events.

At the time of the collision, Lieutenant Philip Potter was a few thousand yards away from the PT 109, commanding the PT 169. Potter recalled spotting the Japanese warship from a distance of about two miles, and that they tried to warn Kennedy of the danger: "We radioed Kennedy to look on his starboard bow. There was a bow wake coming directly toward him. No response. Nothing. And I think Lowrey warned Kennedy. But what amazed us was that we got no response from either of the boats." The PT 109 evidently did not receive this radio warning or the similar broadcast a few minutes earlier by Keresey in the PT 105—either because radio operator Maguire was next to Kennedy in the cockpit instead of at the radio belowdecks, or because the message was not picked up on the 109's often unreliable VHF ship-to-ship radio.

According to Potter, "the destroyer rammed the [PT 109] and it blew up. Just shot into flames." He added, "You could see they went right through the boat. There was an immediate explosion and you knew the gas tanks had exploded." Potter's log recorded he had fired two torpedoes at the *Amagiri,* both of which missed. After circling away toward Gizo, he later asserted he returned to look for Kennedy's boat. "We tried to find the 109 and any survivors," he claimed. "We cut our engines, trying to listen for them. But we didn't hear a thing. Then I told Warfield [by radio] the 109 had been hit and we patrolled around, very slowly, stopping and listening." He gave up the search and withdrew toward the Rendova base.

Potter asserted he spent "thirty to forty-five" minutes searching for survivors of the PT 109 but did not find a trace of them. "I'd say we headed for the base around 3:30 to 4 A.M. We usually liked to get out of that area before daylight because the [U.S. Army Air Forces] planes would take over in daylight. You usually feared them more, if you were in Japanese waters, than you did with the Japanese," referring to the recent friendly fire incidents.

At about the same time Kennedy's boat was struck, lookouts aboard John Lowrey's PT 162 identified a Japanese warship, possibly one of the vessels following in the convoy, speeding north some 700 yards away. Lowrey rotated his boat to fire two torpedoes, but for unknown reasons he did not fire. "The PT 162 finally turned to the south-west upon getting within 100 yards of the warship to avoid collision," Thomas Warfield wrote in his after-action report. By this point, according to Warfield, men on the PT 162 had seen the collision involving the PT 109. And yet there is no record of the PT 162 making any attempt to search for survivors of the PT 109, nor is there evidence Warfield commanded them to do so.

And so, inexplicably, the PT boats closest to the PT 109, the 162 and 169, withdrew toward the safety of the Rendova base. Beyond Potter's alleged cursory check, no one bothered to conduct a methodical search for the crew of the PT 109.

To their horror, the eleven survivors would soon realize no one was coming to save them.

7

LOST AT SEA

★

THE SOUTH PACIFIC
2:40 AM, AUGUST 2, 1943

The ocean floor was 1,200 feet below them.

Eleven American sailors were trapped at night on the fiery surface of the Pacific Ocean, struggling to stay alive. They were surrounded by enemy-held islands.

Gasoline fumes invaded their lungs, causing them to gag, retch, and spiral into unconsciousness. As they thrashed in the water, they gobbled volumes of salt water that made them choke harder. They paddled and treaded water, but there was no visible destination to head for. Their life jackets helped them stay on the surface, but soon their waterlogged shoes and clothes threatened to pull them under.

They had no food, no water, no radio, no life raft, no medical supplies, and, it seemed, no way of getting to safety. Most of them were scattered so far apart they could not see each other—some were so isolated they concluded the rest of the crew was dead. They knew the waters were home to sharks and barracuda.

The eight crewmen in the water saw nothing but blackness all

around, punctuated by pockets of burning gasoline. Their PT boat
had all but vanished.

Those who had been burned were slashed by the agonizing pain
of salt water soaking their wounds. They knew they were helpless
against sharks, or against the Japanese if the enemy chose to circle
back to the impact area, flip on searchlights, and strafe them. Worst
of all, they would have felt utterly alone, adrift in a uniquely hostile
chamber of the universe.

Adding to their despair was the appalling realization that, in
the words of PT 157 skipper William Liebenow, "There was no
well-rehearsed or standard plan for rescue operations at sea, there
was no special training in event we were stuck at sea or fell overboard, and no special training in case we were stuck in the ocean."
They were on their own.

On the portion of the PT 109's bow that remained afloat, John
F. Kennedy attempted to regain control of the situation.

"Who's aboard?" the crippled boat's skipper called out. Only
two of the enlisted men, Maguire and Mauer, replied.

The three sailors were desperately clinging to the floating wreckage of the front end of the PT 109. When it seemed nearby flames
might detonate the remaining gas in the boat's tank, Kennedy ordered his men to abandon ship.

"Over the side!" shouted Kennedy. The three men slid into the
water and swam away from the wreckage. But within fifteen minutes the flames died down, and it appeared much of the spilled
gasoline was pushed away by the wake of the *Amagiri*. Kennedy
summoned Maguire and Mauer back toward the wreck. He then
called out again, trying to reach the other crewmen.

Kennedy ordered Mauer to swing his signal blinker around the
bow as a homing beacon for the others. Then he took off his shirt
and shoes and dove into the water to hunt for the living.

The Dawn of War: John F. Kennedy's daughter and U.S. ambassador to Japan Caroline Kennedy provided the author with this private family photograph of her father as a U.S. Navy ensign in 1942. It has never been published by anyone outside the Kennedy family. (Jacqueline Kennedy Onassis Papers, John F. Kennedy Presidential Library)

The PT 109 crew: Besides Kennedy on the far right, others have been tentatively identified as, top row, left to right: Ensign Al Webb (standing far left, friend of the crew), Leon Drawdy, Edgar Mauer, Edmund Drewitch, John Maguire. Bottom row, left to right: Charles Harris, Maurice Kowal, Andrew Kirksey, Ensign Leonard Thom. All except Webb were assigned to the PT 109. Drewitch, Drawdy and Kowal left the boat before the crash on August 2, 1943.

Seven more men, not pictured, were aboard the PT 109 on the night of the crash: George Ross, Patrick McMahon, Harold Marney, Raymond Starkey, Raymond Albert, William Johnston and Gerard Zinser. Kennedy recalled this photo being taken off Guadalcanal in early July 1943, but it may have been taken the previous month. (John F. Kennedy Presidential Library)

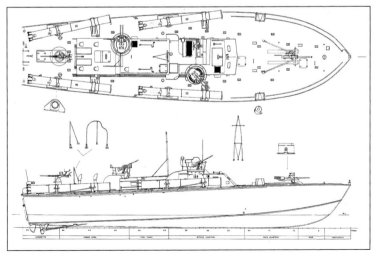

Profile and bird's-eye views of the PT 109.

Kennedy in the cockpit of PT 109. (John F. Kennedy Presidential Library)

This is one of only two known photos of PT 109 in action during Lieutenant (jg) John F. Kennedy's brief command. The photo is heavily water-damaged. The photographer, location and date is unknown, most likely May–June 1943, possibly near Tulagi or the Russell Islands. (Frank J. Andruss Sr.)

Moment of Impact: A 1961 oil painting by official Navy artist Gerard Richardson depicting the moment the PT 109 was rammed by the Japanese destroyer *Amagiri*. (John F. Kennedy Presidential Library)

Captain Frederick Conklin presents the Navy and Marine Corps Medal to JFK at the Chelsea Naval Hospital in Massachusetts, June 12, 1944.

Campaign flyer produced during JFK's presidential run, 1960. Through shrewd marketing and publicity, Joseph P. Kennedy transformed the PT 109 into a chariot that carried his son to the White House.
(Frank J. Andruss Sr.)

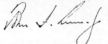

N.º 3

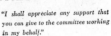

A time for GREATNESS

"I shall appreciate any support that you can give to the committee working in my behalf."

I wish to contribute $.......... (cash, check or money order) to U. S. Senator John F. Kennedy's Presidential campaign fund.

I would appreciate receiving a complimentary replica pin of PT Boat 109.

Please send the free replica pin to:

Name ....

Address ....

City ....State ....

Senator JOHN F. KENNEDY
for President
HEADQUARTERS: 261 CONSTITUTION AVE., N. W., WASHINGTON 1, D. C.

A PT 109–themed "float" (actually a real PT boat, the 796, repainted) carries surviving crew members past the viewing stand of newly sworn-in President Kennedy during the inaugural parade in Washington, D.C., on January 20, 1961.
(John F. Kennedy Presidential Library)

"Without PT 109," said JFK's aide David Powers, "there never would have been a President John F. Kennedy." (Elliott Erwitt, Magnum Photos)

The eight other survivors were scattered and spread out around a wide debris field dotted with pockets of flaming 100-octane fuel. Some were treading water in pools of unignited gasoline. Of those, Zinser, McMahon, and Ross were choking or unconscious from the fumes, and Johnston was retching from gasoline he swallowed while struggling in the water. Three of the eight, McMahon, Zinser, and Johnston, were burned—McMahon the worst of them, having suffered second- and third-degree burns on his upper body.

"Mr. Kennedy! Mr. Kennedy!" shouted Gunner's Mate Charles Harris from a hundred yards away to the southwest. "McMahon is badly hurt!"

Kennedy swam out to meet them. "Is that you, Pops?" he asked the seriously burned McMahon. "How are you, Mac?"

The sailor replied stoically, "I'm all right, I'm kind of burnt." In fact, he was in shock. He couldn't move his arms and hands, and was in no shape to swim.

"How are the others?" asked Kennedy.

"I hurt my leg," reported Harris. Kennedy, who had been on the Harvard swimming team five years earlier, towed McMahon by the strap of his life jacket and headed for the PT 109 wreckage, while simultaneously encouraging Harris, who labored to swim with only one working leg. It was a tough crossing, done against the wind and "very strong current" that were slowly drawing the survivors away from the wreckage.

"McMahon and I were about an hour getting back to the boat," Kennedy remembered of the ordeal.

At one point, Harris despaired, "I can't go any farther," prompting fellow Bostonian Kennedy to wisecrack, "For a guy from Boston, you're certainly putting up a great exhibition out here, Harris!"

"Go to hell," snapped Harris as he struggled in the water.

"I was a good swimmer," explained Harris, who had competed on a Navy swim team. "But I had two problems: my jacket and sweater, and my knee. I hit my knee on something when I went over the side, and I thought it was broken. Kennedy helped me get out of my jacket and sweater, but after that, I made it to the boat on my own."

Elsewhere, machinist's mate Gerard Zinser had awoken in the water to the sounds of crew members' screams and the blinding agony of salt water soaking his burn wounds. He struggled back toward the wreckage.

George Ross regained consciousness some distance from the boat, only to be set upon by an incoherent, babbling Ensign Lenny Thom, who was trying to climb on top of him as if Ross was a log.

"Lenny, Lenny," yelled Ross, "it's me!"

Zinser was floating nearby, and joined Ross in slapping Thom around, hoping he'd regain his senses.

"Mr. Thom is drowning!" yelled Zinser. "Bring the boat!"

On the remains of the PT 109, Edman Mauer and John Maguire heard the commotion and now realized at least two more crew members were alive. They decided to launch a rescue of their own. While Mauer kept swinging the boat's blinker device on the bow as a guiding signal, Maguire fastened a rope to the wreckage and, clutching the free end, swam out into the gasoline-choked water and fumes to search for his crewmates, hollering out their names.

Maguire managed to link up with Gerard Zinser, Barney Ross, and Lenny Thom and guided them toward to the bow's hull. On the way, Zinser screamed, "Please, God, don't let me pass out! Bring the boat!"

"Goddamn it, there is no boat!" Maguire replied.

Lieutenant Kennedy swam over to the group to help escort

Zinser to the boat. But Zinser was at the limits of his endurance. He recalled, "At one point, I wanted to give up, too. My body was terribly burned, and the pain from the swelling and stinging was almost more than I could bear."

Kennedy grabbed Zinser's shoulder, shook him, and shouted, "I will not allow you to die!"

Meanwhile, Ensign Thom, who had by now regained his senses, spotted the semiconscious form of William Johnston. Leaving the group and Maguire's tethered line to attempt a rescue of his crewmate, Thom reached Johnston, who was delirious after swallowing gasoline, inhaling gas fumes, and suffering burns on his neck.

"Come on, Bill, let's go," Thom urged Johnson. "Let's keep paddling." Towing Johnston against the Blackett Strait's swift current, it took Thom as long as three hours to get Johnston back to the wreckage.

Still elsewhere, in the wake of the collision, crewman Raymond Starkey found himself floating on top of a mattress with minor burns on his hands and face, seemingly alone in the middle of the ocean. He was enveloped in darkness, and he was in despair.

"Oh my God, oh my God," Starkey said to himself as he pondered the danger of sharks—the Solomon Islands were home to numerous species, including the feared oceanic whitetip, ten-foot-long marauders of deep water who had preyed on shipwreck survivors for centuries. His thoughts drifted to his wife, Camille, and four-year-old daughter, Shirley. Finally he spotted the wreckage of the PT 109 several hundred yards away and swam over to join the others. Eventually, after enduring a similar ordeal, crewman Raymond Albert found his way to the wreckage as well. (Although Kennedy was later credited in some accounts with personally rescuing three men—McMahon, Harris and Starkey—the evidence suggests he directly saved only McMahon. He did aid Harris, which may or may not have been crucial to the crewman's survival, but Starkey got back to the boat by himself.)

Finally, more than three hours after the collision, eleven survivors were gathered on and around the floating remains of the PT 109. Throughout the dark morning Kennedy and others called out for the two missing crewmen, "Kirksey! Marney!" No reply ever came.

McMahon was suffering from extremely painful burns on his hands, face, arms, legs, and feet. Johnston and Zinser were burned less severely, while other crewmen were variously battered and bruised. Despite their suffering, the survivors were happy to be alive, and they waited for a rescue they were sure would arrive soon. Mauer furtively signaled with the blinker device to summon other PT boats that might be in the area.

But no rescue was coming. The two boats that had been closest to the PT 109, the PT 169 and PT 162, had long ago vanished into the dark. John Maguire recalled bitterly, "We were waiting for the other PT boats to come back. Those sons of bitches ran away from us."

One piece of equipment that survived the collision was the boat's Very pistol, or flare gun. Kennedy decided not to fire it, for fear of attracting the enemy, but this may have been a costly mistake. If he had sent up a distress signal soon after the crash, it might have been spotted by Lowrey, Potter, or Liebenow, and they could have investigated and found the survivors. Harris remembered, "We had a Very pistol, but we didn't shoot it off because we didn't know what had happened yet. We were in Japanese waters, and we didn't want the Japanese coming out after us."

Kennedy added, "We figured the Japs would be sure to get us in the morning, but everyone was tired and we slept."

They drifted south throughout the night in the direction of Ferguson Passage, beyond which was the Solomon Sea—and thousands of square miles of open ocean.

When the sun rose, the eleven survivors still clung to pieces of their crippled boat.

Flanked by enemy-held islands, the floating wreckage of the PT 109 could easily be seen from at least two Japanese outposts. It stuck out, remembered Barney Ross, "like a sore thumb."

Three miles to their northeast loomed the massive shape of Kolombangara Island, which one visitor described as "right out of a King Kong movie." It was home to a garrison of 10,000 Japanese troops. About a mile to the southwest was Gizo Island, the site of another Japanese outpost of more than 200 troops. To the east were the Japanese-held islands of Arundel and New Georgia, and five miles west was Vella Lavella, also controlled by the enemy.

If Japanese spotters were positioned at the proper elevations and positions on either Kolombangara or Gizo, they could see the wreckage with the naked eye; with the aid of field glasses or a telescope, they could have identified the figures as Americans.

The PT 109 survivors were almost within range of Japanese artillery guns based on Kolombangara.

"What do you want to do if the Japs come out?" Kennedy asked his men. "Fight or surrender?"

"Fight with what?" a voice asked. They had little in the way of firepower, only six .45-caliber automatic pistols, one .38, one Thompson submachine gun, a flashlight, a battle lantern, and three knives. They had the flare gun, but they still were reluctant to fire it for fear of alerting Japanese forces, who were becoming notorious for their barbaric mistreatment of prisoners of war.

"Well," asked Kennedy, "what do you want to do?"

"Anything you say, Mr. Kennedy," replied one sailor. "You're the boss."

"There's nothing in the book about a situation like this," said Kennedy. "Seems to me we're not a military organization anymore. Let's just talk this over." He continued: "A lot of you men have families and some of you have children. What do you want to do? I have nothing to lose."

"If they [the Japanese] do come out, we will see them before they get here," suggested Mauer. "If it seems that we have any chance at all, let's fight. But if they send out three or four barges with enough men to overwhelm us, let's surrender. We're no good to anybody dead." But, he added, he would follow any orders Kennedy decided to issue. Zinser agreed, saying they should estimate the size of any approaching Japanese force before they decided what to do.

A more immediate concern was the precarious nature of their "life raft." The daylight revealed the remains of the boat were underwater all the way up to the bow. Some 15 feet of the 80-foot-long boat were poking out of the water at a 45-degree angle, right side up. By 10 A.M. the bow of the wreckage was slowly rolling upside down, still floating, and the two most severely injured crewmen, William Johnston and Patrick McMahon, had to be carefully repositioned on the upturned hull. On Kennedy's order, the others hugged the deck and stayed down as low and still as possible to avoid being spotted by Japanese lookouts. It is not known whether the rear portion of the PT 109 was severed completely by the crash and sank quickly, or if it remained partially attached below the waterline. Naval historians Clay and Joan Blair have speculated the latter was the case: "The rear section, containing the three heavy engines, was badly mangled and sank below the water and the bow lifted to an angle of perhaps 30 to 40 degrees."

"If I ever get out of this," someone quipped, "I'll never ride a PT boat again!" Curses erupted against the Navy, the entire war, and the PT crews who had abandoned them. The men peered hopefully at the southern sky looking for a low-flying American PBY search-and-rescue plane, but none came. As the hours passed, the men were increasingly amazed that it seemed no one was looking for them. The tantalizing sight of Allied-held Rendova Peak was barely visible some thirty-eight miles to the south.

The bow of the boat was rotating such that the smooth, slippery keel was faceup, and soon there was nothing for the men to grasp on to. By 1 P.M. it seemed clear the boat would soon sink, and that there was no rescue under way. The crew would have to seek shelter on land before dark.

"We clung to the unburned bow of the boat for nearly 12 hours," remembered Kennedy, "and we left it only when it was just a foot above water."

The question was where to go.

Kennedy quickly ruled out several islands that looked big enough to contain Japanese troops. Spotting the shape of a tiny island farther away, east of Gizo, Kennedy decided they should head for it, as it looked small enough to be of no practical use to the enemy. Called Kasolo, meaning "Gods of Paradise," by native Solomon Islanders, it had been dubbed Plum Pudding Island by homesick English colonial authorities, who thought its outline vaguely resembled the shape of the traditional English dessert.

"We will swim to that small island," said Kennedy, pointing out their destination. "We have less chance of making it than some of these other islands here, but there'll be less chance of Japs, too."

As Ross remembered, "The boat didn't look like it would make it through another night. That land over there looked pretty good and reasonably attainable. I think we did the right thing. If I had to do it again, I wouldn't stay with the boat."

"I'll take McMahon with me," said Kennedy. "The rest of you can swim together on this plank. Thom will be in charge."

"Will we ever get out of this?" a voice wondered.

"It can be done," declared Kennedy. "We'll do it."

At one point McMahon said, "Go on, skipper, you go on. I've had it."

"Mac," said Kennedy, "you and I will go together."

"I'll just keep you back," countered McMahon. "You go on with the other men—don't worry about me."

"What in the hell are you talking about?" cried Kennedy. "Get your butt in the water!"

"Skipper," pleaded the badly burned McMahon, "I can't make it. Leave me here."

"You're coming, Pappy," replied the officer. "Only the good die young."

McMahon felt death was very near. The prospect of getting back in the salt water with such severe burns must have seemed a needless agony. But Kennedy insisted, eventually persuading him into the water. The PT 109's skipper grasped the strap of McMahon's kapok in his teeth, and at about 2 P.M. began towing him in the direction of the small island, swimming in intervals of fifteen minutes or so, then stopping to rest. "The skipper swam the breast-stroke," remembered McMahon, "carrying me on his back, with the leather strap of my kapok clenched between his teeth."

"How do you feel, Mac?" asked Kennedy during one of their breaks.

McMahon, lying on his back with his face to the sky, replied, "I'm okay, Mr. Kennedy, how about you?" When he asked, "How far do we have to go now?" Kennedy told him they were doing well.

McMahon was amazed by how cool and confident Kennedy

appeared, as if it were a routine maneuver. In later years, Kennedy was fond of quoting Ernest Hemingway's definition of courage as "grace under pressure," and in this moment, as well as many others to come during the ordeal, he would live it.

While Kennedy pulled the wounded McMahon, the other nine sailors gathered around an improvised floatation device they made from two-by-eight wooden planks salvaged from the 37 mm anti-tank gun mount. The nine men attached their shoes and lantern to one of the timber planks, and began kicking and paddling themselves toward the little island in the far distance. Mauer and Johnston, in particular, clung for their lives to the float, as neither knew how to swim.

The two officers in the main group, Thom and Ross, alternatively exhorted and encouraged the others. Still, a few of the men lost hope during the journey.

"If we go on like this, we'll all be lost," griped one of the men.

"As far as I'm concerned, I'm going to stay here," said Mauer. "You swim by yourself if you want to."

Thom countered, "I'm giving orders here. We all stick together."

During the arduous three-and-a-half-mile swim, Ross, who had tied his shoes around his head, lost them as he struggled in the water. Maguire had to let go of the heavy tommy gun, which dropped away into the sea toward the ocean floor more than a thousand feet below.

The longest Olympic swimming event ever staged before then, the men's 4,000-meter freestyle race, was held only once, in 1900. Fourteen of the twenty eight competitors registered a result of "did not finish," and the distance was promptly retired. On the afternoon of August 2, 1943, John F. Kennedy covered that same distance, plus a mile more, over open water, behind enemy lines in broad daylight, fully exposed for four hours to any Japanese lookouts or pilots who happened to look his way. All the while, he bit on to a strap and towed a badly burned sailor along with him. Simultaneously he was charged with leading nine other men, including several injured and several non-swimmers, toward safety. It was a performance Kennedy would rarely talk about publicly, but it was an astonishing feat that his crewmen never forgot. On this day, his leadership and example delivered them the hope, however slim, that salvation may be on the horizon.

After nearly four hours, Kennedy touched solid ground in the shores off Plum Pudding Island, at about 6 P.M., still towing McMahon by the strap gripped in his teeth. The two men's limbs were slashed and bruised on sharp coral as they struggled through shallow water onto the beach. With his feet still in the water, an exhausted Kennedy planted his face on the dry sand, and rested awhile. He had been in the ocean for much of the last sixteen hours, and he vomited repeatedly due to the salt water he ingested while towing McMahon. Neither he or the badly burned McMahon could walk, so they crawled on their hands and knees across ten feet of beach to take cover in the trees and bushes of the tiny island. The other nine survivors arrived soon after. They lay there behind bushes, recovering from the swim, breathing hard, and gazing at the massive outline of enemy-held Kolombangara Island across the passage.

The survivors of the PT 109 had joined the grim fraternity of history's shipwrecked "castaways," the most famous of whom, British buccaneer Alexander Selkirk, was stranded on another South Pacific island for four years and four months before being rescued in 1709, and inspiring Daniel Defoe's novel *Robinson Crusoe*. After a dispute with his captain, Selkirk was abandoned on a rugged

The Death Zone: tiny Plum Pudding Island, the first land reached by the ship-wrecked crew of PT 109. (nativeiowan.wordpress.com)

29-square-mile volcanic island 418 miles west of Chile. He was left with a musket, a pistol, gunpowder, a knife and hatchet, navigation tools, a bedroll, a cooking pot, some clothes, small quantities of tobacco, cheese and rum, and a Bible. He survived largely on prayer, crayfish, local vegetables, and his favorite meal of feral goat broth sprinkled with cabbage palm, watercress, turnips, and black pimento pepper. When he was rescued by another British bucca-neer ship on February 2, 1709, Selkirk was a wild-looking, bearded creature clothed in goatskins. According to one of his rescuers he "so much forgot his Language for want of Use, that we could scarce understand him, for he seem'd to speak his words by halves." Sel-kirk recovered and went back to sea for eleven years, before dying aboard the HMS *Weymouth* off the coast of Africa. His body was dumped overboard.

Curiously, John Kennedy and his crewmen were not the only

American castaways in the area, for on the neighboring, much larger Japanese-held island of Arundel, another dramatic saga was unfolding. There, a shipwrecked U.S. Navy lieutenant named Hugh Barr Miller was hiding in the jungle, living off the land and waging a one-man war against vastly superior Japanese forces. After his destroyer, the *Strong*, was torpedoed a month earlier, on July 4, 1943, Miller scavenged among Japanese barge wrecks for weapons and supplies. He ambushed and wiped out a Japanese patrol with grenades, collected valuable intelligence by observing Japanese movements on nearby Kolombangara, and gathered a satchel full of Japanese documents. A U.S. Marine Corps pilot finally spotted him on the beach on August 16 and realized his red beard marked him as an American. Soon a seaplane landed to pick up Miller, who had lost forty pounds to malnutrition. Under the noses of Japanese forces a mere 2,000 yards away on Kolombangara, Miller struggled out to meet the rubber boat sent over by his rescuers. As he was being evacuated, his arms clutched a cache of Japanese intelligence materials he had captured during his forty-three-day ordeal.

On the other side of Blackett Strait, on Plum Pudding Island in the late afternoon of August 2, the survivors of PT 109 were just beginning their suffering. At least they were on dry land, they reasoned, and it looked like there were no Japanese troops on the tiny island.

Suddenly, however, the men were startled to hear the mechanical hum of a vessel approaching.

They peered through the bushes, and were horrified to see a Japanese barge slowly passing by a few hundred yards off the beach. The American crewmen were in no condition to fight, and they had only a few knives and waterlogged small arms to defend themselves. If the Japanese had seen the PT 109's explosion and were searching for survivors, the Americans had little chance to avoid capture and the inevitable torment that would follow as POWs.

But instead of stopping, the barge glided past them in the direction of the Japanese outpost at Gizo Island. The weak and wounded William Johnston wondered aloud, "They wouldn't come here. What'd they be walking around here for? It's too small."

The survivors slowly fanned out to explore the island, careful to remain hidden behind the foliage.

Nearby, John Kennedy lay sprawled out in the bushes, exhausted.

"If I were a king," wrote the famed American author and journalist Jack London, "the worst punishment I could inflict on my enemies would be to banish them to the Solomons." He added, "On second thought, I don't think I'd have the heart to do it." In 1907, London attempted to circumnavigate the globe from San Francisco in a 45-foot sailboat, but the voyage ended in the Solomon Islands, where London was attacked by venomous centipedes, contracted skin ulcers and malaria, and fell victim to a mystery illness that paralyzed his hands and sent him into months of recovery in an Australian hospital.

At first, the survivors of the PT 109 thought their new Solomon Island home offered a tantalizing promise of survival. Measuring a mere one hundred yards by seventy yards, it was a picture-postcard vision of a balmy South Pacific island floating languidly in azure waters, ringed by a wedding-cake-white beach. A miniature forest of tall casuarina trees promised cover from the enemy, tropical birds frolicked in the branches, and a scattered coconuts could be seen. A few dozen yards offshore, where the coral reef dropped off to 1,000-foot depths, the waters were rich with an array of brightly multicolored fish.

But within minutes of their reconnaissance, it became alarmingly clear to the survivors that if they remained on the island for long, it would kill them. There was no fresh water source on the island. The plant life offered no apparent source of nutrition. There were a handful of coconut-bearing palm trees, but when Kennedy and McMahon cut open some coconuts and tried to eat them, they were sickened. Most of the coconuts they tried turned out to be unripe or inedible.

The castaways had no way of catching the birds that scampered high in the trees other than by gunfire, and given the difficulty of such a shot and the weakened condition the crewmen were in, this would probably only waste ammunition. There were no apparent land animals to hunt and eat, other than some scrawny, skittering land crabs that no one wanted to risk eating. And there was no obvious way for the survivors to catch the countless fish who abounded just offshore. Compounding their predicament was the fact that PT boat officers and crew received little if any specialized survival training. Their knowledge of escape-and evasion techniques or of the skills needed to live off the land in such an exotic locale would have been rudimentary at best.

By late afternoon, the second night of their ordeal was approaching, and the men of the PT 109 were at a loss. How could they could summon a rescue without revealing their position to the enemy? Several aircraft flew over them, but the survivors couldn't make out the planes' markings, in part because Kennedy ordered the men to lie down in the bushes to avoid being spotted. "We didn't do anything to try to signal them," remembered Maguire. "We should have, but we blew it." Ross recalled, "We were paranoid about being seen by Japanese, so in a sense, we were almost fighting rescue."

"How are we going to get out of here?" Kennedy asked the group.

Without water or food, the island was a death trap. The crew was weakening. McMahon was already badly burned on his arms, hands, and face to the point of immobility, and Johnston was, in Ross's memory, "in terrible shape, coughing and retching."

Kennedy was deeply moved by the sight of his injured crewmen, especially McMahon. Kennedy wrote in his unpublished narrative of the incident that "McMahon's burns, which covered his face, body, and arms, festered, grew hard, and cracked in the salt water, and his skin peeled off. McMahon, however, did not utter a word of complaint. His only answer when others question how he felt was a weak, but courageous smile." Kennedy's executive officer Ensign Lenny Thom recalled of McMahon, "You could see he was suffering such pain that his lips twitched and his hands trembled. You'd watch him and think if you were in his place you'd probably be yelling, 'Why doesn't somebody do something?' But every time you asked Mac how he was doing, he'd wrinkle his face and give you a grin."

Once Kennedy fully absorbed the terrible shape his crew was in, he understood he had to act fast. The risks of simply waiting around for rescuers to somehow find them on their forsaken island were too high. At this moment, Kennedy must have felt a deep responsibility to his sailors—they, in turn, looked to him to lead them out of this unfolding nightmare. He decided to take an incredible risk to try to save them. It occurred to Kennedy that for the last several nights, PT boats had patrolled at night through nearby Ferguson Passage. He declared he would swim alone far out into the darkness of Ferguson Passage and try to hail a passing PT boat with their ship's lantern.

McMahon believed it was a suicidal idea. He later explained: "In the first place it was a hell of a long way out to the passage. He'd go out there and float. Now in my mind if the boats had seen a light in the water they'd have blown the light out of the water." Ross also thought it was an absurd idea, and Maguire pleaded with their skipper not to go. But Kennedy insisted. Even though he had just been in the water for more than twelve hours, a harrowing experience he was lucky to have survived just a few hours earlier, he now was planning to return to the ocean, at night, alone for an unknown length of time. Kennedy stripped down to his pants, donned shoes to protect himself from the coral, put on a life jacket, and attached his .38 to a lanyard around his neck.

"I'll take the light out and blink at them," Kennedy told his men. "If I find a boat, I'll flash the lantern twice. The password [for when he returned] will be 'Roger'; the answer will be 'Wilco.'"

Kennedy waded into the water at dusk, hoping the PT boats mustering at Rendova for patrol would come up through Ferguson Passage that night.

As the sun set, the shipwrecked sailors of the PT 109, some on the edge of despair, watched their skipper slowly vanish into the ocean.

LAND OF THE DEAD

★

THE SLOPE OF MOUNT VEVE VOLCANO
AUGUST 2, 1943, 2:27 A.M.

"He's going to get court-martialed for that," thought Benjamin Franklin Nash as he saw the PT 109 erupt in a giant fireball.

Nash was the sole American soldier on the Japanese-held mountain island of Kolombangara. He was stationed in a secret jungle observation post on a slope of the dormant Mount Veve volcano, 1,400 feet above the 10,000 Japanese troops garrisoned at Vila Plantation.

Nash and his superior officer and fellow "Coastwatcher," Sub-Lieutenant Arthur Reginald Evans of the Royal Australian Navy, were watching the final moments of the Battle of Blackett Strait some three miles away through their binoculars, as the phosphorescent wake of a fast-moving ship crossed right into that of a smaller vessel and ignited a fireball flash in the night. Though neither man knew any details of the players involved, Nash was stunned by what he had witnessed, and he felt sure that whoever was on the receiving end of such an explosion was bound to get charged with negligence—if they survived.

U.S. Army Corporal Benjamin Franklin Nash was a stocky, twenty-six-year-old Army radio technician who grew up on in a conservative, patriotic family on a cattle ranch in Colorado. He was awarded a Legion of Merit and a Bronze Star for his actions under fire inside the control tower of Guadalcanal's Henderson Field on February 1, 1943, when he remained at his post to guide aircraft takeoffs and landings during the battle's most violent moments. Now, after convincing his superiors that his radio skills would be an asset to the Coastwatching service, he was on "loan" from the U.S. Army to the Allied Intelligence Bureau as the only American Coastwatcher on the front lines of the Pacific War. The high-risk, cloak-and-dagger nature of the assignment appealed to Nash, who first heard about the Coastwatchers at Guadalcanal. "Their job was to report information on the Japs," he later explained, "and that just intrigued the hell out of me."

Nash and his fellow Coastwatcher, "Reg" Evans, a slightly built, thirty-eight-year-old former steamship accountant and native of Sydney, Australia, had one of the loneliest and riskiest jobs of the Pacific War. Armed only with a few small arms, binoculars, a telescope, a compass, logbook, and canned rations, they and several hundred other Coastwatchers lived behind enemy lines in a network of tiny isolated outposts scattered across a 2,500-mile arc from the west of New Guinea, through the New Hebrides and the Solomons, which alone had twenty-three outposts. Evans was impressed by his new assistant Ben Nash, whom he described as a "quiet, good-humored farming man," who was "so long in the legs, it was quicker to lead a horse under him than ask him to mount it."

The Coastwatchers, overseen by the Royal Australian Navy and the U.S.-run Allied Intelligence Bureau, helped rescue downed Allied pilots and shipwrecked sailors, observed movements of Japanese troops, aircraft, and vessels, and broadcasted coded reports to

American Coastwatcher Benjamin
Franklin Nash. He and his partner,
Australian Reginald Evans, were
startled by a flash of light in the
ocean at 2:27 A.M. on August 2,
1943. (Family of Benjamin Franklin
Nash)

Allied intelligence stations using bulky "Type 3BZ Teleradio" communications equipment that required a team of a dozen natives to
carry. The Coastwatchers' job was to stay hidden, wait, watch, and
report—not to fight. But they were an invaluable asset. By one estimate, 280 American sailors and 321 Allied airmen were rescued
behind enemy lines with the help of the Coastwatchers during the
Solomon Islands campaign.

Many of the Coastwatchers were Australian nationals who had
been living in the islands before war—settlers, plantation manag-
ers, and missionaries—and who chose to remain behind the lines.
The force also included some New Zealanders and British nationals, and in the Solomon Islands, three native Coastwatchers drawn
from the local population. There was just one American, Frank
Nash.

Of the roughly 700 people who served in the Coastwatching service during the war, only 38 were killed, a tribute to the protection

given them by local people—as well as the often impossibly remote locations of their jungle hideaways. "The coastwatchers' working conditions were spooky, lonely, and dreadful," wrote PT 105's skipper, Richard Keresey. "The coastwatcher hid in the hills at a spot with a broad view of the waters of the slot where enemy ships could be seen. Except for the Melanesians [native people], in whose friendship his life depended, he was there alone. He survived mainly on the meager fare of the island. Since their observation posts were seldom near prewar buildings, the coastwatchers often lived in hastily built shacks overrun with rats, and they suffered inadequate netting in their battles with mosquitoes and flies."

On the island of Kolombangara, meaning "Water Lord," Reg Evans and Frank Nash lived in a bamboo hut hidden high up on a mountain slope amid a jungle so rugged that even the few hundred beach-dwelling island natives on the island almost never ventured far inland. The natives built for them two treetop lookout posts, facing west and south, offering them full coverage of Blackett Strait, Ferguson Passage, and the nearby Japanese garrison below at Vila Plantation.

Every night, Evans and Nash scanned their surroundings from their mountain perch, making notes for broadcast to their superiors in the Allied Intelligence Bureau at the Coastwatching base station on Guadalcanal. In summer 1943, Japanese barges were frantically attempting to reinforce garrisons at Munda and Kolombangara's Vila Plantation. Nash recalled, "The barges would come in on the dark side of the moon, and stay as close to the islands as they could, so the PT boats and destroyers in the channel couldn't see them. If you're on the island side looking at the ocean, you can see a silhouette anywhere," but if "you're on the ocean side looking in, you can't see anything."

The previous fall Coastwatchers had secured their reputation by

delivering critical intelligence that turned the tide of the Battle of
Guadalcanal, inspiring U.S. Navy Admiral of the Fleet William
"Bull" Halsey to declare, "The Coastwatchers saved Guadalcanal
and Guadalcanal saved the Pacific." Halsey added, "I could get
down on my knees every night and thank God for [Australian
Coastwatchers] Commander Eric Feldt."

The Coastwatchers, in turn, placed their lives in the hands of
the Solomon Island native people, who were remarkably loyal and
helpful to the Allies. They scouted locations to hide the Coastwatchers, frequently moved them to avoid detection, staged guerrilla attacks against Japanese targets, and fed the Allies a constant
flow of intelligence on Japanese movements. Australian Coastwatcher John Keenan recalled: "If it wasn't for local help I don't
know what we could've done, we wouldn't have lasted 10 minutes."
Many local men and police constables were deputized as armed
and unarmed scouts into the British Solomon Islands Defence
Force.

Before the war, relations between the British colonial authorities and settlers and local people in the Solomons were often cor-
rect but distant, and marred by white attitudes of racial superiority.
But the arrival of frequently heavy-handed and abusive Japanese
troops to the islands in 1942 strengthened the natives' loyalty to the
Allies, and when American forces began retaking the islands, these
attitudes were cemented further. Overall, the Americans seemed
relatively less hierarchical or class-and-color conscious than the
British, and they made a strong positive impression on the Solomon Islanders, with black and white U.S. troops working, eating,
and relaxing side by side with the islanders. One local scout, John
Kari, said the Americans "really went inside the local people," and
another Solomon Islander, David Welchman Gegeo, who helped
conduct a wide range of oral histories with islanders who lived

through the war, observed that the Americans cultivated a mythic image as "generous, egalitarian, wealthy, audacious and rescuers of the Solomon Islands." As a result, Solomon Island natives were highly disposed to help American servicemen in peril.

When the sun came up on the morning of August 2, Coastwatcher Reg Evans spotted debris drifting in Blackett Strait close to where he and Nash had seen the explosion hours earlier. Using the tele-radio gear that Nash meticulously maintained, the two broadcast a dispatch to the Coastwatching office at Guadalcanal: "All four [Japanese warships] went west [at] 0220," and "small vessel possibly barge afire off Gatere and still visible."

Evans received a response at 9:30 A.M. that read: "PT Boat 109 lost in action in Blackett Strait two miles SW Meresu Cove. Crew of twelve [sic]. Request any information."

At 11:15 A.M. Evans replied, "No survivors so far. Object still floating between Meresu and Gizo."

The response: "Definite report PT destroyed last night Blackett Strait between Vanga Vanga [on the coast of Kolombangara] and group of islands SE of Gizo. Was seen burning at 1 AM [sic] The crew numbers twelve possibility of some survivors landing—either Vanga Vanga or islands." (Barney Ross was unaccounted for in the total.)

That afternoon, Evans reported, "This coast being searched. If any landed other side will be picked up by Gizo [native] scouts. Object now drifting toward Nusatupi Island."

Evans put the word out to his network of native scouts to look for survivors, but no sign of them was found along the Kolombangara coast.

John Kennedy and his crew had fallen off the face of the Earth—or at least that's how it seemed to the PT boat officers at the Rendova base.

After daybreak on the morning August 2, when PT 157 skipper Bud Liebenow heard the news at the daily boat captain's meeting that the PT 109 had disappeared with all hands, he was startled to realize that his tent mate was gone. Until now, Liebenow had not connected the flash he spotted in the distance after 2 A.M. to the total loss of a PT boat. "Of course we had lost boats before, but in those cases there had been some of the crew around to tell how it had happened," Liebenow recalled. "This seemed to be a total disappearance with no survivors."

At the morning officers' meeting, one of the PT boat skippers asked Commander Thomas Warfield, "Do you want to send some boats back to look [for the PT 109]?"

"What do you think?" asked Warfield, looking at Potter and Lowrey, the two boat captains who had been nearest Kennedy. "Is there any point in going back?"

"There's no chance they're alive," declared Lowrey, skipper of the PT 162, the boat closest to the PT 109 at the time of the collision. "The boat went up in a ball of fire."

Bud Liebenow remembered, "As far as I know, everybody believed Lowrey when he reported at the boat captains meeting that the 109 was lost, and all hands were dead."

Warfield moved to cut off any discussion of a seaborne search, which angered at least two of the skippers, including Ensign Bill Battle, who like Liebenow was a tent mate of Kennedy. He wanted to return to Blackett Strait immediately and conduct a daylight search, and in fact had already begun fueling-up for the rescue mission. Dick Keresey, skipper of the PT 105, agreed. He recalled,

"There was a whole *group* of us who wanted to do this. We figured that if we didn't take torpedoes, we'd be pretty light and we could really travel fast. We could run in there at high speed before the Japs woke up to what we were doing and run back and forth and find them. But the base commander [Warfield] was not too impressed with this idea. It was extremely dangerous. It exposed a lot of people. I certainly don't fault him for saying it would be hopeless."

Warfield cut them off and ended the discussion. There would be no seaborne rescue mission. Bill Battle was ordered to stop fueling his boat and tie it up back at its berth.

Years later, Keresey recalled bitterly, "The tragedy was that the comrades of the 109 did not go back to look for survivors, even though we saw the search as hopeless. We had not yet learned that hopeless searches should still be made, so that those of us who still had to go out night after night would know that, if we did not return, our comrades would look for us and would fight to save us beyond any reasonable expectation. We should have gone back." Keresey recalled that of the litany of mistakes made during the Battle of Blackett Strait—the withdrawal of all the radar-equipped boats, the rule of radio silence, the orders being issued by Warfield from a bunker dozens of miles away from the action—the worst decision was not to have PT boats return to look for survivors.

Keresey nonetheless did not press the point. As he later explained, he and the others were not thinking straight. They had been up for more than twenty-four hours, enduring the daylight Japanese bombing raid on their base, making two fruitless early morning mass torpedo attacks on the Tokyo Express, and in the case of Keresey and his crew, enduring enemy shelling and float plane attack. Keresey recalled, "All this adds up to a fatigue so severe that thought processes start shutting down. That morning I did not think about the consequence for me, for all boat captains, of failing to look for survivors of the 109. The gain in going back is in the message it sends. Even if you are seen to disappear in a ball of flame, your friends will come looking for you. We should have gone back."

In 2015, PT 107 veteran crewman John Sullivan argued the proper time for a search would have been immediately after the PT 109's explosion around 2:30 A.M., an explosion that was visible, at least in the distance, by several of the PT boats remaining in Blackett Strait. He said, "Nobody went over to look for survivors, nobody. I've just thought of that in the last three or four years—why didn't we go over there and look for survivors? We *should* have! But we didn't."

Ensign Paul Fay wrote a letter to his sister informing her of the death of Kennedy and his crew: "George Ross has lost his life for a cause that he believed in stronger than anyone of us, because he was an idealist in the purest sense. Jack Kennedy, the Ambassador's son, was on the same boat and also lost his life. The man who said that the cream of a nation is lost in war can never be accused of making an overstatement of a very cruel fact."

For the next week, according to Dick Keresey, "I never thought of them nor were they ever mentioned. This was normal; when a man died in combat, he was banished from mind and conversation as if he'd never lived. It made no difference even if he'd been a close friend. Kennedy, Thom, and Ross had been consigned to the dead." Nobody ever talked about who was gone. "That was a subject that wasn't discussed," according to Keresey. "You just did not sit around and say what nice guys they were and how you missed them. You kept all that to yourself. And even in yourself you tried to forget it as soon as possible. You couldn't think about that. You had too many other things to think about."

Commander Thomas Warfield, however, evidently had not totally abandoned hope of finding Kennedy and his crew. Probably spurred to action by Coastwatcher Reg Evans's reports of floating wreckage, Warfield is believed to have dispatched several New Zealand P-40 fighter aircraft to fly over Gizo and Blackett Strait to look for survivors of the PT 109. In the late afternoon of August 2, a formation of P-40s apparently spotted boat wreckage, but no survivors were visible. By then, the shipwrecked PT 109 crewmen were hiding below the trees and bushes of their island refuge.

PT skipper Arthur Berndtson recalled the search planes "flew up over Blackett Strait, saw the bow section floating toward Kolombangara, but said there was nobody on it."

"It was depressing news."

John Kennedy stood alone. Partly submerged on a coral reef, he gazed into the darkness.

He thought of a warning one of his crewmen had offered him before he headed out—"these barracuda will come up under a swimming man and eat his testicles." With this frightful image in mind, Kennedy pushed into the water at about 6:30 P.M. and quickly flipped over into a backstroke. He made it to a tiny piece of land a half mile to the southeast, a sandbar called Leorava Island, which sported a single tree and a patch of bushes. He then crawled and stumbled along a reef that jutted into Ferguson Passage, hoping to hail a passing PT boat on patrol. Stopping periodically to rest on the reef, he cut his knees and shins on the sharp coral.

Kennedy's swim may have been a quixotic, needle-in-a-haystack venture, but he evidentially concluded the alternative—staying put on the island—was hopeless. As skipper of the lost PT 109, he bore responsibility for their predicament, and he must have felt that the burden of getting them out of the death zone rested on his shoulders alone. To remain on Plum Pudding amounted to waiting for starvation or capture. Action was needed, and fast, however long the odds. Perhaps so, but Kennedy's movements also carried severe risks, as historians Clay and Joan Blair reasoned: "The PTs entered Ferguson Passage on full alert. The men manning the guns were, to put it mildly, trigger-happy, as who wouldn't be in enemy waters at night? Suppose Kennedy had seen or heard them, shined his lantern on them, and fired his pistol? The reaction might well have been a reflexive hail of small arms fire in Kennedy's direction." JFK must have appreciated those risks as well as anyone when he entered the water that night.

When Kennedy reached Ferguson Passage around 9 P.M. after a marathon swim of more than two miles, he treaded water and poised himself to fire three pistol rounds and flash his lantern light to attract attention. But there were no signs of PT boats. Instead, he saw flares being dropped by Japanese seaplanes in the far distance, over Gizo Island.

Gripping his lantern, Kennedy tied his shoes to his life jacket so he could paddle better, kept treading water, and searched in vain for rescue. The current apparently began pulling him laterally into Blackett Strait, then in a wide arc back to Ferguson Passage. His fatigue intensified, and his shoes slipped away from him into the ocean.

Eventually, Kennedy gave up and struggled back toward Plum Pudding Island, aided this time by the current. After midnight, Kennedy's men thought they heard him faintly shouting the code word "Roger! Roger!" and believed they saw his lantern flashing. Assuming their skipper had found a PT boat, they were jubilant and rushed out to greet Kennedy. Lenny Thom splashed into the water, yelling, "Jack! Jack!"

But no rescue was coming, and Kennedy, still some distance from the shore, was tiring and helpless to fight the strong ocean current that threatened to pull him past the tiny island. Kennedy drifted away into the emptiness.

Back on the island, with Kennedy gone, his executive officer Ensign Lenny Thom was in charge, and according to several crewman he rallied and inspired them. The outlook, however, was bleak. They could find no fresh water on the island, even when they burrowed down in the ground. When a light rain fell, the men lay on their backs and tried to catch the drops in their mouths. The men licked water off the leaves, and realized the source of its bitter taste. Thousands of birds had appeared after dark in a hail of noise, and added to the island's already thick coating of bird waste. The men soon dubbed their new home "Bird Island." That night few of the crewmen could sleep.

In the morning, the hungry, thirsty survivors despaired when there was no sign of Kennedy. It seemed he was lost, swallowed up in the vast ocean. McMahon's burn wounds were increasingly painful, and Johnston was semiconscious. Harris busied himself with an experiment to disassemble and try to lubricate a pistol with coconut meat, but this only gummed up the weapon instead.

Kennedy floated in the ocean in his trancelike state through the rest of the night. When dawn came after 6 A.M. on August 3, he worried he had lost his mind, because when he looked around, it seemed he had somehow wound up on the reef off the sandbar of tiny Leorava Island, close to where he had started his journey the night before, around the confluence of Blackett Strait and Ferguson Passage. Now barefoot, he suffered cuts and abrasions as he staggered and scrambled along the coral reef. Groping his way onto the sandbar, he collapsed into sleep.

At noon a cry went up.

"Here's Kirksey!" shouted a jubilant Maguire, mistaking the figure coming toward them for one of the two sailors originally lost in the crash. But it wasn't the doomed Kirksey; rather it turned out to be an exhausted, retching John F. Kennedy returning from his fruitless swim over the reefs. He had slept until the late morning, then summoned the strength to swim back a half mile from Leorava to Plum Pudding Island to rejoin his crew. Bearded, hair matted, eyes bloodshot, stripped of any trace of privilege, Kennedy fell in a heap on the beach. Ross and Thom dragged him into the bushes, where he fell into a feverish sleep. He had been in the water for some thirty out of the thirty-six hours since the collision.

Kennedy's harrowing night-long, solitary ordeal in the swirling blackness of Blackett Strait had been desperate, courageous, and perhaps heroic. But it was also futile, and it could easily have cost him his life from exhaustion and drowning, and left his crew without their commanding officer. Nevertheless, their present location was a deathtrap; doing nothing was a poor option. That afternoon, when Kennedy awoke and his crew gathered around, he looked up at Ross and said, "Barney, you try it tonight," before again passing out.

Ensign Ross thought venturing out alone to try to hail a PT boat was a hopeless idea, but he obeyed Kennedy's order. At four in the afternoon on August 3, he swam toward Ferguson Passage onto a section of the reef he could place his foot on, desperately trying to memorize every detail of his surroundings so he wouldn't get lost on the way back. The current pushed him off the reef, but he struggled back into position. In horror, he spotted sand sharks measuring several feet long. When dusk came, Ross waded toward the passage in hopes of summoning patrolling PT boats. He bolstered his courage by recalling Kennedy's swim the previous night, repeating the mantra, "If he can do it I can do it."

Ross apparently treaded water for a short while, pulled out the .38 pistol, and fired three shots into the air at intervals, as a test. The water flattened the noise of the firearm. And for the second night in a row, the PT boats were not patrolling Ferguson Passage, but were instead off the island of Vella Lavella, where Lieutenant Commander Warfield had sent five PT boats on a barge-hunting mission. A column of Japanese barges engaged the PTs in a firefight, killing George Cookman of the PT 107 and wounding two other American sailors.

Ross spent most of the night clinging to the reef. In the morning he made landfall at the Leorava islet, where Kennedy wound up the night before, and likewise collapsed in sleep.

Lieutenant Reginald Evans, the Australian Coastwatcher, spent part of August 2 and 3 following up on Rendova's requests for information on the lost PT boat, and tracking what looked like possible debris from the collision.

Among the native scouts under the command of Coastwatcher Evans were two young men named Biuku Gasa and Eroni Kumana, both about nineteen years old.

At the same time John Kennedy was making his futile swim for help, Gasa and Kumana had spotted Japanese reinforcement troops landing at Kequlavata Bay on Gizo Island. They made the observation from their scout camp on Sepo Island, which was between Plum Pudding and Gizo. Soon they headed toward Kolombangara to deliver the intelligence to Evans.

Along the way, Gasa and Kumana picked through some washed-up debris near Bambanga Island, including a box containing shaving gear and a letter signed by PT 109 crewman Raymond Albert. Stopping briefly at the village of Wana Wana, they gave the items to senior scout Benjamin Kevu, who spoke and read English, but they didn't connect the letter to the PT 109. When they reported to Evans at Kolombangara, the Coastwatcher asked him if they'd seen any survivors of a PT boat, and they said no. Sending them back to Sepo, Evans told them to be on the alert for survivors. The next morning, August 3, Evans messaged Rendova, "No survivors found at Gizo."

At 11:30 A.M. on August 3, Evans received a message from Rendova asking, "Where was hulk of burning PT boat last seen. If still floating request complete destruction [presumably to eliminate any codebooks or clear it as an obstacle to navigation]. Also request information if any Japs were on or near floating hulk."

At 5:05 that afternoon, Evans reported back, "Cannot confirm object seen was floating hulk of PT. Object last seen approx two miles NE Bambanga, drifting south. Not seen since PM Second. P Fortys flew low over it and Gizo scouts have no knowledge object or any Japs that vicinity."

By Wednesday, August 4, there was still no hint of rescue for the men of PT 109. Japanese and Allied planes clashed in dogfights in the distant sky. The survivors again hunkered down in the bushes to avoid being spotted.

Intense thirst slashed at the exhausted castaways of the PT 109. They had eaten nothing since Sunday afternoon except a few unripe coconuts, and drank only what drops of rainwater they could gather. "Hunger didn't seem to bother me too much," remembered Gerard Zinser; "thirst was our main discomfort." Zinser was also tormented by thoughts of his wife not knowing what had happened to him, once the Navy reported him as missing. For his part, John Maguire couldn't shake the feeling that the Japanese had already spotted them and would soon take them into captivity.

Kennedy drew his two officers aside to tell them privately how furious he was at the American commanding officers at Rendova for apparently abandoning them. To the enlisted men, however he projected an attitude of confidence and made occasional reassuring wisecracks to keep their spirits up. At one point, Kennedy announced exuberantly, "We're going to get back if I have to tow this island back!"

"What I would give for a can of grapefruit juice!" Kennedy quipped to Zinser. JFK himself recalled, "I was always thirsty. Guess I drank quite a bit of salt water. Somehow I couldn't get pineapple juice out of my mind and at the time would willingly have paid a year's pay for one can of it."

According to Barney Ross, Kennedy "never allowed us to sit around and mope." They "kept going" thanks to his leadership.

Their most urgent worry, according to Ross, was the severely burned McMahon. "Pappy lay in the water, and the salt water was apparently good for him," despite the initial pain it caused to his wounds. "He kept moving his fingers so that he wouldn't lose the use of his hands," Ross remembered.

But Kennedy knew their outlook was increasingly grim. Zinser's arms were burned and in urgent need of medical attention. Pappy McMahon was in terrible condition, with hideous-looking burn wounds and scabs on his hands and eyelids. If his wounds became infected, McMahon would die before their eyes. Everyone else was growing weaker from thirst, hunger, and exhaustion.

Time was running out.

Somehow, they had to find food and water. To have any chance of being rescued, they figured they had to get closer to Ferguson Passage, past which lay the Rendova PT base. From Plum Pudding Island they could see Olasana—another, somewhat larger islet a mile and three-quarters to the southeast and closer to Ferguson Passage—and it appeared to have plenty of coconut trees. But the men were wary of the long open-water crossing—and afraid the larger island might also contain Japanese troops.

Kennedy decided it was worth the risk. "We're going to that small one," he said, pointing at Olasana. "We'll have to swim for it. Everyone on the log [the planks from the 37 mm gun mount]. I'll take McMahon."

They slowly waded into the water and swam off as a group for Olasana, fighting a strong current. After several hours, Kennedy came ashore first, once again pulling McMahon by gripping the injured man's lifejacket strap in his teeth. When Raymond Albert arrived ahead of some of the others, he yelled back to them so loudly they feared he might have alerted any Japanese on the island, and the men were furious at him.

Once they were all ashore, the eleven men gathered in the shelter of the bushes and discussed in hushed tones whether they should search the island for the enemy. "Why go looking for trouble?" concluded one of the men. And so they stayed put, in a roughly fifty-yard patch of the island.

"The second island was much bigger," remembered Harris. "We were really concerned that there might be some Japs on it. We kept a watch all the time."

Yet again, the shipwrecked sailors of the PT 109 were thwarted. While no Japanese appeared to occupy the island, neither was there fresh water, and the available coconuts in the tiny patch of the island they dared explore sickened a few of the men. Barney Ross tried eating a little snail, but he reported it tasted awful, scaring everyone else off from trying another.

That night, August 4, the weather was too foul for anyone to swim out to Ferguson Passage to try to intercept and hail a PT boat. In keeping with the crew's horrible luck, this unfortunately turned out to be the first night that PT boats returned through Ferguson Passage into Blackett Strait; six boats were patrolling in Blackett Strait by 9:30 P.M.

The next day, Thursday, August 5, one of the disheartened castaways lamented that they were all going to die.

"Aw, shut up," countered William Johnston, echoing a recent exhortation by Kennedy. "You can't die. Only the good die young."

"You guys make me sore," griped Johnston when some in the group began praying. "You didn't spend ten cents in church in ten years, then all of a sudden you're in trouble and you see the light."

Kennedy and Ross were so desperate to procure food and water for their group they decided to make the hour-long swim over to yet another small island located a half mile to the southeast, called Naru (also known as Gross Island or Cross Island), despite observing the ominous sight of a New Zealand P-40 fighter aircraft making a strafing run on the island.

That afternoon, the two American officers surfaced on the four-hundred-yard-wide Naru Island and scampered into the bushes.

They could see the outline of Rendova Peak, agonizingly visible just thirty-eight miles south.

Soon, they explored around the island and were delighted to find a box containing some thirty little bags of Japanese crackers and candy, a fifty-gallon catchment drum of potable rainwater, and a small, damaged one-man canoe. It wasn't much, but after more than three days of exhausting swims and living on little more than a few rotten coconuts and rain drops, it was a victory.

Then Kennedy and Ross froze.

They saw two men out on the ocean paddling a dugout canoe, heading directly toward them.

THE HAND OF FATE

★

NARU ISLAND, AUGUST 5, 1943
4:00 PM

Earlier that afternoon, Biuku Gasa and Eroni Kumana spotted boat wreckage on a reef south of Naru Island, and they paddled their canoe over to investigate.

Their two-man scout team was one of five such tandems under the supervision of Coastwatcher Reg Evans. They were linked by an ingenious network of relief canoes and relay paddlers that formed a communication line between scouts, Coastwatchers, native villages, and Allied outposts in the region.

It was a vital—and demanding—job. Earlier in the war, Gasa helped summarily execute a Japanese pilot who had parachuted out of a disabled plane, and on other occasions, he captured and shuttled Japanese prisoners into Allied custody. "We scouts would paddle out to the small islands—especially this island called Naru," Gasa related in a 1967 oral history. "We would go to stay on the island watching for planes and ships. We would usually stay for one week, when two men would come to replace us, so that Ferguson Passage was always watched. We would also paddle around [the Japanese-held island of] Gizo, always two of us in each canoe."

On this day, after they sighted the remains of a boat run aground on a reef, evidently the remnants of a Japanese barge, they decided to climb aboard to investigate and see what they could salvage. "We found a jacket, a long sword, and a tommy gun," Gasa recounted. "We were about to carry them off when we saw a man watching us from the shore of Naru Island, one of the many small islands in Ferguson Strait. We thought the man was a Japanese and started to paddle off in the opposite direction to get back to Sepo Island." In fact, the man was John F. Kennedy. But from their distant vantage point, the man's unkempt, sunburned appearance and his proximity to a Japanese shipwreck strongly suggested to Gasa that the man was a stranded Japanese soldier or sailor.

By now Kennedy and Ross realized the black men in the canoe were not Japanese, and they watched helplessly as their potential saviors slid away.

But soon something happened in the scouts' canoe, a perfectly ordinary occurrence that may have affected, in a subtle yet profound way, the subsequent course of history. Simply stated, Biuku Gasa's throat was dry. He was thirsty. He wanted a coconut—to cut it open and drink the sweet milk.

And so he and his partner changed direction. Instead of heading straight for their home base at Sepo Island, they took a detour to the usually uninhabited island of Olasana.

"We stopped at the next island [Olasana] because I wanted to drink a coconut," recalled Gasa.

Solomon Islands Scouts Biuku Gasa and Eroni Kumana. (Elliot Erwitt, Magnum Photos)

As Gasa waded toward the shore, he was startled to see a man crawling out from the bushes. "Eroni," he said to his companion, "a Japanese here!" The two scouts pushed their canoe away and prepared to escape.

The man stood up, waved, and beckoned to the scouts in English, "Come!" "No," declared Gasa, "you're Japanese!" "Come, come," said the man, who was joined by a companion stepping out of the brush, "I'm American, not Japanese." Phrases of "Pidgin" (a fragmentary mix of English and local languages) and English were shouted as the castaways tried to explain they were Americans who had lost their PT boat, but the words seemed so broken to Gasa that he could barely understand them. Despite Coastwatcher Evans's recent order to be on the lookout for survivors of a sunken PT boat, Gasa still was convinced the bedraggled men were Japanese. The two scouts understood little English.

One of the Americans held up his arm and said, "Look at my skin—its white."

"No matter skin white or skin red—you Japan!" a skeptical Gasa called back. "No. We are afraid."

"Where are you going?" asked an American. Gasa and Kumana gave a false destination.

"Are you two native scouts?"

"No," replied Gasa and Kumana.

"Are you helping the British or the Japs?"

"No one!" replied the scouts, "We are not helping any country." The scouts tried to push away from the shore with their spears, but were instead carried toward the Americans by a strong current.

"Then another white man crawled out from the bushes" and walked straight toward them, recalled Gasa. It was Lenny Thom, the strapping ensign of the PT 109, sporting a striking blond beard that marked him clearly as a non-Japanese. At first, Kumana reasoned the Nordic-looking Thom must be a German.

"Do you know John Kari from Rendova?" asked Thom. This question proved to be the decisive icebreaker. John Kari was a prominent Solomon Island scout leader who was instrumental in the rescue of many Americans in the area.

"Yes, I know him," replied Gasa, "He's living at my village." "At this point I began to believe the soldiers and to understand what had happened," remembered Gasa. "We went ashore, and our canoe was hidden in the bushes. We were taken to where the other crew members were hidden. It was then about four P.M. Some of the men had burns on their faces. We were told not to shake hands with them because they couldn't move."

Gasa and Kumana shared with the shipwrecked sailors the yams and cigarettes they had with them. The men of the PT 109, according to Kumana, were overjoyed and deeply moved to meet the two potential angels of their deliverance. "Some of them cried, and some of them came and shook our hands," Kumana recalled. Though several of the crew seemed more ravenous for nicotine than they did for food, the PT 109 castaways were fortunate to be given yams as emergency nourishment, as the root vegetable is a highly

Ensign Leonard Thom: Kennedy's second-in-command on the PT 109 had been a football star in Ohio. (National Archives)

nutritious plant loaded with carbohydrates, fiber, potassium, as well as other vitamins and minerals. To Ensign Lenny Thom, however, time seemed to be running out, especially when the scouts pointed to Naru Island, where Kennedy and Ross were, and reported there could be Japanese there. Thom decided he and Ray Starkey would immediately set off for Rendova in the scout canoe, with Biuku Gasa as the pilot. Gasa declared it a bad idea. The boat was too small to carry the former Ohio State lineman Thom and two others, he argued. But Thom insisted, and the three men donned life jackets and set off paddling into the night sea toward

Rendova, which was barely visible in daylight from their island prison.

They made it into Ferguson Passage, where the three men struggled in the dark. The wind whipped up in a churning sea, and waves threatened to capsize the little boat. They were forced to retreat to Olasana.

Thwarted, Thom decided he had to send the two scouts to Rendova the next day by themselves. He took a pencil stub that Maguire had managed to keep in his pocket through the ordeal, and scribbled a detailed distress message on a piece of scrap paper someone had found on the island, a blank invoice, No. 2860, of the Gizo office of the Burns Philp inter-island steamship company—the same company Coastwatcher Reg Evans worked for prior to the war.

The message contained radio signals and call signs, to minimize the chances that Rendova would suspect a Japanese trick:

To: COMMANDING OFFICER–OAK 0
From: Crew P. T. 109 (Oak 14)
Subject: Rescue of 11 (eleven) men lost since Sunday, Aug 1st in enemy action. Native knows our position & will bring P.T. boat back to small islands of Ferguson Passage off Naru IS.

A small boat (outboard or oars) is needed to take men off as some are seriously burned.

Signal at night–three dashes(- - -) Password - Roger -Answer - Wilco

If attempted at day time—advise air coverage or a PBY could set down. Please work out suitable plan & act immediately. Help is urgent & in sore need.

Rely on native boys to any extent

L J Thom
Ens. U.S.N.R. Exec 109

Once again, the crew of the PT 109 collapsed in sleep on a remote island in enemy-held waters. A few nervous members of the crew were suspicious of the nearby Gasa and Eroni and stayed awake to watch them.

Although the PT 109 was only a sad memory for its crew, it was still a preoccupation for Coastwatchers Reg Evans and Frank Nash. At 9:40 A.M. that day, Evans radioed his Coastwatcher base station: "Similar object now in Ferguson Passage drifting south. Position half mile SE Gross [Naru] Is. Cannot be investigated from here for at least twenty-four hours. Now on reef south Gross Is." And still later: "Hulk still on reef but expect will move with tonight's tide. Destruction from this end now most unlikely. In present position no canoes could approach through surf." In late afternoon on August 5, Evans received a report that a "hulk" was examined by an overflying plane and the pilot concluded that it was so "badly damaged it was not worth wasting ammunition on."

It was the last-ever sighting of the PT 109.

After dark on the night of August 5, Kennedy paddled the damaged yet seaworthy canoe that he and Ross had found that afternoon, and headed out into Ferguson Passage to try to summon help. Once again, he found none, so he decided to return to Naru Island, pick up the supplies he and Ross had salvaged earlier in the day, then venture back to his men on Olasana, using the canoe to tow the drum of drinking water. Ross meanwhile stayed on Naru, fast asleep.

After midnight, the crew on Olasana was alerted by shouts from Kennedy that he was making landfall. They called out to him jubilantly: "We're saved! Two locals have found us!"

When Kennedy absorbed the news of the scouts' arrival, he ran to Gasa and Kumana and threw his arms around them. Gasa found it easy to talk to Kennedy, he recalled, "because he knew Pidgin." Kennedy asked if it was Gasa and Kumana whom he had seen off Naru the day before, and as Gasa recounted, "We said 'yes.' And he said, 'Why didn't we come when he waved?' We answered that we thought he was Japanese."

As the fourth day of the ordeal dawned, the crewmen discovered that during the night, one of the men had secretly guzzled all the drinkable water in the can Kennedy had recovered. When they found out, his colleagues swore at him furiously, though they would never reveal the culprit's name to anyone outside the crew. Despair returned. It was as if the loss of the water had brought them back to the reality of how precarious their situation still was.

Spotting the rosary beads draped around John Maguire's neck, William Johnston asked, "McGuire, give that necklace a working over."

McGuire replied, "Yes, I'll take care of all you fellows."

On the morning of August 6, Kennedy wanted to return to Naru to try to hail passing Allied ships or planes. "He was going to swim," recounted Gasa, "but we said we would take him by canoe. We put him in the bottom of our canoe and covered him with coconut leaves." On the way, they intercepted Ross, who was swimming back toward Olasana, and took him over to Naru as well. Once on Naru, the natives revealed to the Americans a secret cache containing a two-man canoe.

The Americans were still nearly forty miles inside enemy waters, and there seemed to be no sure way to evacuate the eleven men in the crew as the available canoes barely had room for four. They had to get a rescue message to friendly lines. But if the scouts got to Rendova without a written message from the PT 109 skipper, they might not be believed. By then, Kennedy and his crew could be dead from starvation, or prisoners of war of the Japanese.

"Kennedy said that he wished to send news to Rendova to tell about the shipwreck," recalled Gasa, "but none of us had paper or pencils."

The magnitude of their predicament seemed to hit Kennedy hard. "Biuku, I'm sorry for my crew. There's no paper."

Considering a nearby coconut tree, Gasa had an idea—a brainstorm that, in combination with Thom's small distress note, offered the possibility of salvation of the crew of the PT 109. He explained, "I remembered that it is possible to cut a message into a piece of coconut husk." Gasa asked his partner Kumana to climb a tree and fetch a coconut for the group to drink, and to save the husk. Showing it to Kennedy, he explained that residents of the Solomon Islands had another way of sending messages: "We natives have lots of 'papers'—you can write a message inside this husk of coconut."

Kennedy made a test carving on the husk and tried in vain to rub it off. It worked. Kennedy gazed in wonder at Biuku Gasa. "Jesus Christ, Biuku," he said. "How did you think of this?"

An impressed John F. Kennedy came over to Gasa, and, according to the scout, "took my head with both hands, twisting it slowly and studying it." Kennedy then grasped the knife and scratched a brief message on the coconut husk:

NAURO ISL

NATIVE KNOWS POS'IT

HE CAN PILOT

11 ALIVE

NEED SMALL BOAT

KENNEDY

The group returned to Olasana, where Gasa and Kumana were given the small paper distress note that had been scribbled by

Kennedy's distress note, carved with a knife into a coconut. (John F. Kennedy Presidential Library)

Lenny Thom, to accompany the coconut, apparently to serve as a backup message.

Kennedy and his crew watched Gasa and Kumana paddle off to the horizon. They had no way of knowing if the natives would make it through to Rendova.

The odds may well have looked bleak. It would be a nearly forty-mile journey through enemy waters by two unarmed teenagers in a small canoe, in an area where Japanese aircraft and surface craft roamed widely. Their risks of being strafed or captured by the enemy were high. If the two natives were detained by the Japanese, the coconut distress message from Kennedy that they carried, as well as the paper note written by Thom, could lead a Japanese force directly to the PT 109 crew. The two young men were, Kennedy would have realized, the slenderest reeds of hope to cling to. Still, the natives offered Kennedy his only visible avenue of salvation.

Gasa and Eroni set off for Rendova, stopping first at Wana

Wana, an island south of Kolombangara and seven miles east of Naru, where they linked up with Benjamin Kevu, a senior Solomon Islands scout under Coastwatcher Evans' supervision. Unlike Gasa and Eroni, he spoke excellent English. At this point, Ben Kevu apparently took three steps that sharply boosted the odds of a successful rescue of the PT 109's crew. He assigned a bigger canoe to the two scouts for their remaining journey; he added to the mission a third man, John Kari—the same John Kari whose common acquaintance to the scouts and Lenny Thom convinced the scouts that the crew were Americans—and Kevu alerted nearby Coastwatcher Reg Evans of the discovery of the PT 109 crew. Evans was in the process of separating from American Coastwatcher Benjamin Franklin Nash on Kolombangara and relocating to Gomu, a small island just north of Wana Wana, to get a better view of events in lower Blackett Strait and Ferguson Passage.

Pushing off from Wana Wana, Gasa, Kumana, and Kari set out in rough seas to attempt their all-night canoe journey.

On the night of August 6, a scout sent by Ben Kevu linked up with Evans at his new secret surveillance post buried in the jungle of Gomu Island, and told him of Gasa and Kumana's astonishing discovery. Eleven lost American sailors were found, some wounded and all starving and dehydrated, on Naru and Olasana Islands.

For four days, Evans had been tracking the fragmentary possibility that the PT 109, or pieces of it, might have survived the explosion he witnessed early in the morning of August 2. So far, he had only negative results to relay to Rendova.

Now Evans finally had confirmation that many of the survivors were actually still alive. The trouble was, he hadn't set up his cumbersome radio equipment, and it would take hours of working through the night to get it and his new headquarters into operation. So Evans decided to transmit the news to Rendova the next morning, August 7, and meanwhile dispatch a canoe to Naru filled with supplies to relieve the survivors, retrieve Lieutenant Kennedy, and ferry him back to confer with Evans. He wrote a note for them to carry to Kennedy:

To Senior Officer, Naru Is.
Friday 11 p.m.

Have just learnt of your presence on Naru Is. & also that two natives have taken news to Rendova. I strongly advise you return immediately to here in this canoe & by the time you arrive here I will be in Radio communication with authorities at Rendova & we can finalise plans to collect balance of party.

Will warn aviation of your crossing Ferguson Passage.

A.R. Evans Lt RANVR

On Naru Island, meanwhile, on the night of August 6, Kennedy decided to make yet another nighttime attempt to intercept passing PT boats in Ferguson Passage, since there was no certainty that Gasa and Kumana would successfully make it to Rendova in time for a rescue to be organized before he and his men began dying or were captured by the Japanese.

Kennedy beckoned Barney Ross to help him push out into the ocean the two-man canoe the natives had furnished them. "Gee, I think we'll tip over, Jack, if we go out," warned a highly skeptical Ross; "it looks a little rough."

Kennedy insisted, "Oh, no, it'll be all right, we'll go out."

The two naval officers paddled out into the ocean, and were promptly pounded by fierce winds, pouring rain, and five-foot waves as they struggled to pilot the little canoe, which soon got swamped, flipped over, and dumped them in the water.

Kennedy shouted to his friend, "Sorry I got you out here, Barney!"

"This would be a great time to say I told you so, but I won't!" was Ross's retort.

They struggled in the swirling surf for up to two hours, at one point becoming separated amid the chaos and darkness.

"Barney!" screamed Kennedy. "Barney!"

He finally found Ross struggling, half-submerged on top of a reef outcropping, which had sliced into his right shoulder and arm and further wounded his already infected and swollen feet. Kennedy had to place oars over the coral in order for Ross to make the torturous step-by-step journey along the reef back to the beach, where the two men collapsed in slumber.

Once again, it turned out, no PT boats went through the Ferguson Passage that night. By now, Admiral William Halsey was fed up with ineffective PT assaults on the Tokyo Express, and that night, August 6–7, he instead dispatched a radar-guided force of six destroyers into action to intercept the Express. In what became known as the Battle of Vella Gulf, not far from the site of the Battle of Blackett Strait, the Americans this time sank no less than four Japanese destroyers carrying 900 soldiers and 50 tons of cargo headed for Kolombangara, including two of the ships involved in the action the night the PT 109 was sunk: the *Arashi*, and the *Hagikaze*. "Awed PT sailors in Kula Gulf 28 miles away sighted the loom of flame," wrote naval historian Samuel Eliot Morison, "and thought the volcano on Kolombangara must have blown its top." The victory ended Japanese attempts to use destroyers to supply their island bases, and they turned to the more difficult method of only using smaller barges instead.

The victory, of course, came too late to mean anything to the men of PT 109. In spite of the hope they placed in the native scouts, they were in as desperate a condition as ever. In the five days since the crash, the castaways had consumed little to nothing: some raindrops, pieces of often-inedible coconut, sips from a cache of fresh water that soon disappeared, a few pieces of Japanese candy that Kennedy and Ross had found on Naru, and the vegetables Gasa and Eroni had shared with them at one meal, which Kennedy was present for but Ross had missed, as he was sleeping on Naru. Zinser thought they would start dying off soon, and believed the wounded Barney Ross would be the first to go.

At 9:20 A.M. on August 7, 1943, Reginald Evans sent an electrifying radio message to Rendova, confirming Gasa and Kumana's discovery of the PT 109's crew: "Eleven survivors PT boat on Gross [Naru] Island. Have sent food and letter advising senior [officer] come here without delay. Warn aviation of canoes crossing Ferguson." The message took several hours to be relayed through the Coastwatching radio network and was passed to Rendova at mid-day.

The same morning, after paddling all through the night on choppy seas, scouts Biuku Gasa, Eroni Kumana, and John Kari finally arrived at a U.S. military outpost at Roviana Island off the island of New Georgia, and came face-to-face with Colonel George Hill, commander of a U.S. Army artillery unit supporting the 43rd Infantry Division. With the help of an officer who understood some Pidgin phrases, Hill deciphered what Gasa was urgently trying to convey: "Americans stranded on island behind the Japs," "One man with feet badly burned or injured and needs help," and finally that Hill, as "Chief for Americans," should "give him rescue boat immediately."

Years later, Colonel Hill retold the story in a letter. "I reported the incident to our Intelligence Section and then tried to remember where I had seen a Navy [boat] pool," he wrote. "I finally thought of Bau Island [Lumbari] back at Rendova. How could I make contact? I had regular intervals for ammo reports from Kokrana by radio so decided for a relay of your copra [coconut] message signed 'Kennedy.' The name at the time meant nothing to me except another joker needing help. I told them [Rendova] the Native Chief [presumably Gasa] was at my command post and could be picked up at Roviana landing pier when a pickup boat was available."

"From this point on the Chief [Gasa] sat on the ground in my tent and just watched my every movement," wrote Hill. "Came noontime and I had a plate of food brought in which didn't interest him too much as he would keep saying, 'Boat where? Man sick!' I had to stall by picking up my field phone from time to time and feign a conversation to someone about a boat. At one point the Chief started swinging his machete in my direction indicating I was not acting fast enough to save your party."

Gasa had finally made it to American lines after paddling for more than fifteen hours, but he was frantic at the seeming lack of action he felt at Roviana. "All the Americans in Roviana were Marines [in fact they were Army soldiers] and they didn't know anything about any Captain Kennedy," Gasa remembered. He added, "we started to feel crazy not knowing what to do" with the written message from Thom and the coconut message from Kennedy, the latter of which Gasa held on to tightly.

"Fortunately about 2:00 P.M. I received word that [the PT] boat pool had received the message and a rescue party would pick up the Chief," Hill later recounted. Hill arranged for the scouts to be transferred by boat to Rendova. He remembered, "Late that afternoon I had to cross to Division Artillery Headquarters on New Georgia when I spotted the Chief in the stern of [a PT] boat."

As the boat passed, Colonel Hill could clearly see Biuku Gasa, headed for John Kennedy's home base of Rendova.

The Solomon Islands scout had a smile on his face.

And he was still gripping the coconut.

Meanwhile, time was swiftly running out for the PT 109 survivors on Olasana Island.

The severe dehydration they were all suffering from could soon trigger a dire cascade of medical crises, as the human body can theoretically survive for weeks without food, but only days without water. At the moment, the nine sailors on Olasana didn't know if Kennedy and the wounded Barney Ross were still on nearby Naru Island or had perished in the ocean overnight. McMahon's wounds were increasingly infected, Zinser and Johnston's injuries were still untreated, and all the survivors were stalked by weakness and despair. They might start succumbing to their fate in a matter of hours or sooner, meaning Olasana Island would be their final resting place.

But then, soon after Kennedy and Ross awoke on the morning of August 7, a vision of salvation appeared on the horizon. It was a long native canoe, filled with cargo and powered by a phalanx of six pairs of powerful arms paddling the boat directly toward the crewmen of PT 109.

It was the rescue canoe dispatched by Reg Evans, manned by senior scout Benjamin Kevu and six more scouts: Moses Sesa, Jonathan Bia, Joseph Eta, Stephen Hitu, Koete Igolo, and Edward Kidoe. Minutes earlier, when they appeared at Naru Island to relay Kennedy and Ross over to Olasana Island, Kevu had strode up to Kennedy and presented him with the message from Evans written on letterhead titled "On His Majesty's Service." Kevu announced in the accented king's English he'd picked up from his British instructors: "I have a letter for you, sir."

Amused by these quaint colonial flourishes (technically the Solomons were still part of the British Empire) Kennedy muttered to Ross, "You've got to hand it to the British!"

At Olasana, the scouts were greeted by a scene of jubilation as the survivors realized their lives were being saved. Kennedy and

Ross exited the canoe, and the men of PT 109 sprang into action to help the natives unload an assortment of life-sustaining supplies. The U.S. Navy's official account of the incident reported, "The natives had brought food and other articles (including a cook stove) to make the survivors comfortable. They were extremely kind at all times." Yams, potatoes, fish, and roast beef hash were prepared by the scouts, water was passed around, and Edman Mauer pitched in to help cook up what must have felt like a royal feast. Cigarettes were distributed. A lean-to was built to shelter McMahon.

After the meal, Kennedy entered the canoe for his trip to meet Coastwatcher Evans. He lay in the base of the boat and the scouts again covered him with palm fronds.

On the journey to Gomu, the canoe was buzzed by a squad of low-flying Japanese planes.

From under the camouflage, Kennedy asked, "What's going on?"

Kevu replied, "Japanese planes, Stay down!"

Kevu stood up and gave the Japanese a friendly wave, and the planes few off.

In late afternoon on Saturday, August 7, the canoe glided up to Evans's new camp on Gomu Island. A barefooted Kennedy emerged from his hiding spot in the base of the canoe, walked across the beach to Evans, reached out for a handshake, and smiled. "Hello, I'm Kennedy," he announced.

"I recall the day very, very clearly," said Reginald Evans in 1961; "he looked like a very tired, a very haggard and a very, very sunburnt young man. It looked as though he'd been through an awful lot." Kennedy's legs and feet were scarred with wounds from sharp coral.

"Come and have a cup of tea," Evans beckoned.

10

THE RESCUE

★

Lieutenant "Bud" Liebenow, the skipper of the PT 157, was stunned.

Like the other PT boat officers at the Rendova base, Liebenow believed Kennedy and his men had all been killed on the morning of August 2. But now, early in the afternoon of August 7, a trio of young Solomon Island natives had appeared at the Rendova dock and handed over a coconut with a message from Lt. (jg) John Kennedy carved on it. As Liebenow examined the object with his torpedoman Welford West, he absorbed the impact of the crude communication—his friend, tent mate, and fellow warrior Kennedy was alive and stranded behind enemy lines with his crew.

Liebenow instructed Welford West to rush the coconut directly into the headquarters tent of base commander Thomas Warfield. Unknown to Liebenow, Warfield himself had just received the message relayed from Coastwatcher Reg Evans reporting the discovery of the PT 109 crew. Warfield was having trouble believing the news and summoned Gasa for a brief conversation.

Studying the coconut husk, Warfield asked, "Who wrote this?"

"Captain Kennedy," said Gasa.

"Who showed him to do this with the coconut?"

"I did," replied Gasa.

Warfield then called a meeting of his boat captains, fourteen of whom crowded into the command tent. According to witness Liebenow, Warfield still was skeptical. *A coconut? Could these natives be trusted? Might it be an elaborate Japanese trick to lure a large American rescue force into a trap?* Warfield no doubt also recalled the unequivocal declaration of Lieutenant John Lowrey, the nearest witness to the PT 109 crash, at the boat captain's meeting hours after the incident: "All hands were lost. They couldn't possibly survive."

And yet there was the coconut, coupled with Coastwatcher Evans's report and the corroborating note from Lenny Thom that the natives also brought with them. It was hard to comprehend, but now Warfield had three sources telling him the same thing: the men of PT 109 were back from the dead.

As for Liebenow, he had no doubt the distress messages were real. He trusted the Solomon Islands natives, with his own life if necessary, and he considered them full allies and brothers-in-arms, as did so many other American servicemen.

Clearly, Warfield had to scramble a rescue force to deliver Kennedy and his men to safety. But in light of the series of recent PT boat disasters and fatalities that occurred under his command, Warfield was willing to commit only as small a force as possible to the rescue operation.

"We can risk one boat for this mission," Warfield announced. Looking at Liebenow, he said, "The PT 157 will go to the Coastwatchers station as we think that there may be a chance that the PT 109 crew has been sighted. Bill Battle's boat [the PT 171] will go out first and first sweep the area with radar to see if there's any Japanese shipping in the area."

In subsequent years, Liebenow downplayed the dangers and difficulties he faced in the rescue, which he called a routine "pickup," but it was an unquestionably hazardous journey into enemy-held waters, with no air cover and no reinforcements in case of attack. It was another dark night with occasional showers and poor to fair visibility.

By coincidence, there happened to be two leading war correspondents at Rendova that day, who each worked for major American press syndicates that served hundreds of newspapers: Frank Hewlett of United Press and Leif Erickson of the Associated Press. Hewlett recalled how he became embedded with the rescue party and boarded Bud Liebenow's PT 157, "I'd known Hank Brantingham from Manila days. I dropped by to see him that day. He said he was going out that night and asked if I wanted to go. I said hell no! I knew the PT's. You went out for about fourteen hours, all night, and maybe shot a few rounds at barges. Never much of a story. Then he told me they were going out to rescue Ambassador Kennedy's son. That was a horse of a different color. I said hell yes! Then I tried my damnedest to ditch Leif Erickson, told him I was going to play poker with Hank or some ruse like that. But he wasn't fooled. So, in the end, we both made the trip."

For his part, Erickson recalled, "I don't remember Frank trying to ditch me, but it wouldn't have worked." Erickson had been tipped off himself by a source on Rendova that they were going out to rescue Kennedy, and recognized it could be a great story, so he hopped aboard, too. They did this with the approval of senior officers at Rendova, who recognized that a successful rescue would generate good publicity.

Finally at 11:30 A.M., a response was relayed to Reginald Evans through the Coastwatchers radio network: "Great news. Commander PT base received a message st [shortly] after yours from survivors by native. They gave their position and news that some are badly wounded and request rescue. We passed the news that you had sent canoes and without wishing to interfere with your arrangements want to know if they [the Rendova base] can assist. They would send surface craft to meet your returning canoes or anything you advise. They wish to express great appreciation. We will await your advice and pass on."

Coastwatcher Evans had suggested the natives take Kennedy alone back to Rendova by canoe via the Wana Wana Lagoon. As for his men on Olasana, they should wait for a PT boat, as recommended by the American officers on Rendova. Kennedy said it was out of the question. He wanted to help pilot a rescue boat over to his men on Olasana, and he wished to be with his men as soon as possible. And so Kennedy and Evans worked out another plan, which Evans radioed to Rendova: "Lieut. Kennedy considers it advisable that he pilot PT boats tonight. He will await boats near Patparan Island. PT boat to approach island from NW Ten PM as close as possible. Boat to fire four shots as recognition. He will acknowledge with same [four shots] and go alongside in canoe. Survivors now on island NW of Gross . . . He advises outboard motor." The pickup of Kennedy and his crew was set for late that night.

But they were not out of danger yet. A perilous stage of the operation was about to begin, as the Americans would try to navigate a round-trip passage, at night, through nearly forty miles of hostile waters, where Japanese float planes and shore batteries hunted PT boats.

Before they went out, Warfield called in the three Solomon Island scouts. He asked Eroni Kumana, Biuku Gasa, and John Kari if they were afraid, or if they were thinking of their families. Warfield stressed that they might enter combat, and that it was fine if they didn't want to go on the mission with the Americans.

"There's no problem," declared Kari, "if they live, we live—if they die, we die."

Warfield then insisted all three scouts sign written statements confirming they were going on the mission voluntarily.

"Light 'em off!" said Liebenow from the cockpit of the PT 157, giving the signal for the engine crew to fire up the boat's engines.

Liebenow gently maneuvered the boat from its dock out to sea, one hand on the wheel and his other slowly pushing the throttle forward to cruising speed.

It was close to 7:00 P.M., just after sunset on the dark, cool night of August 7, 1943. The native men stood close by to help him navigate, and before long he could sense the very faint outlines of islands silhouetted against the black sky.

Don't make a wake, don't make a wake, thought Liebenow, as his boat passed through the water. Liebenow's dilemma was how to reach Kennedy and his men fast enough to execute a swift rescue, yet also travel slow enough as to not give away his position to the enemy. His solution was to travel at about 10 to 15 knots, a bit faster than usual, to engage all three engine mufflers to reduce the noise, and to periodically change course in a zigzag pattern to prevent being zeroed in on by the enemy tracking him from planes or shore batteries. He timed the PT 157's departure and speed to arrive in the target area during the blackest time of night, around midnight.

Liebenow had his full crew aboard his boat, plus several guests. The special rescue party aboard the PT 157 consisted of Solomon Islands scouts Eroni Kumana, Biuku Gasa, and John Kari; Lieutenants Hank Brantingham (Squadron 9 executive officer and Warfield's second-in-command) and Alvin Cluster (in command of Kennedy's Squadron 2); pharmacist's mates Fred T. Ratchford and William J. Lawrence to provide basic medical care to the survivors; plus the two reporters, Frank Hewlett and Leif Erickson. Liebenow's regular crew consisted of executive officer John Ruff; torpedoman Welford West; quartermaster Waldo DeWilde; motormacs Dan Jamieson, Harry Armstrong, and Harry Aust; gunner mates Jimmy Smith, Ray Macht, and Harold Goodemote; and radioman Sam Koury.

"Koury was manning the radio, trying to keep in contact with the 171, which was to furnish radar cover," recalled Liebenow. "We lost contact with the radar boat shortly after leaving the base."

Years later, Liebenow explained, "I've often been asked why a boat with a radar wasn't selected to make the pickup. I'm sure my thinking is prejudiced, however, here it is. A crew with experience and seamanship ability was needed, and most of all, one that wouldn't panic under pressure. This was the crew of the 157. As for the boat, we had been on her since she hit the water at Bayonne [New Jersey] and knew every plank in her. If we went, old 'Aces & Eights' would carry us." The operation required a boat commander and crew with great skill and experience, qualities that Liebenow and the PT 157 crew had in abundance. "We knew the general area of the sinking from the reports of the natives and the dispatches from Evans," Liebenow recounted. "Besides, we had patrolled this area many times."

According to John Kari, Gasa and Kumana became "very weak and seasick" on the journey, as they were exhausted from their epic canoe trip and were unaccustomed to riding in motorized boats. Kari recalled that members of Liebenow's crew "held them like pussycats."

Lieutenant (jg) William "Bud" Liebenow (in T-shirt with binoculars, right) with crew and legendary Squadron 9 Lieutenant Commander Robert Kelly (smoking pipe, center) on a rare daytime patrol, 1943. (National Archives/Bridgeman Carney)

The rescuer: In 2014 and 2015, more than seventy years after the hazardous mission deep in enemy waters to rescue Kennedy and his crew, Liebenow told his story in a series of interviews for this book. Liebenow was an ice-cool, highly skilled boat captain who went on to rescue over 60 American sailors on D-Day. (William F. Liebenow)

For over four hours, the PT 157 gingerly chugged through the dark water, while the native scouts gave Liebenow directions to guide the boat toward Reginald Evans' new Coastwatching station at Gomu Island. As planned, Liebenow raised his .45 pistol and fired four shots to alert Kennedy of their arrival. Kennedy, who paddled out in a native canoe for the rendezvous, fired three rounds from his .38, then realized he was out of ammo for the fourth shot. He picked up a captured Japanese rifle lent to him by Evans and fired a final round in the air, though the recoil was so heavy it nearly dumped him out of the small boat.

As Kennedy approached, a voice called out, "Hey, Jack!"

In a bitter outburst born of the frustrations of past six days, Kennedy's supposed reply was, "Where the hell you been?"

Lieutenant Art Berndtson, who was in the nearby PT 171, re-called that Kennedy's question was hardly welcome: "It was an un-fortunate thing to say, I thought. I know it irked a lot of people on the two PTs. There was a war on. The guys were going out every night, getting killed and wounded. We were busy as hell. I had a patrol to lead that night and I was taking time from it. And then he hit us with that comment, like he was the only guy around!"

Liebenow, however, recalled that the PT 171 was nowhere to be seen, and that a different exchange occurred, one more typical of two junior naval officers exchanging wisecracks in the midst of extreme pressure.

"Hey, Jack: we've got some food for you!" said Liebenow.

"Just what I need," said Kennedy, "No thanks. I just had a co-conut."

"You're probably eating better that we are," joked Liebenow, in a swipe at the monotonous cuisine available at the Rendova base.

Kennedy was hoisted aboard the PT 157 by native John Kari. "Good evening, Lieutenant Kennedy," Kari greeted him in a mellifluous British-accented voice that Lieutenant Cluster described as "out of the Court of St. James's." After hugging some of his saviors, Kennedy then quickly took up a station next to Liebenow and the natives around the boat's cockpit to guide them to the island holding the rest of the PT 109 crew.

Liebenow now got a good look at Kennedy and was shocked at his appearance. His former classmate and tentmate had a thick beard and appeared to weigh "only 110 pounds." "He had made numerous long swims during the week before the pickup trying to intercept our regular patrols," Liebenow later explained. "I'm sure he was in great pain. But physical pain was a part of life in those days; you just kept doing what you had to do. With your shipmates getting killed around you, you felt lucky to be alive and be able to feel pain."

According to Liebenow, on the thirty-minute journey to rescue the rest of the survivors, he faced "tricky navigation through the reefs in the middle of the night and it was dark. We had to feel our way in. We put Welford West, who was our torpedoman and an experienced seaman when he joined the navy, up on the foc'sle [forward bow] with a lead line. It was an old-fashioned way of marking depth in the sea. He would throw it down and it marked distances in fathoms. He called out the depths and we threaded our way through the reefs and shoals. We went right up to the island, we put our nose right up against the shore."

Kennedy's squadron commander Al Cluster, who came up from Tulagi to join the rescue party, was onboard the PT 157 that night. He remembered the scene: "It's a riot in retrospect. The little native got up on the bow of the boat, and we had Jack down below. Each boat had some medicinal whiskey, little bottles of brandy, about the same kind you get on airplanes today."

Kennedy downed one or two of the liquor bottles, and on his

largely empty stomach, the effect was immediate. As Liebenow and West guided the PT 157 directly up to the beach of Olasana Island, an exuberant Kennedy hollered out, "Lenny! Hey, Lenny!" his voice well fortified with alcohol.

"Goddammit," snapped Cluster, "keep your voice down. I don't want to alert the Japanese over on Gizo! Quiet!" Cluster felt the urge to smack Kennedy on the head with an oar if he didn't shut up.

Kennedy was unfazed, and shouted, "Lenny, where are you?"

The PT 109 crewmen were asleep in the bushes.

They had collapsed in exhaustion earlier that night, uncertain of their fate as they began their seventh night in the wilderness. They knew a rescue was underway, but they also appreciated that much could go wrong before they could be evacuated to safety.

At 12:30 AM on August 8, they began waking up to the shouts of their skipper, John Kennedy.

Finally, a voice replied, "Here we are!" It was Ensign Lenny Thom, who, along with the other survivors, did not know the timing and details of the rescue operation. "The boats are here!" someone shouted. Thom joyfully splashed out into waist-deep water to greet Kennedy.

Barney Ross remembered, "Although we'd set a watch all night long, apparently we were all asleep at the critical moment when Jack and the PT boat arrived off of our little haven in the bushes." When salvation came, he recalled, "They were hollering for us to wake, finally we woke up in time to be rescued. I will never forget, I felt sort of foolish—we were all asleep!"

A dinghy was put over the PT 157's side. Liebenow shut the engines off and Welford West, Ray Mach, the 157's rear turret gunner, and Eroni Kumana and Biuku Gasa maneuvered the small boat the short distance to shore. When the most severely wounded crewman, the badly burned Pat McMahon, heard furtive noises in the dark, he declared, "Halt—who goes there?"

"It's me, 'Doc' [Fred] Ratchford!" replied the pharmacist's mate, who was well known and beloved by the sailors at Rendova as the man who routinely dispensed first aid to them, tended to their cuts, bruises, and minor medical complaints, and insisted that they wash their feet every day to prevent tropical ailments.

McMahon, beside himself with joy, crawled out from the shelter of the little hut the natives had improvised for him, stood up, and collapsed into Ratchford's strong arms, tears running down his face.

"Doc Ratchford," McMahon cried, "I knew you'd come for us!"

McMahon was carefully picked up and carried to the boat.

Other crewmen rushed and hobbled to the beach, and waded out to the boat.

By 2:15, according to the ship's log, all eleven PT 109 crew members were aboard the PT 157 and that critical phase of the rescue was complete. Liebenow recalled, "The crew of the 157 still had a job to do. We backed into clear water, spun around and headed for home. It wasn't until we could spot the dark mass of Rendova Island and Todd City that I relinquished the wheel."

"So," Liebenow asked Kennedy during the journey, "what did you do with your boat?"

"Gone," replied Kennedy; "just one of those things."

"Jack," kidded Liebenow, "how in the world could a Jap destroyer run you down? How in the world were you not able to get away from getting cut in two?"

"Lieb, to tell you the truth, I actually do not know. It all happened so quickly. I just don't know how it happened."

The native scouts joined in the gentle teasing of Kennedy, chiding him in Pidgin, "Aren't you an old woman for losing your boat?"

But soon, John F. Kennedy broke down. He collapsed in a bunk belowdecks on the PT 157, and he was crying. "He was very tired," recalled Al Cluster. "There were tears streaming down his face. He was bitter about the skippers who had left them behind. If they had come to look for them, he thought, maybe the other two men lost on PT 109, Marney and Kirksey, could have been saved."

To Liebenow, it appeared McMahon and another wounded sailor, probably Ross, were in shock. They were brought below decks immediately to be tended to with rudimentary first aid by the two pharmacist's mates.

But for the rest of the PT 109 survivors, a feeling of pure, unbounded happiness spread over them. For survivor William Johnston, the overriding emotion was one of joy to be alive, to be found and to be going back to relative safety. He helped himself to some brandy, put his arms around Kumana and Gasa, and loudly sang along with them a Christian hymn the scouts learned in Episcopalian mission school:

> Jesus loves me, this I know,
> For the Bible tells me so;
> Little ones to Him belong,
> They are weak, but He is strong.
> Yes, Jesus loves me; yes, Jesus loves me . . .

According to Liebenow, "We really had a celebration. We broke out the medical brandy, they were all shaking hands and patting

Weather-beaten flag flown by the PT 109 before the crash.
(Frank J. Andruss, Sr.)

our crew on the backs and the natives were screaming [songs] at top
of their voices. I thought the Japs would hear them."

"Let's try to keep it quiet!" Liebenow called out firmly.

At 5:15 A.M. on Sunday, August 8, 1943, Lieutenant William
Liebenow docked the PT 157 at Rendova with the rescued PT 109
survivors aboard.

It was six days and three hours since the *Amagiri* had destroyed
Kennedy's boat. "Kennedy's friends and the crew's friends came
and some cried, they were so happy to see them," Eroni Kumana
recalled. "They gave everybody food. A ship came for us and one
for the crew. We all stood up and shook hands all round."

Kennedy already felt a powerful bond with the two natives who
saved his life. He told Gasa and Kumana that he planned to get another boat to command, and if he managed to not get killed, he
would seek them out in the Solomons sometime later and spend time
visiting them. He owed them everything, but the two men were leaving soon. So in lieu of awarding them a medal, Kennedy presented

Gasa with a gold coin his friend Clare Boothe Luce, wife of Time-Life publishing titan Henry Luce, had given him. Kennedy later wrote to Mrs. Luce to inform her the good-luck piece "did service above and beyond its routine duties during a rather busy period."

Gasa recalled the scene of the festivities: "We had a big feast. The three of us [Gasa, Kumana, and Kari] sat with Kennedy and his crew at one table. Kennedy made a speech thanking us. He said that if he had good luck he would try to come and see us again. Kennedy gave me a 'dime,' and said it was the only thing he could give me at that time. I was also given a ribbon with seven colors, and a Colonel gave me a medal and commended my courage. A canoe from the Wana Wana lagoon came for us and took us home." Years later, Biuku Gasa proudly described his marathon journey through enemy waters by canoe, foot, and barge to rescue John F. Kennedy and his fellow PT 109 survivors as "the quickest and most far-ranging journey ever made by a Solomon Islander in the Western District."

Before they left, Kennedy pulled Kumana, Gasa, and Kari aside and emphatically and repeatedly thanked them for saving his life and the lives of his crewmen. He promised the scouts he would always think of them and would never forget their help and that of Ben Kevu and his colleagues.

In the decades that followed, some PT boat veterans criticized Kennedy's performance during the battle that resulted in the sinking of the PT 109. Years later, PT skipper Hank Brantingham said bluntly: "He goofed off. He got lost. And he got run over." Another leading critic was Thomas Warfield, who said of Kennedy, "He wasn't a particularly good boat commander." Warfield explained, "The nearest thing I can figure out is they got kind of sleepy and weren't too alert and Kennedy was idling with his mufflers closed. He shouldn't have been muffled. He knew the destroyers were coming out. He saw this thing coming at him and got bugged a little bit and shoved his throttles forward [too fast]. And I think he killed his engines."

But even the notoriously difficult Warfield expressed admiration for how Kennedy held his crew together and tried to summon help during their post-crash ordeal, saying, "I think you have to give him a hell of a lot of credit for getting out there and swimming out almost every night, whether it was the most intelligent thing to do or not, you have to give him a hell of a lot of credit for doing that. He was trying to get some kind of action." He added, "It's better than sitting there and starving to death. And if somebody is going to do it, why not the commander of the boat? I think you really have to give him a lot of credit for doing that. He really tried to take care of his boys—he deserves that, no question about it."

According to on-the-scene reporter Frank Hewlett, the PT 109 survivors crew all praised Kennedy "to high heaven." Charles Harris said, "Kennedy was the hero. He saved our lives. I owed him my life. If it wasn't for him I wouldn't be here, I really feel that. I venture to say there are very few men who would swim out in that ocean alone without knowing what was underneath you. Brother, I wouldn't do it. You could give me a million dollars and I wouldn't swim out there. That took a lot of guts. I thought he was great. Everybody on the crew thought he was top-notch."

Although debates over Kennedy's performance in the incident endured for years, as for Kennedy's crew, Bud Liebenow noted that "Not one of them ever had anything bad to say about JFK. And they are the ones who know."

In Hyannis Port, Massachusetts, Joseph P. Kennedy had received word that his son was missing at some point after the crash, but he decided not to tell his wife Rose about it yet. The information must have been devastating to the elder Kennedy, given all he'd done to get John into the PT service. One account has Rose learning of the rescue by phone from a friend, who told her "Jack's been saved!" A mystified Mrs. Kennedy asked, "Saved from what?" She summoned her husband to the phone from his riding stables. According to the August 20, 1943, edition of the *New York Times,* the couple "shouted in joy" when told of their son's exploits. According to the article, "Mrs. Kennedy, first to hear the news by telephone at their summer home, expressed deep sorrow for the two crewmen who lost their lives. 'That's wonderful,' Mrs. Kennedy said when told her son was safe." At the time of their rescue, the PT 109 crew was not yet officially declared as missing, and the news of the PT 109 crash and rescue was delayed for a number of days by wartime censorship.

On August 12, 1943, less than a week after the rescue, Kennedy wrote a reassuring letter to his parents: "Dear Folks; This is just a short note to tell you that I am alive—and *not* kicking—in spite of any reports that you may happen to hear. It was believed otherwise for a few days—so reports or rumors may have gotten back to you. Fortunately they misjudged the durability of a Kennedy—am back at the base now—and am OK. As soon as possible I shall try to give you the whole story. Much love to you all Jack."

In the second week of August the survivors were transferred to Tulagi, where they were examined and treated by Navy doctor Joseph B. Wharton Jr. Many of the crew had bad coral cuts and abrasions that were infected, in addition to fungus and ear infections. As was his custom, Kennedy made a striking impression on Dr. Wharton: "I remember Jack Kennedy at that time quite clearly. He was one of the finest and most brilliant men I had ever met. Very strong and mature for his age. His knowledge was very versatile, everything from poker to philosophy." Kennedy's medical record specified: "Admitted with abrasions, multiple. Patient was on PT boat which was rammed and sunk by enemy destroyer. After being in water about 10 hours landed upon enemy occupied island without shoes, clothing or food. Stayed on island for five days before being rescued. At the present time he shows symptoms of fatigue and many deep abrasions and lacerations of the entire body, especially the feet." The medical officer prescribed "hot soaks and alcohol and glycerine dressings and bed rest. Multiple vitamin tablets and high caloric diet."

After the rescue, the survivors scattered to different assignments. William Johnston and Pat McMahon were evacuated to other hospitals. At Tulagi, Kennedy held a meeting of all the other PT 109 crewmen and told them they earned the chance to rest and recuperate on leave in New Zealand for about a month, or they could choose to stay in the combat zone and go home a month sooner. Everyone chose the latter, so they could get back to the United States as fast as possible. Barney Ross, Gerard Zinser, and Raymond Albert returned to their previous unit, Squadron Ten, based at Rendova. Kennedy, Lenny Thom, John Maguire, Edman Mauer, and Charles Harris stayed at Tulagi awaiting new assignments, along with three crewmen who served on the PT 109 before the crash: Leon Drawdy, Maurice Kowal, and Edmund Drewitch. Ray Lee Starkey stayed with Squadron 9 for the next seven months.

Kennedy closely followed the recovery of his injured men, especially the most badly wounded sailor, Pappy McMahon. In these unpublished passages from his lost 1946 narrative of the incident, Kennedy marveled at McMahon's bravery, and his sense of duty: "When the survivors were finally picked up, McMahon was sent to a hospital at Guadalcanal. He remained at the hospital over four months and on his release, he was ordered back to the United States for release from the service, because of his badly scarred hands. McMahon, however, requested that he be permitted to remain at

Tulagi, Solomon Islands. PT Boat Officers (L-R) James ("Jim") Reed, John F. Kennedy, George ("Barney") Ross [rear], and Paul ("Red") Fay, 1943, likely after August 7, 1943. (John F. Kennedy Presidential Library)

Tulagi and help in the repair of old engines. Because of the great shortage at that time of experienced engineers and because of McMahon's persistent requests, he was allowed to stay for nearly six months more. He worked every day—explaining to the new engineers the intricacies of 1800 horse power Packard engines, and frequently disregarded the doctor's advice and worked on the engines himself. I saw him often with the thin skin of his hands cut and bleeding at the end of a day's work. But he still had that smile. McMahon's courage was an inspiration to us all."

On Tulagi, when Kennedy's buddy Johnny Iles first had heard the PT 109 was lost, he asked a Catholic priest to "say some masses for Kennedy." When Iles eventually greeted Kennedy on his return to Tulagi, he remembered, "I gave him a big hello. Then I happened to mention about the mass. He was furious! He read the riot act to me. He said he wasn't ready to die just yet and why the hell had I given up hope?"

John Kennedy's war could have ended here. By losing his boat and enduring his agonizing ordeal of survival, he had earned himself a one-way ticket home to the safety of shore duty, to a long rest and recuperation in the United States, and back to the sybaritic, globe-trotting life of a super-rich bachelor with a golden future.

But John F. Kennedy made a surprising decision.

He chose to stay in Solomon Islands, keep himself in the line of fire—and fight.

11

LIFE AND DEATH AT THE
WARRIOR RIVER

★

SOLOMON ISLANDS
FALL 1943

"If your boat was sunk, you'd get new assignments in the States," explained Kennedy's squadron commander and close friend, Al Cluster, of the Navy's informal custom during World War II. But Kennedy would not hear of it, despite his recent harrowing ordeal.

It seemed Kennedy wanted revenge, in Cluster's view, as if he wanted to strike back hard at the Japanese. Cluster thought Kennedy was haunted by the deaths of Kirksey and Marney, ashamed for losing his boat and not sinking the Japanese destroyer that instead destroyed his own vessel. "I think all these things came together, and he wanted to get back at them," reflected Cluster.

Back in the United States, however, the PT 109 incident generated a brief flurry of national attention, in which Kennedy was transfigured almost overnight into a war hero. It was exactly the image his father hoped would propel his son to prominence after the war. On August 19, Navy censors approved stories written by the two wire service reporters, Leif Erickson and Frank Hewlett, who witnessed the rescue; the articles appeared with headlines such as KENNEDY'S SON IS HERO IN THE PACIFIC and KENNEDY'S SON SAVES 10 IN PACIFIC. Al Cluster followed up with a letter to Joe and Rose Kennedy on September 18, telling them the stories of their son's courage were true. "Kennedy did a fine job," he told them. "He's in my squadron and is one of the finest officers I have. He did very commendable work in getting his crew out O.K. and we're all very proud of him."

Joe Kennedy, his eyes always on the lookout for a "main chance" to thrust his family into national prestige, sprang into action and tried to get *Reader's Digest* to run a story on the PT 109 in their hugely popular national magazine. But he got nowhere. The magazine wasn't interested. The story of the PT 109 came and went, and soon was lost in the flurry of thousands of other stories of war heroics.

On August 22, 1943, despite the utter failure of the August 1–2 Battle of Blackett Strait, Commander Thomas Warfield launched another nearly catastrophic mass PT boat raid from Rendova. This one, incredibly, was scheduled for the daylight hours, its target several cove entrances on Kolombangara. "I did all I could to prevent the attack being made," wrote Sub-Lieutenant Reginald Evans, the Coastwatcher who had helped save the lives of the survivors of PT 109, in his after-action report. He continued: "Machine guns covered the entrance to both coves and a small coastal gun opened fire from Kukkuli Pt. The P.T. boats retired at high speed under a smoke screen. I was later informed that the U.S. casualties were 3 killed and 5 wounded. Had the Japs been good gunners they would have sunk half the boats." Evans was shocked by "the absurdity of the attack" by eight PT boats in broad daylight, which gave the Japanese a half an hour to prepare a counterattack. American participants in the operation called it Warfield's "suicide mission."

Back at the Tulagi PT base, on September 1, 1943, just three weeks after the rescue of the PT 109 survivors, Al Cluster gave a barely recuperated John Kennedy the command of another boat, the PT 59, a 77-foot Elco design that was slightly older than the PT 109. So far, PT boats had proven mostly ineffective in sinking Japanese capital ships, and Cluster and Kennedy decided to pursue Admiral William Halsey's idea of converting them into barge-hunting gunships.

Cluster recalled, "I guess you could say we were in a kind of miniature arms race with the Japs. They armed the barges with big guns and protected them with armor. Then we responded by creating what we called a gunboat, a radical departure for the PT force." On the PT 59, Cluster and Kennedy decided to remove two depth charges, the four torpedo tubes, and the 20 mm Oerlikon cannon, and install bigger guns, including ten .50-caliber machine guns and two 40 mm Bofors cannon, one of which was retrofitted with Japanese motorcycle handlebars that had been salvaged at Guadalcanal.

Additionally, Cluster recalled, "We reinforced the decks with armor plate. They were really very heavily armed little boats." Typically, Kennedy pitched himself into the tough physical work. "I don't think I ever saw a guy work harder, longer hours," said Cluster. By the time they finished, the boat was bristling with heavy firepower.

The new experiment in PT gunboats took place as the Allies were slowly pushing north through the Solomon Islands, having finally captured the Munda airfield, landing on Vella Lavella on August 15, and occupying the islands of New Georgia and Gizo. The Japanese were falling back to the islands of Choiseul and Bougainville, and were preparing to evacuate their large garrison on Kolombangara, which they completed at the end of September.

On October 8, Kennedy was promoted to full lieutenant. But he still needed a crew for the newly refitted gunboat PT 59, now stationed at Tulagi, off Guadalcanal. One day, two volunteers appeared on the dock and greeted Kennedy. He looked stunned. There before him were two fellow survivors of the PT 109 disaster, Edman Edgar Mauer and John Maguire.

"What are you doing here?" asked Kennedy.

"What kind of a guy are you?" they replied. "You got a boat and didn't come get us?"

Kennedy became choked up; according to Maguire, it was "the nearest I ever seen him come to crying." No less than three other crewmen who had previously served under Kennedy on the PT 109 before the crash also volunteered: Maurice Kowal, Edmund Drewitch, and Leon Drawdy. "Have a picked crew, all volunteers, and all very experienced," Kennedy wrote proudly of his new crew. "Every man but one has been sunk at least once, and they all have been in the boats for a long time."

Kennedy's executive officer, Lieutenant (jg) Robert Lee "Dusty" Rhoads, remembered, "What impressed me most about Jack then was that so many of the men that had been on PT 109 had followed him to the 59. It spoke well of him as a leader, I thought." Similarly, John Klee, who was a gunner on the PT 59 under Kennedy's command in November 1943, recalled in a 2014 interview that he was struck by how "not a single one of the those PT 109 men ever had a bad word to say about Kennedy." Klee was also impressed by the quality of the sexy "pinup" photos Kennedy kept of some of his girlfriends posted in the boat's captain's quarters.

Gunner's mate Glen Christiansen, who became chief petty of-

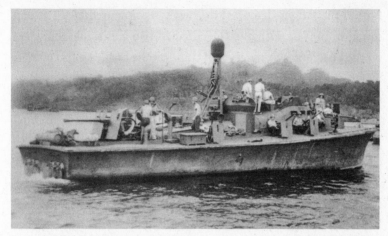

Kennedy's Revenge: PT 59, which Kennedy converted into a gunboat. He was so hell-bent on attacking the Japanese that one of his crew despaired to a senior officer, "My God, this guy's going to get us all killed!" (John F. Kennedy Presidential Library)

New guns installed by Kennedy on PT 59. (Frank J. Andruss Sr.)

ficer of the PT 59, described the newly reconfigured boat: "It had so many guns on it that we literally had two crews: one that lived on the boat, and one that would come on the boat. We had sixteen men and three officers, whereas normally, a PT boat, a seventy-seven-foot Elco, would have eight men and two officers."

At Tulagi, Kennedy continued his habit of organizing discussions on politics, history, and current events. One sailor remembered seeing Kennedy wading through back issues of the *New York Times* piled up in his bunk. Using copies of popular magazines like the *Saturday Evening Post, Life,* and *Collier's* as discussion guides, Kennedy and his friends debated world affairs in his tent, as Kennedy exhorted his colleagues to read, to form opinions, and to understand, in the words of Red Fay, "why the hell we're out here." Fay added, "He made us all very aware of our obligation as citizens of the United States to do something, to be involved in the process. Yet side by side with this seriousness he had a great sense of humor—that laugh of his: the laugh was so contagious that it made everybody laugh. You'd tell a story or a joke and then that laugh would come out, he just had everybody laughing."

Despite the ordeals of the PT 109's sinking and his chronically fragile health, Kennedy retained the powerful charisma that would eventually help propel him into the Oval Office. A Catholic priest who met him in the fall of 1943 wrote that John Kennedy was a "fine, upstanding lad, guts, brains, courage to give away, generous, worshipped by his lads." James Reed marveled of his friend Kennedy, "He always had that sense of leadership: quietly assertive. Not at all flamboyant. And that magical quality that everybody liked him. But I tell you this about Jack, he never complained. He always had a terrific humor, a really acute sense of humor. He was very self-deprecating." After joining several patrols on Kennedy's PT 59, Commander Thomas Warfield's intelligence officer, future

Kennedy strikes a jaunty pose in a photo believed to be taken at Tulagi after his rescue. (John F. Kennedy Presidential Library)

Supreme Court justice Byron "Whizzer" White, recalled, "I began to get a strong feeling about what kind of fellow he was. He proved himself to be very intelligent in the way he ran his boat, as well as cool and courageous under fire."

Kennedy's health, however, was increasingly precarious. His weight was plunging toward 150 pounds, his chronic back trouble was intensifying, and he was limping around with a cane. The Navy needed live bodies in action, and he qualified, just barely. After a routine medical exam required for promotion to full lieutenant on October 20, he wrote to a friend: "I looked as bad as I could look . . . [but] I passed with flying colors, ready 'for active duty ashore or at sea' anywhere, and by anywhere they mean no place else but here. They'd give you twenty-twenty with no strain. Everyone is in such lousy shape here that the only way they can tell if he is fit to fight is to see if he can breathe. That's about the only grounds on which I can pass these days." The following month, the Tulagi medical officer conducted X-rays of Kennedy and diagnosed an "early duodenal ulcer."

In letters to his family and friends from September through November 1943, Kennedy revealed flashes of bitterness and disillusion at the war. "The war goes slowly here, slower than you can ever imagine from reading the papers at home," he wrote. "Munda or any of those spots are just God damned hot stinking corners of small islands in a group of islands in a part of the ocean we all hope to never see again." In a letter to Inga Arvad, he expressed guilt over one of the men he lost, Andrew Jackson Kirksey: "He told me one night he thought he was going to be killed. I wanted to put him ashore to work. I wish I had."

In another letter to his parents, he reassured them of his intention to come home to enjoy the pleasures of family vacation life: "After this present fighting is over will be glad to get home. When

I do get out of here you'll find that you have a new permanent fix-
ture around that Florida pool. I'll just move from it to get into my
sack. Don't worry at all about me, I've learned to duck."

On October 18, 1943, Kennedy moved from Rendova up to Lambu
Lambu Cove, site of a primitive, rat-infested, new advance PT base
on the northeast coast of Vella Lavella Island. The mission of the
PT 59 and the handful of other PT boats at Lambu Lambu was to
harass and attack Japanese barge traffic, as Allied forces geared up
for a critical landing on the Japanese stronghold of Bougainville
island and smaller diversionary landings on the island of Choiseul,
where up to 5,000 exhausted Japanese troops awaited evacuation.
The ultimate target was the Japanese military's regional headquarters on the island of Rabaul.

For the next month, October 18 to November 18, Kennedy
commanded the PT 59 gunboat in a total of thirteen patrols from
Lambu Lambu to the nearby island of Choiseul. Kennedy's boat
was bombed several times by Japanese floatplanes, and it shot up
some apparently unmanned Japanese barges. In a replay of his PT
109 experience, he never engaged in combat with Japanese surface
craft, with the exception of the night of November 5–6, when the
PT 59 opened fire on three barges, which quickly vanished. "The
59 experiment was a failure," recalled his executive officer Dusty
Rhoads. "The theory was to provide one gunboat with each section
of PTs. The gunboats, screened by the PTs, would move in and
attack the barges. Unfortunately, by the time we got the three boats
converted, the barge threat was gone. We never fought anymore.
We only certainly saw barges on one night. They were coming out
of Choiseul and they went right back in. So everything we were
built for, barge fighting, we never did."

On the night of November 1–2, 1943, however, John F. Kennedy had an opportunity to save the lives of ten American servicemen, this time in a daring emergency rescue mission in the midst of combat. It was an operation for which Kennedy received no medals or special recognition, and he rarely ever talked about the event again. But Kennedy's actions meant salvation for ten U.S. marines.

In the midafternoon of November 1, Lieutenant Kennedy was abruptly asked by Lieutenant Arthur Berndtson, executive officer of Squadron 10 and temporary base commander at Lambu Lambu, if he could support an operation to evacuate a trapped force of eighty-seven exhausted Marines from the island of Choiseul, where they were engaged in a campaign aimed at diverting Japanese attention from the American's real target, Bougainville.

The PT 59's fuel tank was less than half-full. Kennedy did not expect to go on a mission that night, and he had confirmed this with the planners at the Lambu Lambu PT boat office. Refueling the boat was a laborious, time-consuming process. Berndtson recalled, "It was a hell of a place to try to refuel. All by hand. Jack had about seven hundred gallons. That was not enough to get over and back. He needed at least one thousand gallons. I asked him if he would go anyway. I was sending two other PT boats along. If Jack ran out of fuel, one of the other boats could tow him home. He was disconcerted, but he agreed to go." Kennedy had good reason to be fearful, as he was embarking on a sixty-five-mile journey into the night, with less than half a fuel tank and with only a compass bearing to navigate by.

"Let's go get them," Kennedy declared to his crew. "Wind her up!"

The three PT boats rushed out from Lambu Lambu toward Choiseul at 4:35 P.M., stopping along the way at Voza Village, where the marines had established an outpost on Choiseul, to pick up a marine officer and Navy officer as guides. Kennedy was surprised to see his friend from Rendova, Richard Keresey.

"What the hell are *you* doing here?" Kennedy asked Keresey.

"Never mind that, we have to haul ass up the coast," snapped Keresey, jumping aboard the PT 59. "There's a bunch of marines trapped!"

They found the mouth of Choiseul's Warrior River at about 6 P.M., following the faint sounds of gunfire and screaming. It was dark and rainy as Kennedy's PT 59 pulled up toward the beach, joining one other PT boat and three steel amphibious landing craft, or LCPLs (Landing Craft, Personnel, Large). The marines had splashed into the water and were struggling aboard the LCPLs as Japanese troops poured heavy fire toward them from the shore. One of the landing craft was maneuvering to race the marines back to Voza. But the other overloaded LCPL had scraped its hull open on a coral reef, stalled, and was sinking some 250 yards from shore. "There were Japs on the shore and the marines were in the water, shooting at them," recalled PT 59 crewman Maurice Kowal in an interview decades later with PT boat historian Frank J. Andruss Sr.

"Here's a PT boat!" shouted one of the marines. Kennedy placed the PT 59 between the shore and the crippled landing craft, and his crew pulled some ten marines on board, several of them wounded. Kennedy's gunners were poised to rip up the jungle with suppressive counterfire but were prevented from doing so by fear of hitting friendly forces in the darkness.

Minutes earlier, Corporal Edward James Schnell of Wilmette, Illinois, was critically wounded by a bullet in his chest. As the medic helped carry him to shore, Schnell beseeched him, "Doc, don't leave me."

The medic, a Lieutenant Stevens, assured him, "I'm not going to leave you, Jimmy."

As he lifted Schnell aboard the PT 59, Stevens said, "Lieutenant, I've got a man in bad shape here."

"We'll find a place for him," replied Kennedy from the cockpit. "Any left?" When it was clear all the marines were aboard, Kennedy headed back to Voza. On the way there, Kennedy checked in on the severely wounded Corporal Schnell, who was laid out in Kennedy's bunk as medic Stevens readied a plasma bottle and sutures to treat him.

"Am I all right, Doc?" asked Schnell.

"Jimmy, don't worry about it," replied Stevens, "you're going to be all right."

At Voza, most of the marines were moved over to landing craft for the final trip over to the Lambu Lambu base on Vella Lavella Island. Schnell, however, couldn't be moved and stayed aboard Kennedy's PT 59.

At 1 A.M. on November 2, as the medic held his hand, Corporal Schnell died.

Two hours later, the PT 59's engines went dead, having burned through the last of the fuel. PT 236 slowly towed it the rest of the way to Lambu Lambu, where the marines were offloaded to safety. Glen Christiansen, the PT 59's chief petty officer, remembered a tragic episode during the last stage of the operation: "We called for air cover. We were sitting out there vulnerable as hell, out of gas. As I remember, they sent us a bunch of Australian P-40's [to provide air cover]. Either four or six of them. Well, none of them came back. They all got shot down. It wasn't our fault: we'd been ordered out, and they knew we'd run out of gas, but there was a big stink about it."

Despite the tragic loss of the Australian flyers, Kennedy was energized by his rescue of the marines. In the span of three months, he had played a starring role in saving twenty American lives. Now he fantasized about leading an extremely dangerous, daylight mission back to the same island to attack Japanese positions. "What would you think of this?" Kennedy asked Christiansen, explaining the idea to him.

"Jesus Christ, Mr. Kennedy," said Christiansen, "there's no way. We don't know what's up there!"

Christiansen was so alarmed at Kennedy's idea that he went around Kennedy to appeal to Kennedy's superior officer and squadron commander, Al Cluster, who was visiting the Lambu Lambu outpost. "I hope he doesn't go through with this, because we're going to get slaughtered up there!" despaired Christiansen. "Mr. Kennedy was very gung ho," recalled Christiansen years later. "He had this vendetta or revenge thing on his mind." He reasoned, "We had terrific firepower, and could have raised hell in the river, but I had read a report on the Kolombangara raid [Warfield's "suicide mission" of August 22] where all those people got killed. The problem was, they got inside the river and couldn't turn around. It was real hairy. I couldn't see risking our lives. I felt we ought to try to do something to get at them, bomb them with aircraft or something, but let's not go up the river ourselves."

According to Cluster, "Jack got very wild." Some of Kennedy's men, he related, "said he was crazy and would get them killed." Cluster squashed Kennedy's plan for a daylight gunboat raid up the Warrior River. But Custer observed that the Warrior River rescue on November 1–2, 1943 was a turning point in JFK's life, signaling a "change of seriousness" that that made him "grow up emotionally." Previously, according to Cluster, "We were kind of a happy-go-lucky bunch down there in the Solomons, 'knights of the sea' and all that crap, going out and attacking these large ships with all that glamour: whereas in reality it had become a dirty, minor war in which you just had to do the best you could." Now, after the PT 109 crash and the rescue of the marines, Kennedy was a seasoned warrior.

In Kennedy's final performance report in December 1943, Cluster gave him a perfect 4.0 for his leadership as PT 59's commanding officer, writing that Kennedy "demonstrated a cool effectiveness

under fire and exhibited good judgment and determination in entirely strange conditions. His cheerful attitude and initiative qualify
him to be the exec. officer of a PT Squadron." For Kennedy's actions
in wake of the PT 109 crash, Cluster remembered recommending
him for the Silver Star, the Navy's third-highest award after the
Medal of Honor and Navy Cross, both of which are awarded for
exceptional heroism in combat. Instead, Kennedy, Ross, and Thom
were each given the Navy and Marine Corps Medal for their actions.
The medal is a "lifesaving" medal, not a combat decoration.

In a 1944 review of the action, the Navy ruled that no other
medals were warranted, since the "heroism" at issue did not involve
actual engagement with the enemy—this despite the fact that the PT
109 was participating in a combat operation at the time of the sinking, and the crew's post-crash ordeal obviously took place in a combat
environment, in areas that were controlled or contested by the enemy.
The enlisted men of the PT 109, some of whom were involved in
lifesaving efforts as heroic as the officers, received no medals, though
they made no public complaint or comments on this point.

The final citation for Kennedy's Navy and Marine Corps Medal,
signed by Secretary of the Navy James V. Forrestal and dated May
19, 1944, read: "For extremely heroic conduct as Commanding Officer of Motor Torpedo Boat 109 following the collision and sinking of that vessel in the Pacific War Theater on August 1–2, 1943.
Unmindful of personal danger, Lieutenant (then Lieutenant, Junior
Grade) Kennedy unhesitatingly braved the difficulties and hazards
of darkness to direct rescue operations, swimming many hours to
secure aid and food after he had succeeded in getting his crew
ashore. His outstanding courage, endurance and leadership contributed to the saving of several lives and were in keeping with the
highest traditions of the United States Naval Service."

The rescue of Kennedy and his crew occurred at almost exactly the moment the Allied drive against the Japanese in the Solomons gained a critical burst of momentum. Historian John Prados wrote of August 8, 1943: "While that day marked the end of an ordeal for Jack Kennedy and his men, it also framed the moment Japan tumbled over the edge into an abyss."

Through 1943, the Japanese were expelled from much of the Solomon Islands as the Allies pushed inexorably north and west, and Japanese aircraft and supply losses escalated to intolerable proportions. "So it was that the Solomons became the grave of Japan's dream," wrote Prados. "Here the pendulum of the Pacific War began to swing against Tokyo. The Battle of Midway robbed the Japanese of momentum and stripped their aura of invincibility. But after Midway the pendulum hung in balance. Japan retained numerical superiority and some distinct qualitative advantages. The dream was still attainable. In the Solomons the war was fought to a decision." After the war, Rear Admiral Sokichi Takagi of the Naval General Staff admitted that when the Allies invaded the Solomons, he said to himself that if Japan lost there, "all roads would lead to Tokyo." And so they did.

Physically, Kennedy was a wreck by November 1943.

His back was paining him, and he would soon be diagnosed with both malaria and colitis, or inflammatory bowel disease. He was severely underweight. On November 18, Lieutenant Al Cluster relieved Kennedy of command of PT 59 and sent him to the hospital at Tulagi. Bidding an emotional farewell to his sailors, Kennedy shook each of their hands and told them, "If there is ever anything I can do for you, ask me. You will always know where you can get in touch with me."

At Tulagi, X-rays were given and "chronic disc disease of the lower back" was added to his medical record, as well as the diagno-

sis of an ulcer. (A year later he would be given a medical discharge
from the Navy for physical disability and placed on the retirement
list, which was finally made official on March 1, 1945. The reason
for his discharge was colitis.) In late December, 1943 it was clear
Kennedy would not recover, and Cluster officially detached him
from duty with his PT squadron: JFK's war was over.

Kennedy left the South Pacific from Espiritu Santu on December 23, 1943 aboard the escort carrier U.S.S. *Breton,* for passage via
Samoa and Pago Pago back to San Francisco. He remained in the
United States for the rest of the conflict.

John Kennedy had begun the war as a pampered, globe-trotting
young man barely out of college. But now, after seven months in
the combat zone, the PT 109 crash and the rescues of his crewmen
and the marines at Warrior River, Kennedy had proven to himself
and to others that he was capable of leadership and command, and
possessed considerable courage under fire.

12

THE WINGED CHARIOT

But at my back I always hear
Time's winged chariot hurrying near;
And yonder all before us lie
Deserts of vast eternity.

"To His Coy Mistress," Andrew Marvell (d. 1678),
Excerpted by John F. Kennedy in his 1951 travel diary

John F. Kennedy returned to the United States from the Pacific War in January 1944, landing in San Francisco, then making a brief stop in Beverly Hills to see his old girlfriend Inga Arvad, now a syndicated columnist and reporter for the North American Newspaper Alliance. Though it became clear to both their romance was over, Arvad interviewed Kennedy for her column, and Kennedy gallantly rejected any claims of self-aggrandizement. "None of that hero stuff about me," he declared in the story, which was picked up on the front page of the *Boston Globe*. "The real heroes are not the men who return, but those who stay out there, like plenty of them do, two of my men included."

Kennedy headed for a checkup at the Mayo Clinic, then to his family's Mediterranean palazzo-style estate in Palm Beach, Florida, where he spent several weeks relaxing in idyllic splendor after nine months in the war zone. His mother wrote in her diary, "What joy to see him—to feel his coat & to press his arms," "to look at his bronze tired face which is thin & drawn." On February 5, Kennedy flew to New York City for a few days' stopover en route to his assignment back at the PT boat training center at Melville, Rhode Island, and then to a Navy posting in Miami for much of the rest of the year.

Once in Manhattan, Kennedy headed straight into the arms of a new girlfriend, freshly divorced model and fashion editor Florence Pritchett. He took her for a night on the town that started at the world-famous Stork Club, on East Fifty-Third Street just off Fifth Avenue. The club, presided over by a colorful character named Sherman Billingsley, was a mecca for the rich and famous of the era—and for American military servicemen as well, who were welcomed to the club as honored guests. When soldiers returning from overseas were asked where they were headed, many would gleefully exclaim, "The Stork Club!" The nightspot became a cultural icon for the music, liquor, food, and female companionship that soldiers and sailors yearned for when they came home. One wartime photograph of John Kennedy at the Stork Club shows him on the dance floor with an exotic beauty, a delirious smile plastered on his face.

On a given night at the Stork, one could bump into J. Edgar Hoover, Fred Astaire, Lana Turner, Frank Sinatra, Alfred Hitchcock, or Helen Keller, as GIs and sailors hobnobbed with millionaires and starlets. "From the late 1930's to the mid-1950's, Billingsley's place at 3 East 53rd Street was the headquarters of what was called cafe society: the social merging of the children of the old rich with movie stars, gossip columnists, prewar Eurotrash, politicians, judges, some favored cops, a few good writers and a sprinkling of former bootleggers," wrote Pete Hamill. "These were people who did not stay home at night; they went out to see and be

A skeletal Kennedy, showing the effects of multiple illnesses and eight months in the tropical combat zone, back in the United States in 1944.
(John F. Kennedy Presidential Library)

seen, to audition for one another, to scheme and lie and laugh, to drink hard, to pick up men or women and above all, in the Stork Club, to be socially ratified. Admission to the holy place, along with a good table, was an achievement; rejection was a humiliation. Billingsley always had the last word."

One evening in 1940, Ernest Hemingway paid a bar bill at the Stork Club by cashing in the $100,000 check he'd just earned for selling the movie rights to *For Whom the Bell Tolls*. On another night, Hemingway punched out the warden of Sing Sing prison, laying him flat out on the club's floor. "If you were at the Stork, you would not have to think at all," Hemingway happily recounted. "You would just watch the people and listen to the noise."

Patrons entered the Stork Club under a green canopy guarded by a whistle-blowing doorman uniformed in blue. Past him flowed a veritable parade: "men in black tie and silk hats, servicemen in uniform, and veiled ladies in capes and furs and seamed stockings, black stiletto heels going tap-tap-tap over the glistening pavement," wrote author Ralph Blumenthal. One then descended to the seventy foot long by thirty foot wide barroom, topped by a full length mirror, which "allowed Billingsley to look up and keep an eye on everything and patrons to admire themselves and one another under softly flattering lights—the ultimate entertainment at the Stork Club."

Ahead, the velvet-draped, crystal-chandeliered main ballroom echoed with rattling ice, popping champagne corks, and rhumba music, as telephones were whisked to V.I.P. tables by waiters in white jackets and Billingsley's photographers fired off publicity shots to be rushed to the society columns. Finally, through a far door, was the holiest of inner sanctums, the Cub Room (some called it the "Snub Room"), where tables were reserved for only the most fabulous guests. The head waiter there was nicknamed Saint

Peter. As society columnist Lucius Morris Beebe explained, "To millions and millions of people all over the world, the Stork symbolizes and epitomizes the deluxe upholstery of quintessentially urban existence. It means fame, it means wealth; it means an elegant way of life among celebrated folk. The Stork is the dream of suburbia, a shrine of sophistication in the minds of thousands who have never seen it, the fabric and pattern of legend." For all its remove from the events that unfolded 8,500 miles away in Blackett Strait, it was here in this unlikely setting that the PT 109 saga would take a decisive turn.

One night in early February 1944, John F. Kennedy took Flo Pritchett to the Stork Club on a double date with the Time-Life correspondent John Hersey, whose World War II novel *A Bell for Adano* would be awarded the Pulitzer Prize the following year, and his wife, Frances Ann Cannon, herself a former Kennedy girlfriend. In the course of the evening, Kennedy, remembered Hersey, "began to give an account of this adventure he'd had" in the Solomon Islands. Instantly, the writer was intrigued. The tale seemed to have all the elements of a great magazine feature.

"What appealed to me about the Kennedy story was the night in the water, his account of floating in the current, being brought back to the same point from which he'd drifted off," recalled Hersey. "It was the same kind of theme that has fascinated me always about human survival, as manifested in the [eventual] title of the piece ['Survival']. It was really that aspect of it that interested me, rather than his heroics. The aspect of fate that threw him into a current and brought him back again. And that sort of dreamlike quality. His account of it is very strange. A nightmarish thing altogether."

Kennedy said he'd think over the possibility of cooperating with Hersey in recording an account of the PT 109. The next day, Kennedy telephoned his father and told him of the idea. Joseph

Kennedy, who had failed to interest *Reader's Digest* in the story the previous August during the brief flurry of attention generated by the United Press and Associated Press bulletins, naturally was delighted by the idea. A piece in *Life* magazine, the biggest media showcase in America at the time, could work magic for his son's career. John Kennedy told Hersey he would cooperate, provided Hersey speak first with several PT 109 crewmen who by now were posted back at the Melville, Rhode Island, PT base, so he could get their account of events. Hersey set up the assignment with *Life* magazine and got to work.

On February 23, according to Hersey, he interviewed Kennedy in New England Baptist Hospital in Boston, where Kennedy was being examined for back pain. "His insistence that I see the crew first struck me very favorably," Hersey remembered. "It didn't seem to me to be self-serving. There was a real kind of officer modesty about it. He had a kind of diffidence about himself that seemed to be genuine at that time. So in a joking way he wondered how he looked to them. They were wildly devoted to him, all of them. Absolutely clear devotion to him by the crew. No reservation about it. They really did like him." Hersey recalled spending all afternoon and part of the evening interviewing Kennedy in his hospital bed, adding, "He drew me a map of the area particularly to illustrate the night he got off the reef and was in the water all night long and was carried out by the current. And also to illustrate the actual collision that took place."

The story gave Hersey a perfect opportunity to pursue his emerging creative goal of "using novelistic techniques in journalism." When Kennedy first reviewed Hersey's draft, however, he spotted a delicate problem. After their rescue PT 109 crewmen Raymond Albert had been killed in a separate incident later in the war. Evidently, Hersey referred to a moment when Albert lost his nerve during the ordeal. "I realize, of course, that his fate is ironic and dramatic and that his lack of guts is an integral part of war—and one that probably is not mentioned enough," wrote Kennedy to Hersey. "I feel, however, that our group was too small, that his fate is so well-known both to the men in the boats and to his family and friends that the finger would be put too definitely on his memory, and after all he was in my crew. To see whether or not I was being oversensitive on this I asked two officers to read the story, and they both, independently of me, brought up the matter." Kennedy advised, "it should be omitted." Hersey cut out the reference in the final version.

Kennedy also insisted the phrase "Kennedy saw a shape and spun the wheel to turn for an attack" be kept intact. It was clearly important to Kennedy that he be portrayed as a man of action who was hit in the course of attempting to attack, rather than as a completely helpless victim. Heeding Kennedy's request, Hersey kept the line in.

To Hersey's surprise, *Life* rejected the article, for reasons unknown. The magazine, which had been covering the war on a nearly real-time, weekly basis, may have considered the story too old. Undaunted, Hersey sold it to the literary weekly the *New Yorker,* which had a much smaller audience than *Life.* John Kennedy seemed only somewhat disappointed to Hersey, but his father was clearly highly dissatisfied. The *New Yorker* spoke to a slice of the American intelligentsia, not to the voting masses capable of propelling a Kennedy into political office, as the elder Kennedy foresaw.

Then Joe Kennedy had an idea that proved to be a masterstroke. He proposed to the mass-audience monthly *Reader's Digest* that they run an unprecedented condensation of the *New Yorker* piece, with Hersey agreeing to donate his author's fee to Mrs. Andrew Kirksey, the widow of one of the two men who died in the PT 109 incident. Neither magazine had made such a deal before, and at first both publishers, the *New Yorker*'s Harold Ross and *Reader's Digest*'s Paul Palmer, flatly refused. But after a sustained pressure-and-charm offensive by Joe Kennedy, they both relented and a deal was struck in June 1944 that would make John Kennedy a national hero.

On June 17, 1944, less than two weeks after D-Day, John Hersey's article on PT 109, simply titled "Survival," appeared in the *New Yorker*. The long-form, five-thousand-word piece was a vivid, precise blend of narrative, dialogue, and scene-setting that put the reader at the center of the surreal experience along with Kennedy and his crew. It was a detailed sketch of the essential facts of the story, with some points collapsed and others obscured by wartime censors. The roles of Coastwatchers Reginald Evans and Ben Nash were eliminated for security reasons, as Coastwatchers were still on dangerous, highly secret duty in the Pacific. Evans's identity was changed to a fictional New Zealand infantry officer named "Lieutenant Wincote." The names of the natives who helped rescue Kennedy were not mentioned in the article, and neither were those of Kennedy's American rescuer Lieutenant (jg) Liebenow of the PT 157 and his colleagues. The roles of Ensign Lenny Thom and other members of the crew seemed diminished in comparison to Kennedy's, and no mention was made of either Thom's written note that accompanied the coconut to Rendova, or the furtive efforts of Commander Warfield at Rendova to follow up on the Coastwatcher reports of the possible PT 109 wreckage. Instead, Hersey left the impression that Rendova had totally given up on the PT 109, writing "back at the base, after a couple of days, the squadron held services for the souls of the thirteen men," a poignant scene for which no firm evidence has been found.

For Joe Kennedy's campaign of family self-promotion, the Hersey feature was a perfect instrument. The article was not a typical propaganda piece of combat derring-do, but an authentic meditation on human endurance against the primal forces of nature:

Kennedy, home from the war, on a date with fashion editor Florence Pritchett, at New York City's swanky nightclub the Stork Club. Kennedy encountered writer John Hersey, who asked if he could write about the PT 109 incident. Immediately, Kennedy checked with his father, and soon, a classic piece of New Journalism was created, along with a heroic saga that helped propel Kennedy into the U.S. House of Representatives. (Photograph courtesy of Stork Club Enterprises LLC)

darkness, the ocean, hunger, and thirst. "Hersey's 'Survival' produces John F. Kennedy as a hero, but not in the sense of a model person seen as a performing great exploits; the hero of Hersey's narrative is rather a youth who has enormous bravery and energy but who is transformed by chastening experience," wrote Ohio State University's John Hellmann, author of *The Kennedy Obsession*. "More complexly, the production of Kennedy as hero begins in his transformation into the narrative sense of that term, the protagonist or main character of the story with whom the reader is positioned to identify. As a true-life 'character,' Kennedy then walks off the page into the text of a political production in the media age."

The Hersey article conjured the classic dramaturgy of myth-telling later described by Joseph Campbell as "the standard path of the mythological adventure of the hero": the rites of passage of separation (the PT 109 sinking), initiation (the ordeal on the islands and abandonment to death), and return (the rescue). Campbell outlined the basic elements of heroic mythology in terms that closely evoke the structure of the saga unveiled in "Survival": "A hero ventures forth from the world of common day into a region of supernatural wonder," "fabulous forces are there encountered and a decisive victory is won," and "the hero comes back from this mysterious adventure with the power to bestow boons on his fellow man." Hersey's "Survival" parallels the "Hero's Journey" described by Campbell in other key ways, including the "threshold crossing," the "night-sea journey," the "rescue" and "resurrection," and even the "helper," who can be seen as Eroni Kumana and Biuku Gasa, and the "elixir," which can be interpreted as the symbolic coconuts that nourished the crew (just barely) and bore the message that delivered them from the underworld back to the world of the living. In short, Hersey's article became the founding document of the

John F. Kennedy mythology, helping firmly establish him as a hero in twentieth-century American political culture.

One survivor of the crash was surprised when he read the *New Yorker* article. Speaking for himself and his fellow survivors, George "Barney" Ross recalled, "Our reaction to the 109 thing had always been that we were kind of ashamed of our performance. I guess you always like to see your name in print and that Hersey article made us think maybe we weren't so bad after all. We'd never gone around saying, hey, did you hear about us? But suddenly your name's in print and Hersey made you sound like some kind of hero because you saved your own life. So I suppose my reaction to the article was to be pleased with myself. I had always thought it was a disaster, but he made it sound pretty heroic, like Dunkirk."

The condensed version of the article, the editing of which further sharpened Kennedy's role, appeared in the August 1944 issue of *Reader's Digest,* reaching millions of readers. At the age of twenty-seven, John Kennedy was a budding pop culture icon.

Until the PT 109 incident, John Kennedy had lived in the shadow of his high-achieving older brother, Joseph Jr., the obvious leader of the pack of eight children and dynastic heir apparent to the larger-than-life father, who was already grooming Joe Jr. for a future in national politics. With the flurries of attention that John's adventures generated in August 1943, in January 1944, and then in the summer of 1944 with the *New Yorker* and *Reader's Digest* articles, this family calculus was thoroughly scrambled, as John was now both a decorated war hero and a bestselling author, as well as a media star.

"What I really want to know," wrote Joe Jr. peevishly to his brother John after reading the *New Yorker* piece, "is where the hell were you when the destroyer hove into sight, and exactly what were your moves, and where the hell was your radar?" (The PT 109 of

course had no radar.) The intensely competitive Joe Jr., a naval avi-
ator based in England, had already piloted thirty-five missions; as
his brother later wrote, "he had completed probably more combat
missions in heavy bombers than any other pilot of his rank in the
Navy."

Having done more than his duty, Joe, Jr. was eligible to return
to the United States. But in August 1944 he volunteered for an ex-
quisitely complex and dangerous operation to bail out of a PB4Y
Liberator aircraft stuffed with 12 tons of explosives that would be
guided by radio signals to crash into a German rocket complex. If
successful, the assault could help slow the onslaught of German
rockets on London, and earn Joe, Jr. medals and fame to rival those
of his younger brother. He took off from an RAF base in England
on August 12, 1944. Eighteen minutes into the mission, his aircraft
blew up over Newdelight Wood near the Suffolk hamlet of Blythe-
burgh, instantly killing Kennedy and his single crew member,
Lieutenant Wilford John "Bud" Willy. "Driven by a hunger to
redeem the Kennedy name from his father's errors of political and
moral judgment," noted historian Alan Axelrod, "by lifelong com-
petitiveness with his younger brother, Lieutenant (jg) John F. Kennedy, hero of PT 109, and, more selflessly, by a passionate desire to
spare London further V-weapon devastation, Joseph P. Kennedy Jr.
answered the call."

The heavy mantle of Joseph Kennedy Sr.'s political ambitions
now landed squarely on the fragile shoulders of a sickly John F.
Kennedy. "I'm now shadowboxing in a match the shadow is always
going to win," John despaired to a friend. Through 1944 and 1945,
John suffered through continuing health crises and was detached
honorably from the U.S. Navy in December 1944, after which he
briefly pursued an inconsequential stint as a war correspondent for
the Hearst News Service in 1945, and spent months in the Arizona

sun trying to rebuild his strength and health. During this time, Joe Sr. and John Kennedy appear to have reached an understanding that John was the family's "anointed one" and that politics would be his destiny.

"I can feel Pappy's eyes on the back of my neck," John said to a friend during the Christmas holiday of 1944, adding, "I'll be back here with Dad trying to parlay a lost PT boat and a bad back into a political advantage. I tell you, Dad is ready right now and can't understand why Johnny boy isn't all engines ahead full."

Years later, John told a reporter, "It was like being drafted. My father wanted his oldest son in politics. 'Wanted' isn't the right word. He demanded it. You know my father." On another occasion, Kennedy explained: "My brother Joe was the logical one in the family to be in politics, and if he had lived, I'd have kept on being a writer."

Joseph Kennedy Sr. confirmed John's account of the succession, asserting matter-of-factly to a journalist in 1957, "I got Jack into politics. I was the one. I told him Joe was dead and that it was therefore his responsibility to run for Congress. He didn't want to. He felt he didn't have the ability and he still feels that way. But I told him he had to." Another time he said simply, "I thought everyone knows about that. Jack went into politics because young Joe died. Young Joe was going to be the politician in the family. When he died, Jack took his place."

In a series of private father-and-son conversations held through 1945, Joseph P. Kennedy and John F. Kennedy agreed that in 1946, the initially reluctant son would take up the family mission for national political office, and run for the U.S. House of Representatives from the Eleventh Congressional District in Massachusetts.

Evidently, they also agreed, at least tacitly, that the PT 109 story and the veteran's angle would be front and center in the campaign's marketing and publicity. It was a strategy born of obvious necessity, as the young Kennedy's war record was about all he had to run on, but in the context of a campaign set in the immediate aftermath of the war, and against primary and general election opponents with little combat experience, it proved decisive.

In December 1945 Kennedy founded a new Veterans of Foreign Wars post named for his brother Joe. Bankrolled as always by his father's vast supply of cash, he began building a campaign staff that was packed with young war veterans. Joseph P. Kennedy Sr. arranged for his son to be made president of the upcoming national VFW convention, which would host twenty thousand veterans, and arranged for the appointment to be widely publicized.

On April 22, 1946, John Kennedy made the formal announcement he was running for the U.S. Congress. The first press release anchored his campaign firmly in his war record, dramatically claiming that Kennedy's inspiration for entering politics stemmed from a promise he made aboard the combat-tossed PT 109 itself. The press release read: "In the Solomon Islands, when ships were sinking and young Americans were dying all around him, John F. Kennedy made a solemn pledge to himself aboard the battle-scarred PT he commanded. The pledge was to serve his country in peace as well as in war—no matter what the cost to his own ambitions in private fields or the discomfort that might be his at the hands of any who are politically ambitious in a strictly mercenary way."

In the 1946 campaign, Kennedy honed a stump speech that focused on the heroics of his PT 109 crew, while shyly downplaying his own role. It was a humble, yet clever, strategy that Kennedy pursued for the rest of his career: he approved the widespread use of the PT 109 story and imagery in his campaigns and interviews; but assuming the part of "bashful American hero," he maintained a reserved, "aw shucks," "I'm not a hero" attitude toward his own exploits. This air of modesty, combined with his own increasing fame, made audiences love Kennedy even more, especially since they already knew the essentials of the PT 109 story thanks to his father's marketing and publicity muscle. His 1946 campaign ads showed a picture of a war veteran father gesturing toward a picture of Kennedy and saying proudly, "There's our man, son."

Campaign worker John Galvin recalled, "No one was ever unaware of [Jack] Kennedy's war record and injury, it was played up all the time."

In 2014, former Kennedy White House aide Dan Fenn recalled of Kennedy, "He wasn't much of a braggart, he wasn't much for self-psychoanalyzing either. He didn't like campaigning so much. The Hersey article was a hell of a story that became well known thanks to the efforts of his father." Fenn noted the 1946 contest "was a real fight, because there were a lot of local pols that seemed to have the edge" in the campaign, and while Kennedy was already "a pretty appealing candidate," his war service and the fact that his brother was killed in the war "added a sheen, a luster that was important right after the war."

Another Kennedy campaign aide, William J. Sutton, recalled the powerful effect the PT 109 story had on voters, even before the formal announcement. "I remember the New England Hardware Banquet at the Statler," he said in an oral history for the John F. Kennedy Library. "He gave his first speech there on the PT 109 incident, which was an extremely well-delivered speech for a newcomer. But, at that time, I knew he was captivating people with the story of his episode in the Pacific. That was his speech that day and at the end of the speech practically everybody in the hall, mostly a male attendance, came up and shook his hand. Even then, I heard that they wanted to do something for him, although he hadn't announced for Congress, at that time." At an American Legion hall event once the campaign was under way, Kennedy said, "I think I know how all you mothers feel because my mother is a Gold Star mother [of a fallen serviceman], too." He was met with a wave of approval and affection.

Early in the campaign, Kennedy sometimes seemed to be a nervous, hesitant, and generally poor public speaker. But telling the PT 109 story was his touchstone, and he later traced his confidence in his own political future to these speeches and to how well audiences responded. Privately, Kennedy wisecracked to a friend about the story's universal appeal, "My story about the collision is getting better all the time. Now I've got a Jew and a nigger in the story and with me being a Catholic, that's great."

Late in the campaign, mastermind Joe Kennedy administered a coup de grâce. He blanketed key election neighborhoods with thousands of copies of the John Hersey *Reader's Digest* article in pamphlet form, along with a press release of support signed by PT 109 crewman William Johnston, now a truck driver in the Dorchester section of Boston. One source placed the distribution at 15,000 copies in East Boston, another widely quoted estimate was at least 100,000 copies in total, and yet another account put a copy in the hands or mailbox of every single voter in the district. "Christ!" exclaimed campaign worker John Galvin. "We had millions of them!"

Kennedy insiders Dave Powers and Kenny O'Donnell later wrote of the marketing significance of the PT 109 story in launching Kennedy's political career. "Blanketing the district with copies of Hersey's account of Kennedy's wartime heroism was an obvious but highly effective promotional move," they wrote. "His well-known display of incredible courage in the South Pacific gave him an aura of glamour that overshadowed his political inexperience and the charges that he was a carpetbagger whose father was buying him a seat in Congress."

Kennedy easily won the primary and coasted to victory in the November 1946 general election, securing nearly 72% of votes. In January 1947, John F. Kennedy headed to Washington, D.C., to be sworn in as a member of the U.S. House of Representatives. Finally, it seemed Joseph Kennedy's burning desire for national political prominence for his family would be fulfilled.

Over the next six years though, John Kennedy compiled an undistinguished record as a carefree bachelor-playboy congressman. His health was a greater concern. He was sometimes mistaken for a skinny young Senate page or elevator operator. In 1947 he was diagnosed with Addison's disease, a collapse of the adrenal glands that could trigger fevers, weight loss, weakness, and death if not correctly treated. From 1950 on Kennedy relied on cortisone treatments for relief, and he hid the diagnosis from the public for the rest of his life. His congenitally malformed back, aggravated by PT boat life and possible football and tennis injuries, greatly troubled him as well.

At first, John Kennedy seemed destined to languish in Congress as a backbench-warming bit player. The path to higher office was blocked by Kennedy family archrival U.S. senator Henry Cabot Lodge Jr., a liberal Republican mandarin, decorated World War II veteran, and grandson of a man who had beat Kennedy's own maternal grandfather in a clash for the U.S. Senate in 1916. Lodge was at the peak of his power and popularity, and was looking forward to an easy election win in 1952 for a third term. To outside observers, Kennedy had hit a brick ceiling surprisingly early in his career; at the same time, his ever-fragile health was on the rocks. The Kennedy's father-and-son ambitions appeared doomed to disappointment.

But as usual, Joseph P. Kennedy Sr. had an idea, and it was a big one. He believed his son could beat Lodge. In 1950, he began quietly launching polls, opposition research, and long-range planning for John F. Kennedy to capture a seat in the United States Senate. Following his own adage that "things don't just happen, they are made to happen by the public relations field," Joe Kennedy decided his son should boost his credentials as an expert on global affairs and foreign relations as befitting a Senate contender, so he sent John on an around-the-world fact-finding trip, accompanied by two of his siblings.

The trip would climax, the elder Kennedy decided, in Japan, for a startling photo opportunity designed to generate headlines and attach his son's name and face to a historic image of grace, humility, and mature diplomacy.

John F. Kennedy would go to Japan, track down the former commanding officer of the Japanese Imperial Navy destroyer *Amagiri*—and embrace the man who nearly killed him.

13

MISSION TO TOKYO

★

JAPAN
NOVEMBER 2, 1951

John F. Kennedy stepped off a plane at Haneda Airport just outside Tokyo, a dusty traveler on the last leg of a three-week trip that had taken him to Pakistan, India, Thailand, Malaya, Indochina, and Hong Kong.

Along the way, his father had intercepted him with publicity suggestions in cables sent from the United States: "If possible try and get some news service to report your activities each location. Good for buildup here." "Have interview National Hookup probably night of 15th. Write me names important people you talked with for newspaper publicity and air [radio] talks."

At the request of local American officials, Kennedy was greeted in Tokyo by Gunji Hosono, a distinguished Japanese international-law professor and director of the Japan Institute of Foreign Affairs, who escorted the young congressman and his traveling companions, brother Robert Kennedy and sister Patricia, to the capital city.

Hosono was a seasoned globe-trotter himself, having visited London during the same time the Kennedy family lived there in 1940, and having earned degrees at the University of Southern California and New York's Columbia University.

Tokyo was in its sixth and final year of post-war U.S. military occupation. The city was rebuilding from the ashes of World War II, and it played host to a seething cauldron of ambitious merchants and businesspeople, fledgling democratic politicians and union activists, black market bosses, communist spies and gangster-paradise nightclubs, all very loosely overseen by Allied occupation authorities working out of the giant former Dai-Ichi ["Number One"] Insurance building overlooking the Imperial Palace grounds, now referred to as "GHQ," or "General Headquarters."

Earlier that year, General Douglas MacArthur left his post as Supreme Allied Commander and viceroy of the American occupation in a wave of popular emotion and gratitude, which he clumsily destroyed in testimony before the U.S. Congress when he described his Japanese subjects with a dismissive remark: "by the standards of modern civilization, they would be like a boy of twelve as compared with our development of 45 years." The comment was widely viewed by Japanese as an insult and embarrassment, and the image of MacArthur quickly disintegrated from that of a demigod in the Japanese memory.

Once in Tokyo, Robert and Patricia Kennedy began sightseeing, while Professor Hosono took the likeable Congressman John Kennedy to lunch at Kacho, a restaurant in the Tsukjii district, home to the largest fish market in the world. As he surveyed his guest's appearance, Hosono was struck by the thirty-four-year-old American's height, a reaction no doubt accentuated by how thin Kennedy was after a lifetime plagued by injury and illness. But Hosono's impression would also have been by colored by the inevi-

The Ginza district, Tokyo, the capital of U.S. occupied Japan in 1951, the year
John Kennedy came to the city in search of the man who nearly killed him in the
war. Instead, Kennedy was hurled again upon the gates of death. (Werner Bischof,
Magnum Photos)

table comparison to how stunted the average Japanese adult's stat-
ure was after decades of war and privation. As lunch was prepared,
John Kennedy revealed a surprising wish—he wanted to seek out
and meet the captain of the Japanese destroyer that sank the PT
109 in August 1943, killed two of his crewmen, and missed ending
his own life by a few feet. He wanted to meet this captain, whoever
he was, and pose for a picture with him.

"Can you help me find him?" Kennedy asked Hosono.

Kennedy had no information to go on, other than a time, a
date, and the names of the Solomon Islands near the crash site. It
was a needle-in-a-haystack request. Finding someone in the chaotic
landscape of postwar Japan would be hard enough under any cir-
cumstance. But the American war veteran didn't know the name of

the man he was looking for, the name of his ship, or what part of Japan he lived in.

Despite the difficulty of the assignment, Hosono said he would try his best. As it happened, Kennedy picked the perfect man for such a daunting task. Hosono was so well connected, GHQ official John Gardiner, also a guest at the luncheon, considered him "the best 'finger man' in Japan," who must have "a machine who can locate anyone in Japan."

After lunch, Hosono rushed across the city to the office of the Fukuinkyoku, or Navy Demobilization Bureau, the Japanese government ministry that kept records of the Imperial Fleet and Japanese veterans. Officials there could not remember a case of a Japanese destroyer running over an American torpedo boat, but Hosono insisted that clerks rifle through the files and search with the few clues Kennedy gave him.

Before long, the clerks struck gold: the object of Kennedy's hunt was Kohei Hanami, a retired commander of the Japanese Imperial Navy. In 1943 he was the thirty-four-year-old commander of the destroyer *Amagiri,* or Heavenly Mist, which reported colliding with and destroying a small American vessel. His listed address was a family farm at Shiokawa, a remote hamlet in Fukushima Prefecture more than two hundred miles northeast of Tokyo. This was unfortunate for the purposes of a reunion with John Kennedy, since it would take some time to set up a meeting and Kennedy was due to leave Tokyo in a matter of days. Hosono considered trying to call Hanami on Kennedy's behalf, but Japan's telephone service to rural areas was too rudimentary at the time.

Suddenly, however, matters took a dire turn.

The precise details of what occurred next are shrouded in mystery, as Kennedy never talked publicly about the event, and the files at the John F. Kennedy Presidential Library are strangely devoid of almost all records of the Tokyo portion of his trip. But key parts of the story can be reconstructed from fragments that survive in the files at Kennedy Library and in clues identified by researchers over the years.

John F. Kennedy abruptly experienced a severe medical crisis at some point between his lunch with Professor Gunji Hosono and his departure from Tokyo on November 8, 1951, when he returned to the United States via San Francisco. According to Kennedy's doctor at the time, Dr. Elmer Bartels, the crisis was triggered by his Addison's disease and exacerbated by the strains of his long voyage. Bartels claimed that Kennedy "had not been properly taking care of himself on the trip."

In Tokyo, Kennedy collapsed with a fever so alarming that his brother Robert arranged for his emergency air evacuation to a U.S. Army hospital on Okinawa for treatment. There, Robert sat by John's bedside as the fever spiked to over 106 degrees, the point at which hallucinations and convulsions can appear, followed by coma, brain damage, and death if the fever has not broken. A priest was brought in to administer the last rites of the Catholic Church to John F. Kennedy. In the only public reference Robert Kennedy ever made to the event, he noted, "They didn't think he would live."

Contacted by phone in the United States, Dr. Bartels prescribed penicillin and adrenal hormones, and eventually, the fever receded. Kennedy recovered in time to leave on a flight out of Tokyo on November 8. Likely guided by Kennedy family spin control, Boston newspapers announced Kennedy "cut short" his trip "after being taken ill in Okinawa," with a condition that "may have been malaria"—once again a calculated nod to his wartime service in the Pacific, where he had first contracted the disease.

Kennedy returned to the United States in time to make a nationwide half-hour radio broadcast report on the trip from New York on November 14, 1951. He made little mention of Japan. Photos taken of him around this the time reveal his almost skeletal frame.

Since John Kennedy would disguise the details of his Addison's disease for the rest of his life, it is possible that those Kennedy family members with knowledge of his Tokyo crisis chose not to talk about it—other than Robert Kennedy's brief comments about the fever's climax in Okinawa, which omitted any mention of Addison's disease. John Kennedy's detailed personal diary of the trip contains no mention of his experience in Tokyo, as he may have been too tired, busy, or sick by then to make notes.

Kennedy's hasty departure from Tokyo dashed any hopes of a reunion photo with Kohei Hanami, and the matter lay dormant for the next nine months. Then in the late summer of 1952, Hosono read in *Time* magazine that John F. Kennedy was running for a seat in the U.S. Senate to defeat Henry Cabot Lodge Jr. Hosono, who had dropped the PT 109 project when Kennedy abruptly left Tokyo in November 1951, had a brainstorm. Why not, Hosono thought, see if he could help Kennedy become a senator? He probably couldn't get Kennedy and Hanami physically together on such notice, but why not introduce them by telegram and letter? Hosono immediately tracked down Kohei Hanami's address again and sent a message to Hanami at his remote farming village. He asked Hanami to write Kennedy a note endorsing his Senate bid.

When Kohei Hanami began reading the message, he was, in his word, "flabbergasted."

He clearly recalled the moment of impact that occurred eight years earlier when he ran over a small American craft after departing from Kolombangara. But ever since then, he had assumed all the Americans were killed in the crash.

As he read the letter, former commander Kohei Hanami was stunned to learn that not only did some of the enemy sailors survive, but one of them, the captain of the boat, was a member of the United States House of Representatives. Hanami's mind, which had until now been preoccupied with the welfare of his crops, was swept back in time.

"It had been years since I had even thought of the incident involving my ship in the Solomons," he explained. "I could recall every detail, the sound of the collision as my ship raced over the PT boat, the feel of the damp night air and the smell of the gasoline flames that leapt higher than the deck, scorching the *Amagiri*'s paint. It had seemed impossible that anyone aboard the other ship had survived. Mr. Hosono's letter filled me with relief and gratitude that so many Americans had come through that engagement of so long ago."

After reading Hosono's message, which felt to Hanami like "a ghostly visitor from the past," he sat down and wrote Kennedy a letter of friendship, in which he recalled the war and the PT 109 incident from his point of view. He ended the note by endorsing Kennedy's U.S. Senate candidacy.

Hanami sent the letter to Hosono in Tokyo, along with a wartime picture of himself and a photo of the *Amagiri*. On September 26, 1952, Hosono relayed the letter to Jack Gardiner, the former State Department official in Tokyo who had attended the November 1951 lunch in Tokyo with Kennedy and Hosono. Hosono instructed Gardiner, now living outside Boston, to give Hosono's message to Kennedy "immediately." The purpose of the letter, wrote Hosono, was to help Kennedy's election campaign in November. Hosono added, "our friend will be sure to win against Senator

Lodge," and "Kennedy must be the hope of the Democratic Party in [the] future."

Almost two weeks later, Gardiner hand-delivered the letter to Robert F. Kennedy at the Kennedy campaign headquarters in Boston. The younger Kennedy was now acting as campaign director for his brother's race, under the close direction of their father. Grasping the potential significance of the note, Robert told Gardiner he would take immediate action. When informed of the development, Joe Kennedy realized it was a story that could shore up his son's foreign-affairs credentials against the experienced incumbent Lodge, by projecting the narrative that John Kennedy was a seasoned war hero, world traveler, and international-affairs expert.

On October 19, 1952, in the thick of the Kennedy-Lodge electoral clash, the Kennedy campaign issued a press release that reprinted the full text of the Kohei Hanami letter, leading with the passages that supported Kennedy's bid for the U.S. Senate. The campaign simultaneously released the photos of a smiling Hanami and his destroyer. The press release added, "Soon after the war, recovered from serious injuries he suffered in the sea battle, Kennedy toured most of the world, including Japan, where he took the trouble to find out who commanded the destroyer and almost succeeded in meeting him. Kennedy thought a hand of friendship to a former enemy might win a staunch Japanese spokesman for the United States. The gesture was instinctively understood by Hanami."

The story was picked up in the Boston newspapers and by *Time* magazine in its November 3, 1952, issue. The impact of the campaign, according to John F. Kennedy was "very beneficial." It was a "rather unusual" endorsement, remembered Robert F. Kennedy, "but it helped."

Photograph of Kohei Hanami, sent by Hanami to John F. Kennedy in 1952 and subsequently released to American media during JFK's senate campaign. (John F. Kennedy Presidential Library)

Henry Cabot Lodge Jr., who had won four straight national election victories since 1932, originally thought he would crush John F. Kennedy by 300,000 votes. But he ran a weak campaign, stumbled in a debate with Kennedy, and ultimately lost the November general election by a narrow margin of 70,737 votes out of 2,353,231 votes cast.

"I felt," Lodge remembered, "rather like a man who has just been hit by a truck."

On February 18, 1953, John F. Kennedy sent a warm letter of thanks to his former enemy Hanami, the man who had been responsible for the greatest trial of his life. Kennedy's letter was written on the stationery of a newly inaugurated United States senator. In the years that followed, Kennedy and Hanami maintained a friendly personal correspondence, exchanging greetings at Christmastime and special occasions. In 1953, when he heard of Kennedy's marriage at age thirty-six to twenty-four-year-old Jacqueline Bouvier, Hanami offered his best wishes. After Kennedy entered the hospital for back surgery, Hanami penned a message of encouragement. Kennedy wrote back affectionate notes to thank Hanami. In an interesting parallel, like Kennedy, Kohei Hanami entered elective politics. In 1954 Hanami was elected councilman of Shiokawa, a group of villages totaling thirteen thousand people. He was elected mayor in 1962.

14

THE GREATEST ACTOR OF OUR TIME

★

Kennedy's most characteristic quality is the remote and
private air of a man who has traversed some lonely terrain of
experience, of loss and gain, of nearness to death, which
leaves him isolated from the mass of others.

NORMAN MAILER, 1960

In 1953, John F. Kennedy settled into the life of a United States
senator and a rising star in American politics. The PT 109 episode
assumed a central position in his press and campaign images. In his
Senate office in Washington, D.C., he kept a model of PT 109 on a
shelf directly behind his work desk, and a plastic memento case
containing the now-famous "rescue coconut" on his desk.

In 1956 Kennedy narrowly missed being selected to run for vice
president on the ticket with Democratic presidential nominee Adlai
Stevenson. He had two serious operations on his back, and published *Profiles in Courage,* a book that was awarded the Pulitzer
Prize for biography in 1957. His first child, Caroline, was born that
year. Also that year, he was selected to serve on the prestigious
Senate Foreign Relations Committee, and in 1958 he was easily
reelected to a second term in the Senate.

In 1957, Kennedy agreed to serve as "technical advisor" on an episode of a CBS TV show called *Navy Log* that reenacted the PT 109 incident. When Kennedy visited the set of the production at Santa Monica, California, he was spotted by a gossip columnist, who described him as "giddy" with excitement as the cameras rolled. The low-budget production, when aired, was laughably inaccurate, but it did serve to present the "war hero" senator to a television audience and helped build the ambitious politician's national profile.

When John Kennedy ran for the ultimate prize—the presidency—in 1960, the PT 109 story was again exploited as an essential piece of campaign biography. The tale formed a critical foundation of Kennedy's appeal as a presidential candidate, and the details of Kennedy's personal rescue of a fellow sailor and his leadership of the surviving crew in a combat zone gave him a credential that few other presidential candidates have enjoyed, that of a certified action hero. Thousands of "PT 109 tie clasps" were mass-produced and handed out as campaign talismans, the John Hersey article was again widely distributed by the Kennedy campaign, and some of Kennedy's PT 109 comrades and other PT veterans pitched in to campaign with Kennedy.

At a speech at the Alamo in San Antonio, Texas, on September 12, 1960, Kennedy welcomed a crewman from his PT 59 command: "it is a source of pride to me that my friend, Vivian Scribner, who served with me on a PT boat, who I have not seen since 1944, drove up the Rio Grande Valley 250 miles to be with us on this platform." On October 3, 1960, Edman Mauer appeared with Senator Kennedy at a campaign rally at Augustine's Restaurant in Belleville, Illinois. "We have the good fortune to have a member of my crew who was on my torpedo boat in World War II who lives in this area of East St. Louis," said Kennedy. "I would like to have you meet my friend, Mauer. Would you stand up and take a bow?" The crowd

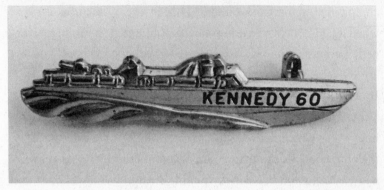

A PT boat pin from JFK's presidential campaign, 1960. Through shrewd marketing and publicity, Joseph P. Kennedy turned the PT 109 incident into a chariot that carried his son to the White House. (Hubbard Collection)

enthusiastically applauded. "He was on a merchant ship that got sunk in the Solomon Islands and he had the bad fortune to then come on my boat which got sunk." Kennedy paused while the crowd laughed. "I am glad to see him today. It is the first time I have seen him for 17 years. We are delighted he is here." Appearing at the same event were Gerard Zinser's mother and father, who also lived nearby. In Garden Grove, California, PT 109 survivor Ray Starkey, now an oil worker, acted as a local Kennedy campaign chairman.

One Kennedy aide who served on JFK's 1960 campaign, Richard Donahue, recalled in a 2015 interview that several of the PT 109 veterans asked Kennedy for help in looking for work, making themselves "a pain in the ass," in Donahue's words. Kennedy did recommend them for jobs, though they were rejected for various reasons according to Donahue.

Despite the prominent use of PT 109 as a campaign marketing device, Kennedy "was neither a professional warrior nor a professional veteran," wrote JFK aide Theodore Sorensen. "He never boasted or even reminisced about his wartime experiences. He never complained about his wounds." During the Wisconsin primary, when a young man asked him how he came to be a war hero, Kennedy famously quipped, "It was easy—they sank my boat."

In May 1960, Kennedy faced a critical point in his quest for the White House—the West Virginia Democratic presidential primary—for which his wartime service would play a crucial role in the outcome. His campaign once again was run by Robert F. Kennedy, with Joseph P. Kennedy pulling strings, writing checks, and offering strategic advice to his sons, as always. Kennedy's main rival was Hubert Humphrey, the junior senator from Minnesota. Until then, Kennedy seemed to be emerging as the front-runner for the nomination, while Humphrey, Adlai Stevenson, and Lyndon B. Johnson remained potent rivals.

But Democratic Party bosses and political pundits were increasingly doubting whether a Roman Catholic could gain Protestant votes, especially in a heavily Protestant state like West Virginia, which some considered a bastion of anti-Catholic bigotry. Kennedy was the only Catholic in the race, and no Catholic had ever been elected president. A firestorm of questions was erupting over whether Kennedy's loyalties would be split between America and the Vatican. If Kennedy lost in West Virginia, he might well have been perceived as unelectable because of his religion, and been knocked out of the race. He had to win, but his support was suddenly collapsing. Weeks before the primary, Kennedy trailed Humphrey, a Protestant, by 20 points in the West Virginia polls.

The Kennedys' solution was to double down on their trump card, the saga of PT 109. "The only thing we had was the 109," recalled Richard Donahue, then a Kennedy campaign aide. "We used that." West Virginia, recalled Donahue, was an intensely patriotic state that led the nation in the proportion of its population

PT 157's Bud Liebenow helps JFK campaign for president in Grand Rapids, Michigan, 1960. The two men were amused by how many people in campaign crowds shouted out that they were on the boat that rescued Kennedy. (William F. Liebenow)

who were Gold Star Mothers, or mothers who had lost sons in the war. "And of course he [Kennedy] was a Gold Star Brother," he noted, adding, "it was the only thing we could do to take the sting out" of the religious issue.

Charles Peters, then a county campaign manager for Kennedy in West Virginia, remembered in 2010, "The military experience, being a hero, in West Virginia, that just meant so much. Military service was highly honored, heroism even more. And so in my county alone we distributed 40,000 copies of that *Reader's Digest* article about Kennedy's war experience. Well, that had a big effect."

Kennedy regained his footing and launched an effective coun-terattack on the religious issue, framing it as a question of tolerance versus intolerance. He declared, "Nobody asked me if I was a Cath-olic when I joined the United States Navy." He noted, "Nobody asked my brother if he was a Catholic or a Protestant before he climbed into an American bomber to fly his last mission." On April 25, he told a statewide West Virginia audience, "I refuse to believe that I was denied the right to be president the day that I was bap-tized."

A low blow was delivered for Kennedy on April 27, two weeks before the final vote, when Kennedy's friend Franklin D. Roosevelt Jr., himself a decorated World War II Navy veteran, attacked Hum-phrey by saying, "I don't know where he was in World War II," and even handed out leaflets claiming Humphrey was a draft dodger. It inferred cowardice on the part of Humphrey, who did not serve in the war for medical reasons, despite trying to enlist. Roosevelt later said "of course, Jack knew," referring to the smear.

When reporter David Broder asked John Kennedy if he thought Humphrey's lack of military service was a legitimate campaign issue, Broder was struck by Kennedy's "super-cool, almost cold-blooded reaction." Kennedy replied, "Frank Roosevelt is here making his speeches, and I'm making mine." For his part in the dirty trick, said FDR Jr., "I always regretted my role in the affair. Humphrey, an old ally, never forgave me for it. I did it because of Bobby." According to Roosevelt, "RFK was already a full-blown tyrant. You did what he told you to do, and you did it with a smile."

On the Sunday night before the vote, Kennedy delivered a speech that journalist Theodore H. White called "the finest TV broadcast I have ever heard any political candidate make." In conclusion, Kennedy declared that when a president takes the oath of office, he swears on a Bible to support the separation of church and state. "And if he breaks his oath," said Kennedy, "he is not only committing a crime against the Constitution, for which the Congress can impeach him—and should impeach him—but he is committing a sin against God."

Kennedy administered a crushing defeat to Humphrey, winning 60.8 percent of the West Virginia primary vote. That night, Humphrey pulled out of the race. The showdown proved a Roman Catholic could win in a bastion of Protestant voters. It was a landmark victory for Kennedy, as it cleared his path to the Democratic presidential nomination, which he would win on June 13, 1960. It was also victory for religious tolerance in America, as it proved that a non-Protestant, a Catholic, could make a legitimate claim to the White House.

In the fall general-election campaign against Republican nominee and sitting vice president Richard M. Nixon, the PT 109 saga served as a vivid counterpoint to Nixon's experience in World War II. Like Kennedy, Nixon was also an officer in the U.S. Navy who served honorably in the South Pacific, but Nixon's service became better known for his poker-playing skills and management of a hamburger stand rather than any combat heroics. The backdrop of PT 109 was so powerfully reinforced in Kennedy's campaign materials that Kennedy had little need to refer to it himself, in keeping with his "bashful hero" image.

One day during the 1960 campaign, U.S. Navy veteran Lawrence Ogilvie squeezed into an elevator in Spokane, Washington, came face-to-face with candidate John F. Kennedy, and introduced himself as a veteran of the PT 162, which was the boat closest to the PT 109 when it was hit by the *Amagiri*.

Years later, Ogilvie recalled, "The Jap destroyer, later known as the *Amagiri,* came from our starboard side about 250 feet in front of our 162 boat, and hit the 109 on the starboard side, looked like right in the center. Gas tanks on the 109 exploded, lighting up the whole area. The can sliced through the 109 and never slowed down at all, then disappeared into the night. We were stunned and never fired a shot, trying to realize what had happened. We didn't think anyone from the crew could live through that and Lt. Lowrey took us out of there. The crew wanted our Skipper to go back, but we couldn't see the 109 any longer out there, and we never did go back."

When John F. Kennedy learned he was talking to a man who was on the PT 162 that night, he briefly stepped out of his supremely cool, confident, and poised image and revealed a glimpse of how, for all the value the PT 109 episode provided him as a candidate for the nation's highest office, the ordeal in the Blackett Strait still haunted him somewhere within.

"Where in the hell did you guys go?" Kennedy snapped. It was all he had to say to Ogilvie.

On October 10, 1960, in the thick of the extremely hard-fought presidential contest, an eighteen-year-old man named Jack Kirksey stood outside the late Franklin D. Roosevelt's "Little White House" in Warm Springs, Georgia.

He was waiting to meet John F. Kennedy, the skipper of the boat on which his father, Andrew Jackson Kirksey, was killed seventeen years earlier. The only memories of his father Jack had were from photos and stories told by family members. Beside him was his mother, Kloye, Kirksey's widow.

The two had never met John F. Kennedy before, but Kennedy had been a guiding force in their lives ever since the tragedy. Shortly after the loss of the PT 109, Kennedy had warmly written to Kloye,

"If a boat captain is fortunate, he finds one man in his crew who contributes more than his share and through his leadership, builds morale and *esprit* up throughout the boat. With us, Jack Kirksey was that man—and he did a superb job." Kennedy told the widow of her husband's final days. "During the last weeks when the going was tough," he wrote, "Jack never lost his courage or his cheerfulness. Yet the thought of you and your son was always with him. He talked of you often and he frequently showed me the pictures that you sent of your son—with tremendous pride." Of the tragic events in Blackett Strait, Kennedy recounted to Mrs. Kirksey that "we could find no trace" of her husband "and no one reported seeing him." Kennedy acknowledged he was "truly sorry that I cannot offer you hope that he survived that night."

In March 1944, when Kennedy was back in the States and posted in Miami, he again wrote Kloye, who had a son with Kirksey and two sons from her previous marriage, to ask how she was doing. He enclosed a copy of a group photograph of Kennedy and part of the PT 109 crew on the boat's deck, taken off Guadalcanal in early July 1943—just prior to their move to Rendova. "The picture, unfortunately, is poor—the heat spoiled the negative but it is good of Jack." Kennedy explained he had "been wondering if all Jack's affairs with the Navy have been worked out satisfactorily and if there is anything that I can do in this regard. I hope that you will write me and let me know if things aren't going well for you. Your husband was a great friend of mine, and I will feel it a privilege if there is something I could do."

When John Hersey's *Reader's Digest* article appeared, Kennedy arranged for two thousand dollars to be sent to Kloye Kirksey, and the same amount to be forwarded to Harold Marney's family. In the months and years that followed, Kennedy personally advised

During the 1960 presidential campaign, Kennedy stopped in Warm Springs, Georgia. There, for the first time, he met the widow (center) of his lost PT 109 crewman Andrew Kirksey and their son Jack (right). She described the encounter as the greatest day of her life. After the picture was taken, they went to a private room and had a conversation that changed Jack Kirksey's life. (Andrew Jackson Kirksey Family Collection)

Kloye on how to apply for, maximize, and manage her veteran survivors' benefits, in a way, explained her son Jack, that she "was taken care of for the rest of her life."

Hoyt Grant, Kloye's son from her previous marriage, recalled, "Kennedy wrote Mother several letters and kept in touch with her to make sure all of her affairs with the Veterans Department were taken care of, and even made a 'hot line' call to the Director of the Veterans Administrations, asking him to call Mother to make sure she knew all of her benefits. Jack was listed as missing in action for a year, before my Mother received her checks, and it was slim pickings there for a while. My brother and I both worked and helped her. She was sent $2,000 by the author of the article that was published in the *Reader's Digest*, and she purchased a home out on Warm Springs highway."

For all of Kennedy's help, explained Jack Kirksey in 2014, his mother "was in total awe of" JFK, and when Kennedy invited her to meet him at a campaign stop at Warm Springs, not far from her home, Kloye was "totally, utterly excited and elated about meeting him" for the first time.

Ever opportunistic and eager to sell their Yankee candidate to southern constituents, the Kennedy campaign saw a publicity opportunity in the admiring PT 109 widow. An article about her appeared in the *Atlanta Constitution* with the headline "War Widow Tells of Kennedy's Help." In the article, Kloye was quoted as saying of Kennedy, "My husband always said he was the kind of person that you wouldn't know had a dime in his pocket." She added, "He's just a down-to-earth, honest-to-goodness person and I think he'd make us a fine president."

When Kennedy and his entourage swept into the "Little White House" in Warm Springs, where Franklin D. Roosevelt had held court decades earlier while recovering from polio, JFK was mobbed by well-wishers who were gathered to hear him make a speech from the front steps of the house.

Kennedy was ushered to meet Kloye and Jack Kirksey. "I couldn't hardly talk to him," the younger Kirksey remembered, dazzled by the moment.

"I'm so glad to see you," Kennedy told Kloye, "and I'm very glad to meet your son." She gave Kennedy a present of a small hand-carved sculpture of a Democratic donkey braying at a Republican elephant. The three went to a private room and Kennedy put them at ease.

"It was almost like a family member asking what you'd been doing and how you'd been doing in school," Jack Kirksey remembered. "He was mostly interested in asking questions about my schooling and my life. He wanted to know if anyone had contacted me about veterans' education benefits, which they had not. He was interested in my mom and how she was doing and if everything was OK. He just was extremely interested in people. He was an extremely compassionate man. He was such a caring guy. If you had any personal contact with him, you couldn't help but be bowled over. He was bigger than life." A photograph taken of the meeting captures a haunted look on Kennedy's face as he shook the hand of the son of his lost crewman, as an emotional Kloye Kirksey looks on adoringly.

On November 8, 1960, after an epic campaign clash the *New York Times* called "one of the closest and most contentious elections in American history," John F. Kennedy beat his fellow naval veteran of the South Pacific and Republican presidential nominee, Vice President Richard Nixon, by a margin of just 0.1 percent of the popular vote.

Joseph Kennedy's dream had finally come true: a Kennedy

would be president. It was the culmination of an eighteen-year quest that started with the father's summit meeting at the Plaza hotel in 1942 with Commander Bulkeley to maneuver John into the PT boat service, followed by the sinking of the PT 109, a brief burst of national publicity in the weeks that followed, the publication of Hersey's landmark *New Yorker* article the following year, and the deployment of massive amounts of the father's cash to support JFK's campaigns for the House of Representatives in 1946, the Senate in 1952, and the White House in 1960. In each of the campaigns, the mythology of PT 109 played a central, and possibly decisive, role. As longtime aide Dave Powers, who served as JFK's "Special Assistant" once they reached the White House, put it, "Without PT 109, there never would have been a President John F. Kennedy."

JFK invited his surviving PT 109 crew members to Washington, D.C., to attend the inaugural festivities on January 20, 1961. The former sailors climbed aboard a float that featured a replica of their now-famous lost torpedo boat. In fact, it was the PT 796, a Higgins PT boat painted to represent PT 109. (This boat has been restored and is now housed in Battleship Cove, Fall River, Massachusetts.) "All the crew rode on the PT 109 float in the parade as a surprise to the skipper," recalled Pat McMahon. "As we passed by the presidential reviewing stand, Kennedy stood up, grinned, whipped off his silk top hat, and gave us the skipper's signal: 'Wind 'em up, rev 'em up, let's go!'" A delighted Kloye Kirksey and her son Hoyt came up from Georgia to attend the inauguration as JFK's guests.

One day not long after the inauguration, the director of the Atlanta, Georgia, office of the U.S. Veterans Administration was shocked to hear his secretary tell him, "The White House is calling!"

John F. Kennedy was on the line, ordering him to send a car to the Kirkseys' home, bring Jack to his office, and explain his educational benefits to him. When Jack got there, it looked like the director "almost had a stroke" in the wake of a direct call from the president of the United States. Benefits were arranged and Jack attended college accounting courses that launched his career. In late April 1961, Kennedy sent Kloye Kirksey an aerial photograph of the American cemetery in Manila, where the name of her late husband was inscribed on a memorial wall. If she ever came to Washington, the president wrote, he "would like very much to have the White House and other public places here shown to you."

When John Kennedy was planning his inaugural celebrations, he remembered Professor Gunji Hosono and the quiet, behind-the-scenes role the Japanese man played in his political ascension, and so he invited his Japanese friend to the inauguration.

As the parade passed by the White House reviewing stand, Kennedy spotted Hosono and his daughter Haruko, and beckoned them to join him and Robert Kennedy at the seat of power. President Kennedy placed the professor directly behind himself, his wife, and Vice President Lyndon Johnson to watch the parade.

Few if any of the onlookers would have had the slightest idea what a white-haired elderly Japanese man and his attractive daughter were doing standing with the president of the United States on the day of his inauguration.

On January 25, 1961, Gunji and Haruko Hosono entered the Oval Office as Kennedy's first foreign visitors in the White House. Sitting beside the president's desk with his daughter, Professor Hosono presented Kennedy with a message of congratulations from Japanese Prime Minister Hayato Ikeda. He also gave Kennedy an ornate, ceremonial scroll that wished the new president success. It was signed by seventeen Japanese men. They were veterans of the *Amagiri*, the Japanese Imperial Navy destroyer that destroyed PT 109.

At 8:50 A.M. on his first full day as president, John Kennedy sat alone in the empty Oval Office, flinching at the freshly painted green walls, pressing buzzers, and inspecting his desk drawers, which were empty except for a printed instruction sheet detailing a plan of action in case of a nuclear attack.

Soon he called in an aide and said, "What the hell do I do now?"

The Oval Office soon filled up with mementoes of the PT 109, talismans from the event that paved his path to power: the SOS coconut from the PT 109 rescue refurbished as a paperweight, a ten-inch glass ornament etched with a likeness of PT 109, and his navy ID card encased in a glass ashtray. On his desk there appeared a plaque from Admiral Hyman Rickover given to commanders of Polaris nuclear submarines bearing a Breton fisherman's prayer: OH GOD, THY SEA IS SO GREAT AND MY BOAT IS SO SMALL.

Time magazine's Hugh Sidey watched the early transformation of the room: "There were the marks of a navy vet: on the walls flanking the fireplace hung two naval pictures showing the 1812 battle between the *Constitution* and the British frigate *Guerriere*, and on the mantel was a model of the *Constitution*."

Early in 1961, Kennedy met in the Oval Office with journalist Robert J. Donovan, who wished to write a book about PT 109. Recalling the chaos of the incident, Kennedy tried to talk him out of it. "Oh, Bob," he said, "don't get into that. You'll be flogging a dead horse." Referring to the article by John Hersey, he recalled: "Every time I ran for office after the war, we made a million copies of that article to throw around." He added, "That operation was more fucked up than Cuba." The recent failed CIA-backed exile

TOP As president, Kennedy filled the Oval Office with nautical items, including a replica of the PT 109 in a glass case on his desk (foreground of photo), and the famous distress coconut enclosed in a case (far right of photo). (John F. Kennedy Presidential Library)

BELOW President John F. Kennedy accepts a model of PT 109 from a young Luke Flaherty as he greets the crowd gathered at Great Falls High School Memorial Stadium, Great Falls Montana, September 26, 1963. Kennedy had less than 2 months to live. (John F. Kennedy Presidential Library)

invasion of Cuba at the Bay of Pigs had delivered a body blow to Kennedy's young presidency, and he must have seen parallels between that fiasco and the Battle of Blackett Strait seventeen years earlier, both of which were plagued by poor planning, communications, and coordination.

Donovan persisted, and obtained Kennedy's cooperation in hastily writing *PT 109: John F. Kennedy in World War II,* an essential account of many of the basic facts of the PT 109 incident, published in the fall of 1961. Donovan traveled to the Solomon Islands and Japan to interview participants, and he spoke with several of the surviving PT 109 crewmen. As an "authorized" account produced in cooperation with a sitting president, the book was highly favorable to John F. Kennedy. According to Kennedy's press secretary, Pierre Salinger, JFK was pleased with the Donovan work, which became a major bestseller. Joseph P. Kennedy himself couldn't have better crafted the opening line of the *New York Times* review: "This is a book that should be read by any American who is worried how John Fitzgerald Kennedy will react in time of deep, terrifying crisis."

A Hollywood film adaption of the Donovan book was fast-tracked into production by legendary mogul and Warner Bros. studios co-founder Jack Warner. From the start of the movie's development in 1961, John F. Kennedy and his father, the former movie studio czar, tightly controlled key aspects of the project, demanding (and obtaining) veto power for approval of script, director, and cast. Joe Kennedy personally negotiated Donovan's book option contract with Warner Bros. and stayed involved in the movie's development until a December 19, 1961, stroke incapacitated him for the rest of his life. It was an unprecedented level of White House involvement in a movie production, and it was the first time a major studio had made a feature film about a sitting president. JFK went so far as to make suggestions to star Cliff Robertson on how he should comb and color his hair. Jackie Kennedy wanted Warren Beatty to play Kennedy, but Beatty correctly sensed the project was doomed.

Indeed the *PT 109* movie was dogged by script problems, production delays, and directorial turmoil. At one point, while auditioning director candidates by screening films in the White House movie theater, a disgusted President Kennedy ordered the projector stopped, saying to his press secretary, "Tell Jack Warner to go fuck himself." The original director was fired while shooting was under way in Florida (standing in for the Solomon Islands), and his successor, veteran director Leslie Martinson, was better known for his TV work. No PT boats similar to Kennedy's survived, so standing in for them were several 85-foot U.S. Air Force crash rescue boats, converted to resemble PTs. Operating within the iron grip of both Jack Warner and the White House, Martinson did an admirable job in finishing the picture under difficult conditions.

Released in 1963 and starring Cliff Robertson as JFK, the movie flopped, earning only $5.5 million in worldwide revenue versus a $6.5 million production budget, for a net loss of $1 million. Studio chief Warner, who thought he had a blockbuster classic on his hands, was baffled, and wrote, "I don't understand why it missed." At a Hollywood party, Kennedy said to Warren Beatty, "You were right about that movie." Author Robert Donovan later agreed, telling a historian, "I didn't think it was a good movie. I was disappointed." Of the script, Cliff Robertson despaired: "I'm like a painter who is given three pots of paint and told to come up with twelve colors." *Newsweek* pronounced the screenplay "agonizingly bad." *Look* magazine dismissed the film as "just this side of the Bobbsey Twins."

Looking back on the affair in 2014, historian Nicholas J. Cull of the University of Southern California put part of the blame on presidential-level interference in the script process. "To borrow a metaphor from the incident which started the whole thing," wrote Cull, "they were at sea in a flimsy craft and were broken in two by the impact of a powerful oncoming vessel; ironically, in the case of the movie that vessel was the Kennedy White House."

A few weeks after his inauguration, Kennedy received a surprising, emotional message from his past. It was a letter from his Solomon Islands savior Biuku Gasa, who wanted to share his feelings on Kennedy's entering the White House. "This is my joy that you are now President of the United States of America," wrote Gasa. "It was not in my strength that I and my friends were able to rescue you in the time of war, but in the strength of God we were able to help you."

Kennedy wrote back a fond letter that read, "I can't tell you how delighted I was to know that you are well and prospering in your home so many thousands of miles away from Washington. Like you, I am eternally grateful for the act of Divine Providence which brought me and my companions together with you and your friends who so valorously effected our rescue during time of war. Needless to say, I am deeply moved by your expressions and I hope that the new Responsibilities which are mine may be exercised for the benefit of my own countrymen and the welfare of all of our brothers in Christ. You will always have a special place in my mind and my heart, and I wish you and your people continued prosperity and good health."

Kennedy continued to think of his old brothers-in-arms Biuku Gasa and Eroni Kumana, and he held on to the hope that he could see them again someday.

In the Oval Office, John F. Kennedy also still thought of Japan and of former captain Kohei Hanami of the *Amagiri*. Ten years after his abortive and near-fatal stay in Tokyo, JFK began considering of the possibility of returning to Japan to meet with Hanami and his fellow *Amagiri* veterans.

It was a trip Kennedy's friend Gunji Hosono had also suggested in a series of letters to Attorney General Robert F. Kennedy, and so in February 1962, RFK and his wife traveled to Japan on their own state visit, as the first stop on an around-the-world goodwill tour. RFK's Japan trip was also to serve as a testing of the waters for a possible JFK presidential visit that would follow, perhaps in the presidential election year of 1964.

On the afternoon of February 6, 1962, Robert F. Kennedy and his wife, Ethel, entered a packed auditorium at elite Waseda University in Tokyo, on the second day of a planned eight-day visit to Japan.

A riot was erupting at their feet.

Standing before a giant pair of Japanese and American flags, Robert Kennedy took the stage and faced an audience of thousands of Japanese students in a state of utter bedlam, packed into an auditorium designed to hold less than half as many. Thirty-five hundred students were jammed into the hall, and four thousand others surrounded the building.

There was shouting and screaming as pockets of communist agitators spread through the crowd, bent on throwing RFK off the university grounds. Much of the buzzing crowd was welcoming, but smaller sections were chanting insults at Kennedy, and at each other, including, "Okinawa!" "Cuba!" "Kennedy go home!" "Shut up and sit down!" Scores of reporters and photographers swarmed around the stage, encircling Kennedy and his party, which included rising young Japanese politician Yasuhiro Nakasone, who later became prime minister of Japan.

A live national TV feed was broadcasting the scene to millions in Japan who had recently bought their first-ever black-and-white

TVs from Sony and other fast-rising Japanese manufacturers. Across the country, horrified Japanese citizens, ordinarily polite and gracious hosts, could see that their distinguished foreign guest, the brother of the president of the United States, no less, was being gravely insulted by a crowd that was out of control.

RFK had with him no personal security other than a few nearby U.S. government aides. There were no uniformed police or security guards anywhere in sight, as by tradition they were not allowed on the grounds of the university. Ethel Kennedy and their State Department translator stood by his side, equally defenseless.

Robert Kennedy had been sent to Japan by his brother President John F. Kennedy, as a prelude to what they both thought would be the first-ever trip there by a sitting American president. The presidential visit would culminate in the "photo op" JFK and his father had wanted to stage for more than ten years—of an emotional reunion between the survivors of the PT 109 and veterans of the destroyer, *Amagiri,* that sank her. Another memorable photo eleven years earlier of General Douglas MacArthur towering jauntily over a formally dressed Emperor Hirohito had made the point, in dramatic fashion, that the two countries were at peace and working together, with Japan clearly as the vanquished junior partner. This new photo would enshrine the postwar relationship of the two nations as full partners in a way that no proclamation or treaty could. In the meantime, media images of Robert Kennedy and his wife barnstorming through Japan could project a young, vigorous image of America to all generations of Japanese.

The visit was inspired in part by the persistent enthusiasm of the Kennedy's old friend from Japan, Gunji Hosono. Robert Kennedy later explained, "Every few weeks I would receive a letter [from Hosono] stressing the importance of a trip to his country, and about every ten days a visitor from Japan would arrive in my office, armed with an introduction from Dr. Hosono. He would shake hands and sit down and immediately begin to urge that I go to Japan as soon as possible."

But now, on just the second day of RFK's trip, not only did everything seem about to unravel, but it appeared Kennedy could be in immediate physical danger. In fact such a reception was not unprecedented. Two years earlier, when Dwight Eisenhower's press secretary, James Hagerty, arrived in Tokyo to plan a trip to Japan by President Eisenhower, he was attacked by protestors, evacuated by helicopter, and promptly fled the country. The Eisenhower trip was canceled.

The local CIA station in Tokyo warned RFK of fresh intelligence reports predicting the situation at Waseda could become dangerous and urged him to cancel the event. One report said that mobs of students would snake-dance around the auditorium, another account predicted picketers would link arms to blockade Kennedy. Forewarned, RFK nevertheless decided to brave the crowds and try to enter the university for a scheduled forum with students. Outside the auditorium, a mob of three thousand young people surged around Kennedy and his party, and there they all seemed friendly and joyous.

Inside, however, the story was very different. Kennedy recalled: "the building seated about 1,500, but 3,000 were jammed into the hall. They filled the aisles, the orchestra section, the balcony and spilled out into the corridors." The disrupters in the crowd may have been small in number, but their shouts of "Free Okinawa" and other slogans echoed the frustration of many Japanese who still resented the postwar U.S. occupation that ended ten years earlier, were humiliated by the continued American occupation of Okinawa, and worried that Cold War tensions would pull Japan into a war between the Soviet Union and the United States. The Japanese, of course, knew better than any other people the stakes of nuclear conflict.

As flashbulbs popped and the crowd applauded in welcome, Robert Kennedy began speaking into a table-mounted microphone. Screams of protest erupted, along with a thunderous stomping of feet. Toward the front of the audience, a student activist named Yuzo Tachiya began yelling at the top of his lungs. He had helped distribute thirty thousand fliers around campus earlier in the day to draw students to the event, and he had worked out with the faculty how the event would be structured and translated. Tachiya objected to Kennedy breaking the agreed-upon format, by using his own translator and making a speech. Tachiya wanted a debate instead. And he wasn't going to shut up until he got it.

RFK remembered, "At first I thought if I ignored him he would subside."

So he continued right through the shouting: "The great advantage of the system under which we live—you and I—is that we can exchange views and exchange ideas in a frank manner, with both of us benefiting. . . . Under a democracy we have a right to say what we think and we have the right to disagree. So if we can proceed in an orderly fashion, with you asking questions and me answering them, I am confident I will gain and that perhaps also you will understand a little better the positions of my country and its people."

But "bedlam was spreading," recalled Kennedy aide John Seigenthaler. "The Communists were yelling 'Kennedy, go home.' The anti-Communists were yelling back, and the others were yelling for everyone to keep quiet. So Kennedy stopped talking."

RFK said, "There is a gentleman down in the front who evidently disagrees with me. If he will ask a single question, I will try to give an answer. That is the democratic way and the way we should proceed. He is asking a question and he is entitled to courtesy." He beckoned to Tachiya, "You sir, have you something to tell us?"

Robert F. Kennedy, during a grand tour of Japan in 1962 intended to pave the way for a planned presidential visit by his brother, faced a chaotic scene at Waseda University. Pandemonium reigned, but Kennedy remained calm, inviting lead heckler Yuzo Tachiya (pictured) onto the stage. (John Dominus, Time-Life)

Yuzo Tachiya was pushed up onto the stage. Kennedy shook his hand, and then did something that may have astonished and impressed the multitudes of Japanese citizens watching spellbound on network TV. At the center of the stage, in a gesture of respect, Robert F. Kennedy politely bowed to his heckler.

He took Tachiya's hand and led him carefully to the microphone. The crowd roared its approval. "Bob treated him with great friendliness," remembered Seigenthaler. RFK was "so cool," recalled U.S. State Department official Brandon Grove, "so cool."

"I'm glad to see you," said Kennedy. "I wonder if we couldn't see if you have a question you'd like to ask. I know that you must believe in free exchange and have something to say. Perhaps you could make your statement and ask me a question and then give me an opportunity to answer."

Like a patient older brother, RFK put his hand on the young Tachiya's shoulder and said, "You go first."

As millions of Japanese citizens looked on and an interpreter whispered the translation in Kennedy's ear, the attorney general of the United States politely held the heavy microphone for Yuzo Tachiya, as the student, who RFK noted was "taut and tense and filled with contempt," raced through a ten-minute diatribe on a long series of hot-button issues: the risks of nuclear war, the occupation of Okinawa, Article 9 of the Japanese constitution (renouncing armed forces), the CIA's involvement in the Bay of Pigs invasion, and America's embryonic intervention in Vietnam.

Finally, when Tachiya finished his oration and Kennedy took his turn to speak, he was cut off. "Immediately every light in the house went out as the power failed," remembered RFK, "and the microphone went dead. For fifteen minutes there was complete chaos. I attempted to speak without a microphone. It was not possible. Everyone now began to yell—at me, at each other, at the school authorities. This only added to the confusion."

Some students were pitching chairs at each other. But Kennedy sensed correctly that even though the auditorium power was dead, the live national TV feed remained plugged in. He could still speak directly to the entire country of Japan. RFK stood his ground and patiently endured the spectacle for nearly twenty minutes as some lights were restored and university officials scurried around to salvage the affair. A battery-powered bullhorn was discovered beneath the stage and given to Kennedy. The U.S. ambassador to Japan, Edwin O. Reischauer, a highly respected Harvard University Japan scholar with an accomplished Japanese wife, moved to the front of the stage, held up his hands, and beseeched the multitude in fluent Japanese to quiet down and listen to their guest.

The bedlam subsided and Kennedy proceeded, without notes, to give the students and the TV audience of Japan a point-by-point reply to the arguments of the Yuzo Tachiya, still beside him. The remarkable extemporaneous speech was a vivid demonstration of democracy in action. "We in America believe that we should have divergences of views. We believe that everyone has the right to express himself. We believe that young people have the right to speak out and give their views and ideas. We believe that opposition is important. It's only through a discussion of issues and questions that my country can determine in what direction it should go."

"This is not true in many other countries," Kennedy argued. "Would it be possible for somebody in a Communist country to get up and oppose the government of that country?" He explained: "I am visiting Japan to learn and find out from young people such as yourselves what your views are as far as Japan is concerned and as far as the future of the world is concerned."

"The audience erupted in cheers and the incident became one of the biggest press stories about our trip," recalled journalist Susie Wilson, who accompanied the Kennedys to Japan. "I had never seen such a raw display of courage before, and I understood, in that moment, the risks one takes as an activist and what is required to sway an audience." According to witness Brandon Grove, Kennedy "was not ruffled, or angry," "he knew what he wanted to say," and "he spoke from the heart about what he thought was right."

Robert Kennedy's impromptu display of eloquence in the midst of chaos was so moving, recalled Grove, that his own eyes were filling with tears. He looked over at another American aide, John Seigenthaler, and saw that the same thing was happening to him, too. They were witnessing America at its finest on the world stage, a glimpse of their country's potential to inspire the world through its words, its example, and its courage in inviting criticism and other points of view while holding firm to its own ideals.

RFK welcomed other students to ask questions, and as he wrapped up his remarks he closed with a burst of soaring rhetoric that anticipated the heights he would later achieve in his 1968 U.S. presidential campaign: "We are facing many of the same problems in the United States that you face in Japan. The solution for all of us is to join as brothers to meet these difficulties. There are great problems. There are great challenges. The age of greatness is before us and we, joined as brothers, can meet our responsibilities and obligations and make this world a better place for ourselves and for our children."

At this, a voice in the audience began singing a traditional Japanese children's folk song called "Akatombo," or "Red Dragonfly," about a child's memories of seeing dragonflies at twilight. More and more student voices joined in, and soon the entire auditorium was roaring through the melody in a sentimental serenade for their guests.

> *Dragonflies, as red as sunset,*
> *Back when I was young*
> *In twilight skies, there on her back I'd ride*
> *When the day was done*
> *Mountain fields, in late November*
> *Long ago it seems*
> *Mulberry trees and treasures we would gather*
> *Was it only just a dream? . . .*
> *Let's go back,*
> *Let's go back together*
> *Let's go back to childhood,*

Let's go back to the sweet old days . . .
Dragonflies, as red as sunset,
Back when I was young
Now in my eyes, when I see dragonflies
Tears are always sure to come.

In the audience a tall teenage boy stood up and shouted a declaration to Robert and Ethel Kennedy.

Kennedy thought it might be more verbal abuse from an angry communist, but the translator whispered that the boy was apologizing for the previous behavior of some of the students. He was the school's cheerleader in chief, and he bounded through the crowd and launched himself up onto the stage next to Kennedy and his wife.

Holding his white-gloved hands straight in the air to signal the crowd to launch into the Waseda school song, "Miyako No Seihoku," the cheerleader swung his hands back hard and fast on the first note, and accidentally delivered a hard blow with his left fist directly to the stomach of a stunned Ethel Kennedy, sending her backward, doubled over in pain. During an interview for this book more than a half century later, Ethel Kennedy remembered, "In his exuberance he flung his left arm out and he caught me in the stomach. Of course at the time I was pregnant and I didn't know it. He just knocked the wind out of me." In a film of the encounter she winces hard, then quickly recovers with a smile to join the students and their American guests in the chorus of shouting, "Waseda! Waseda! Waseda!" Until the day he died in 1968, Robert Kennedy delighted in singing and shouting the song for friends.

It was, remembered Ambassador Reischauer, nothing less than "one of the most dramatic live TV programs in history." He wrote, "I cannot overemphasize what a tremendous success the Attorney General's visit was, especially the incident at Waseda University. While the latter skirted the thin edge of disaster, it turned out to be a resounding triumph that may well have a lasting effect on the student movement in Japan." Reischauer also recalled: "At the time we did not realize what a tremendous victory we had just had. Although the microphones were dead in the hall, they were operating on all the television hook-ups, so that the whole of Japan had been electrified by [the scene]. Bobby's calm, reasoned, even humorous presentation had come through in sharp contrast to the ranting of the Communist students. He had become in one brief moment a sort of youth hero, recognized by all Japanese, and the rest of his trip was virtually a triumphal procession."

It was an overwhelming media and public relations coup for Robert and Ethel Kennedy, who were greeted by enormous crowds and glowing media coverage for the rest of their trip, during which they visited Japanese farms, factories, schools, and temples, toured Osaka and Kyoto, rode the Tokyo subway, held hands and plunged onto a crowded Tokyo skating rink, ate succulent Kobe beef, and watched judo and sumo displays. At the great Todai-ji temple complex in the ancient Japanese capital of Nara, they lit incense and viewed the world's largest bronze sculpture of Buddha. At a sake bar in Ginza, RFK mingled with customers and sang what he remembered as "a very off-key rendition" of "When Irish Eyes Are Smiling." Thousands of people lined rural roads as the Kennedys' motorcade passed through the country.

In Osaka, schoolchildren mobbed the couple, calling "Kennedy-san, shake hands!" At a Matsushita Electrical Industrial Company factory, *Time* magazine reported, "the Attorney General sat down at a workers table and chatted about Communism while munching manfully on a whale steak." In Kyoto, Kennedy sipped sake in a small back-alley bar and chatted about world affairs with university professors. He sought out audiences with ordinary Japanese, especially students and labor representatives.

"The Kennedys had such a disarming way; they really charmed people, and were so genuine," remembered the journalist Susie Wilson, who joined her friend Ethel on the trip, during in a 2014 interview. The thirty-three-year-old Ethel Kennedy proved enormously popular, projecting an attractive aura of informality, enthusiasm, and friendly fascination with Japanese culture. "Ethel loved people," recalled Wilson. "She chatted with any and all of them, and they responded to her genuineness, and her concern for them and their cares."

Few people realized at the time that Ethel Kennedy had her own intimate personal family connection with Japan, through her father, industrialist George Skakel, the founder of Great Lakes Carbon Corporation, one of the largest privately held companies in America. In a 2015 interview for this book, Mrs. Kennedy explained, "My dad had a business association with Mitsubishi, for which during the war he had a terrible guilt trip, because he supplied tankers to the Japanese before the war." The giant Mitsubishi group of companies was a bedrock of the modern Japanese economy, and also of Japan's economic and military expansion during World War II.

After the war was over, Ethel Kennedy recounted, "Daddy called the head of Mitsubishi and said, 'Well, we passed through this terrible stage. But now it's only right that we turn things around. So let's go about our business together.' The head of Mitsubishi said, 'No, George, I can't do that. We are destroyed. We have no factories, we have nothing.' Dad said, 'I'll send a tanker over tomorrow. That's my present to you to help you get back on your feet again.' And that was really the start of Mitsubishi's return."

Fifty-three years after her triumph in Tokyo with her husband, Ethel Kennedy's memories of their visit to Japan were vivid and powerful. "What was wonderful, I think, about Bobby on that trip was he wasn't afraid to hold back. He talked about the differences in our country, and how Americans were free to state their beliefs. What's very fascinating is that despite the language barrier, it seemed to me that the philosophy that Bobby represented and talked about, such as about labor unions and how much they helped the people, really left their mark. It seemed to me it was a concept they hadn't believed in before. You could see them thinking about what he was saying. They just were stunned. Because I think he felt he did in fact get through about our labor policies, which were totally almost unknown territory for them. When he brought up minimum wage and decent circumstances, everything that American labor unions stand for, I do think he affected what would later be tremendous change."

For his part, Robert F. Kennedy recalled, "We left Japan with a certain sadness. We had eaten snails and seaweed for breakfast and whale meat for lunch. We had slept on floors, lived through an earthquake, been thrown to the ground by judo experts and had gone ice-skating before breakfast. We had had meetings at 6:30 in the morning and at 11:30 at night. We had visited farms and factories and sake houses. We had met government officials and factory workers. We had learned a great deal and enjoyed ourselves tremendously in the process."

The visit's ultimate aim, of course, was to pave the way for what Robert Kennedy and his brother John had hoped would be an even greater triumph: a presidential visit to Japan to occur early in the

election year of 1964, a voyage that would culminate in an emotional reunion between JFK and his fellow survivors of the PT 109
disaster, and the surviving veterans of the Japanese warship that
attacked her. But in reality RFK achieved something far greater
and more lasting than a fleeting photo op.

Through their travels in Japan, Robert and Ethel helped trans-
form the previously troubled postwar embrace of Japan and the
United States into a new relationship defined by youth, energy,
dialogue, and mutual respect and equality.

As Dartmouth professor of government Jennifer Lind wrote,
"Robert Kennedy's visit, and the networks and institutions it created, helped knit the U.S. and Japanese societies closer together.
Two countries once dismissed as impossible allies forged, through
careful and persistent diplomacy, a durable and warm relationship."
The trip, she added, "heralded a new era in U.S.-Japanese relations."

On February 7, 1962, the third day of RFK's visit to Japan, the
attorney general was greeted by a special visitor.

In a reception room at the Japanese Institute for Foreign Affairs
in Tokyo, a door slid open and a distinguished middle-aged man
was ushered in to greet Kennedy. He was the mayor of a small town
in the Japanese countryside. His name was Kohei Hanami, and
during World War II, RFK learned, he was commander of a destroyer called the *Amagiri*.

He was, Robert Kennedy realized, the man who had nearly
killed his brother. Kennedy unhooked his own PT 109 tie clasp
and gave it to Hanami, and Hanami gave Kennedy a painting of
Mount Fuji. Like few others, the two men would have understood
how strange the currents of history were that brought them together at that moment.

As commander in chief, John Kennedy forged bonds of intense affection with many of those who served in his administration, a connection that evoked the powerful ties felt by his PT 109 crewmen.

"He was an incendiary man who set most of the people around him on fire," remembered Kennedy's secretary of state, Dean Rusk. "It was really fun to work with him." Rusk identified one of Kennedy's strongest executive strengths: a personality enriched by immense personal charm, intellectual integrity, and often self-deprecating humor, traits that forged his staff into a Shakespearean band of brothers. Budget director David Bell explained that inside the Oval Office, "Kennedy was a magnificent natural leader. He was like a red-haired Irish sea-raider. Everyone had the natural feeling they'd follow him anywhere. He was quick and funny, and committed to all the right purposes. He was the guy you'd want to follow into the machine-gun fire." State Department official Pedro Sanjuan remembered simply, "When he came into the room he was like the sun: he radiated confidence and victory."

Kennedy's special counsel and longtime speechwriter Theodore Sorensen, first among equals in the band JFK brought into the White House from the Senate, recalled Kennedy's tactics for building an effective team, instincts Kennedy may have first developed during his wartime service: "He treated us more as colleagues or associates than employees. He made clear that we were there to give advice as well as take orders." Domestic affairs assistant Myer Feldman said, "I can't imagine a better boss. He gave you enough discretion, but at the same time you knew you were going to have his support even if you did something a little bit wrong. He wouldn't criticize you in front of anybody else." Staff assistant Ralph Dungan recalled, "Everybody on the staff really liked and respected him. You'd really knock yourself out doing anything you could for him. He was terrific."

A story was told of Kennedy, working late in the Oval Office on a freezing-cold night, looking out and seeing a Secret Service officer shivering at his post in the garden just outside the windows. He opened the door and called out, "I don't want you out there in that terrible cold," and ordered him to "come in and get warm." The officer refused, saying such was his job. Kennedy soon came out with a heavy coat and announced, "I want you to put this on. You're not warm enough, I can tell. 'A few minutes later the president came out again, this time with a couple of cups of hot chocolate, and persuaded the agent to join him. The two sat down on the cold steps outside the Oval Office and sipped their mugs together. Years later the agent wept as he told the story.

For much of his presidency, John F. Kennedy lurched from emergency to emergency as simmering domestic and international crises began detonating around him. An emboldened Soviet premier Nikita Khrushchev, after smelling blood at Kennedy's poor performance in the Bay of Pigs disaster and after bullying him at a summit meeting in Vienna, geared up for showdowns in Berlin, Laos, Vietnam, and Cuba.

The civil rights movement, excited by Kennedy's sympathetic rhetoric, entered a new phase of action, and major crises erupted in Mississippi, Alabama, and elsewhere as black Americans asserted their rights as citizens. One of these crises, over the attempt by James Meredith to enter the segregated University of Mississippi in October 1962, required John and Robert Kennedy to micromanage the emergency deployment of more than 10,000 federal combat troops to rapidly stage what amounted to a lightning invasion of northern Mississippi to rescue Meredith and stop an extremely dangerous riot from spreading.

When the operation proceeded slower than JFK liked, he mut-

tered a complaint that echoed his observations of military ineffi-
ciency during the war: "They always give you their bullshit about
their instant reaction and split-second timing, but it never works
out. No wonder it's so hard to win a war."

Beyond the campaign dividends it paid, the PT 109 incident
may have critically shaped Kennedy's attitude toward the military
and the projection of military force, and shaped the way he made
decisions during his brief, tumultuous time in the White House.
Like many men who had served as junior officers in World War II,
he developed a sharp skepticism toward military bureaucracy, and
a seasoned view of the fallibility and periodic incompetence of "the
brass": the commanders, generals, and admirals whose arrogance
and mistakes were often paid for in blood by younger men, and
who now were reporting to him as commander in chief. Kennedy
White House assistant Dan Fenn said, "My own feeling is that the
wartime experience had a terrific impact on his view of military
leadership and that played a major role in a lot of decisions."

Clint Hill, a Secret Service agent on the Kennedy detail from
1960 to 1963, agreed that JFK's wartime experience was a crucial
influence on his presidency. In a 2015 interview, he recalled, "I am
sure that wartime experience had a great deal to do with decisions
he made as president, especially decisions relating to foreign relations and the United States military. I don't think there's any question about that. It gave him an understanding of the military, but
also about how things can go wrong, how at a moment's notice,
things can go from better to worse. It really made him understand
how a group that big has to work together to be successful at whatever they're doing. It helped him form a better basis for being president; he had that experience behind him that many people didn't
have. He knew what it was like to be in combat, and under fire,

and I'm sure that made him apprehensive about putting anybody else in that position."

John Kennedy's youngest brother, Edward Kennedy, saw the PT 109 episode as a defining event in JFK's perception of himself, as he passed through an extreme test of physical endurance and survival. The younger Kennedy said, "It really made an impression on himself about his own steel and his inner toughness. I think it had a really important impact in terms of how he perceived himself for the rest of his life. I think he was a different individual. It made a very important mark on his character."

While president, Kennedy presided over a booming economy, a steel crisis, the launch of the Peace Corps and NASA's quest for the moon, the projection of a positive, inspiring image of America around the world, and a secret war against Cuba that saw his brother the attorney general receive at least one personal briefing on sabotage attacks and multiple assassination attempts against Cuban head of state Fidel Castro.

From August to November 1963, John and Robert Kennedy also presided over a chaotic mélange of American involvement and noninvolvement with various coup plots in Saigon, a slow-motion nightmare that culminated, to JFK's shock and dismay, in the gangland-style machine-gun rubout of American ally and South Vietnamese head of state Ngo Dinh Diem and his brother. "He's always said that it was a major mistake on his part," said RFK in 1964 of JFK's authorization of support for the coup plots. "The result is we started down a path we never really recovered from." The final plunge of America into the abyss of Vietnam may have occurred under Lyndon Johnson at the Gulf of Tonkin in 1964, but it started on Kennedy's watch with the assassination of Diem the year before.

If some stories are to be believed, Kennedy, who continued to suffer from fragile health during his presidency, also is alleged to have conducted high-risk affairs with a large number of women other than his wife. His cabinet secretary Fred Dutton asserted that Kennedy behaved "like God, fucking anybody he wants to anytime he feels like it." British prime minister Harold Macmillan famously quipped that Kennedy spent "half his time thinking about adultery, the other half about secondhand ideas passed on by his advisors."

In the weeks before Kennedy died, Congress had blocked most of his domestic program, and his popularity had plunged from 83 percent after the Bay of Pigs to 57 percent, due in part to growing southern resistance to civil rights. One victory was the Senate's 1963 passage of the JFK-supported Nuclear Test Ban Treaty, the first arms control agreement of the nuclear age.

The zenith of Kennedy's brief presidency was the peaceful resolution of the Cuban Missile Crisis in October 1962, when he and his brother Robert stared down some of their own hawkish military and civilian advisors and found a way out that did not involve the catastrophic detonation of nuclear warheads. In JFK's secret White House tapes of the crisis, Kennedy's calm, rational discussion and decision-making style shines clearly through as that of a man who has, to use his own inaugural phrase, been "tempered by war," a man whose character was forged in the cauldron of combat, military disaster, death, endurance, and survival.

The memories and the lessons of PT 109 may never have been far from Kennedy's mind.

EPILOGUE: THE RISING SUN

Shortly after John F. Kennedy's assassination on November 22, 1963, journalist I. F. Stone wrote, "He died in time to be remembered as he would like to be remembered, as ever young, still victorious, stuck down undefeated, with almost all the potentates and rulers of mankind, friend and foe, come to mourn at the bier. For somehow one has the feeling that in the tangled dramaturgy of events, this sudden assassination was the only way out. The Kennedy administration was approaching an impasse, certainly at home, quite possibly abroad, from which there appeared to be no escape." The following year, the *New York Times'* James Reston mused, "He always seemed to be striding through doors into the center of some startling triumph or disaster. He never reached his meridian: we saw him only as a rising sun."

As president, John Kennedy projected an incandescent image of a brilliant, funny, diligent young executive facing titanic crises with Hemingwayesque "grace under pressure," confidence, wisecracks, and existential cool. One scholar, John Hellmann of Ohio State University, saw Kennedy's imagery as that of a self-created bashful American war hero and sensitive rebel, striking chords of Lord Byron, Henry Fonda, Jimmy Stewart, Gary Cooper, and Cary Grant, all powered by the foundation myth of PT 109. As Hugh Sidey wrote in 1983, "He was the greatest actor of our time, dimming those mere celluloid performers like Ronald Reagan."

Even if he had somehow dodged potentially catastrophic personal scandals like the Ellen Rometsch affair, a tabloid-style alleged-hooker-and-spy story that may have been on the verge of detonating publicly at the moment he died, it is obviously impossible to know if Kennedy would have managed the blossoming crises of the 1960s any better than his successors did.

Whatever the judgments of historians and pundits, JFK towers above his competition with one crucial audience: the American people. He had the highest average Gallup approval ratings while in office of any president; his 70 percent beat his closest competitor, Dwight Eisenhower, by 5 percentage points. In 1996, after thirty-three years of posthumous criticism, revisionism, and alleged sex and mafia scandals, Kennedy won again, this time in a *New York Times*/CBS poll that asked which president Americans would pick to run the country today. Kennedy's winning 28 percent was more than double the number-two choice (Reagan at 13 percent), and he buried FDR, Truman, and even Abraham Lincoln, who shared a three-way tie at 8 percent.

Similar results were found by a Gallup poll published in November 2013, on the fiftieth anniversary of Kennedy's death, in which American adults rated JFK higher than any other president who has held office after him. On November 15, 2013, Andrew Dugan and Frank Newport of Gallup reported: "Kennedy has usually appeared in the top group of presidents when Americans are asked in an open-ended format to name the greatest U.S. president in American history. That includes a 2000 measure, in which Kennedy was at the top of the list, eclipsing Abraham Lincoln, Franklin Roosevelt, and Ronald Reagan."

Then, as now, many Americans may look at John F. Kennedy and see, despite his human failings and contradictions, images of what they would like themselves to be, and what their leaders should be as well: a man of action who was also intelligent, diplomatic, curious, compassionate, comfortable with himself and with criticism; an American who had a confident and ambitious vision for his country's destiny yet understood the power of leading by example rather than by bluster; and a leader of immense charm who, as the men of the PT 109 repeatedly attested, possessed the strength to persevere through incredible trials.

When John Kennedy died, then U.S. ambassador Edwin Reischauer reported, "The Japanese response to the assassination was overwhelming." The U.S. embassy in Tokyo was deluged with condolence letters, and thousands of people flocked to a memorial mass for the fallen friend of Japan.

In a small Japanese town early on the morning of November 23, 1963, Kohei Hanami, the former captain of the *Amagiri*, was awakened by a phone call. "I have terrible news," cried a neighbor. "Your friend, the American president, has been assassinated."

"Nonsense," replied Hanami. "How do you know?"

"I stayed up to watch the first television program from the United States relayed by satellite. The program was interrupted for a news flash."

"I don't believe it," Hanami retorted. "Assassinations may occur in some countries, but not in the United States." Soon after, a reporter called Hanami and confirmed the terrible news.

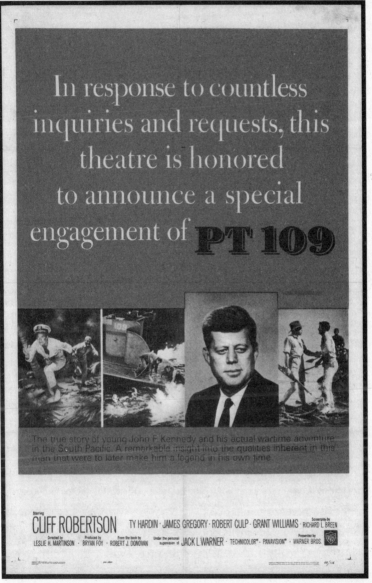

Warner Bros. poster announcing special screenings of *PT 109* following Kennedy's assassination. (Warner Bros.)

Hanami was devastated. "Who will lead the world to peace?" he wondered. "What will happen to all of us?" He felt sympathy for Kennedy's wife and little children. If only Kennedy had come to Japan instead of going to Dallas, Hanami thought, his life might have been spared.

Hanami was seized with a feeling of *zannen*—a Japanese word that describes emotions of melancholy, pity, and disappointment— over the idea that Kennedy escaped death in war by a few inches, but fell victim to a violent death in peacetime. Hanami's neighbors called upon his home offering condolences as if one of his family members had died. A few days later he traveled to Tokyo by train, attended memorial ceremonies, and paid his respects at the American embassy.

In the decades following Kennedy's assassination, his popularity steadily soared in the wake of the largely broken and failed presidencies of Lyndon Johnson, Richard Nixon, Gerald Ford, and Jimmy Carter, but the cultural memory of JFK's moment of destiny, the PT 109 episode, gradually faded.

In 2002, Robert F. Kennedy's son Maxwell Taylor Kennedy journeyed to the Solomon Islands to meet and thank the native men who rescued his uncle John and the survivors of the PT 109. He was invited to join a National Geographic Society expedition to find the wreckage of the boat led by oceanographer Robert Ballard, and he jumped at the chance.

In an interview for this book in 2015, Max Kennedy reflected, "PT 109 was really etched in my life since I was a small child. We were raised in Virginia, but grew up on Cape Cod. Whenever there was some kind of dangerous situation or difficulty or challenge on the water, I would always think of President Kennedy on the PT 109 and the extraordinary bravery that he showed. And then we'd just kind of suck it up and do our best to get through whatever storm or difficulty we were facing when we were children."

Over the years, Max had talked to his cousin John F. Kennedy Jr. about the possibility of trying to find the PT 109. The president's son "was a great scuba diver, and he had scuba-dived all over the Pacific Ocean," remembered his cousin, but he died in a plane crash in 1999, before he was able to search for the wreck. Now Max Kennedy would make the trip, representing the whole Kennedy family.

When Max Kennedy arrived in the Solomon Islands, he linked up with Richard Keresey, JFK's wartime friend and former skipper of the PT 105.

Wondering about his uncle's repeated nocturnal attempts to hail passing PT boats in Ferguson Passage, Max Kennedy asked Keresey, "What would you have done if you had seen the lantern or heard the pistol?"

Keresey replied, "We would have fired every gun and made sure anybody there was dead."

"Did Jack know that?" asked a surprised Kennedy.

"He absolutely knew that," acknowledged Keresey. "But we also would have checked, and then we would have found his body. And we'd know that he did it because his crew was still alive, and we'd go find them." It was then that Max Kennedy absorbed the full impact of his uncle's struggles, and he realized the "extraordinary sacrifice" he was willing to make for his crew.

When Max Kennedy was finally brought face-to-face with the now-elderly Eroni Kumana, one of JFK's two initial rescuers, on a remote island in the South Pacific, he was not prepared for the wave of emotion that overcame himself and Kumana, nearly sixty years after the rescue triggered by Kumana and his partner Biuku Gasa. "It had been way, way, way too long," Kennedy recalled. "It had just been too much time for them to have gone without meeting Jack, or my father, or some member of my family."

The two men embraced each other in a long, close hug, and Eroni Kumana began to cry, loudly and freely. "It was so unbelievably moving," recalled Kennedy. "We very quickly had a connection at an extraordinarily deep level. My God, he was so sweet."

Kennedy remembered, "I had read all the World War Two books as a kid, and I heard all the stories about what the Japanese army had done to people who helped the United States in the Pacific and the terrible atrocities these guys faced. They cut off their private parts and did terrible, terrible things. That's what these guys [scouts like Kumana and Gasa] faced and they knew that's what they faced. They knew that if they were caught they would be tortured horribly for two or three days until they were dead. And yet they did this! They risked their lives, they risked everything. There's no reason that they had to do that. And they truly saved the lives of all of the men who survived that sinking."

When the two men first met, Max Kennedy recounted, "I started moving my right hand slowly toward his stomach. And he immediately knew I was going to try to tickle him. Which nobody would know! It wouldn't even occur to somebody that they were going to get tickled at a moment like that. He and I tickled each other constantly for the next week. Sneaking up on each other. It sounds like such a silly thing, but having a physical connection, as well as having such a beyond-belief, genetic and spiritual connection was one of the most moving things that's ever happened to me. I knew it would be incredible to meet them. But I've met so many people who knew Jack and my father, and I'm somewhat jaded at that kind of thing. I really wasn't ready for the outpouring of emotion that came for me personally, as well as them. And it was really shared in a way that doesn't usually happen."

Max Kennedy was delighted to see Kumana wearing a T-shirt reading "I Rescued JFK." The shirt design was popular in the Solomons, said Kennedy, "but in his case—it's true!"

Kennedy held a reunion with both Eroni Kumana and Biuku Gasa, who hadn't seen each other in years, and presented each with a bust of his uncle. He read aloud to them a letter written by JFK's last surviving brother, U.S. senator from Massachusetts Edward M. Kennedy. The note read, "President Kennedy often spoke of the great courage of those who came to his aid and he never forgot them. Not a day goes by that I don't think of him and miss him. And it means a great deal to know that my brother is still remembered with affection in the Solomon Islands."

Meeting the two men had a moving personal impact on Max Kennedy, who recalled the encounter as a pinnacle of his life. "I've just never seen people with so much heart, so much honesty. They were completely incapable of even making an effort to hide their feelings or their emotions. It was just a remarkable outpouring of emotion when we finally met. They really lived a biblical life, because they had no electricity, no refrigerators. They ate fish and rice and beans and coconuts. So when they go out fishing they only catch enough fish for one day because they have no way to preserve them. They never worry that they're going to run out of food. There's not even a hint of worry about it. Every day they go out and they catch the fish they need. More than any other people I've ever met in my life, and I've met people all over the world, they do not worry about the next day. They live completely in the moment, and I think that's why you see that extraordinary outpouring of emotion when we met because everything is moment to moment for them. They were able to concentrate one hundred percent on where they were, with me."

Max Kennedy spent days visiting with Eroni Kumana and

Biuku Gasa, as they explored the islands, shared food and laughter, and told each other stories about their lives.

"God, we had so much fun together," Kennedy remembered wistfully in 2015. "They were just incredible men."

Robert Ballard's 2002 National Geographic expedition used photos and sonar to identify a PT boat's port forward torpedo and launch tube on the ocean floor of Blackett Strait that the U.S. Navy concluded was "probably" from the PT 109, but the expedition was unable to recover any of the wreckage. It is still not known exactly which pieces sank at what times after the crash, and what the precise pattern of impact and damage was on the boat.

Today, the wreckage of the PT 109, if any still exists, still lies somewhere more than a thousand feet below the waves at the bottom of the ocean in Blackett Strait in the Solomon Islands.

In August 2007, Eroni Kumana was invited aboard the USS *Peleliu,* a U.S. Navy aircraft carrier that was visiting the Solomon Islands on a humanitarian and diplomatic mission in the wake of a devastating earthquake and tsunami that killed more than fifty people and damaged Kumana's house. The *Peleliu's* commanding officer, Captain Ed Rhoades, presented Kumana with an American flag and an assortment of gifts. "I mourned for a whole week upon hearing of my friend's [John Kennedy's] death," Kumana said. "I can now be at peace since through my friend's legacy, people have come to know me, my people and my country, the Solomon Islands." According to Kumana's friend and local businessman Danny Kennedy (no relation), "The family was absolutely ecstatic and Aaron [Eroni] was running on adrenaline the whole time" during his 2007 encounter with the U.S. Navy. "It was probably the happiest day of his life." Kumana stayed overnight on the ship, and met U.S. Navy secretary Donald Winter, who was visiting Gizo. "This is an individual who has had a very significant role in the history of our nation and the world," said Winter. "It was an honor to meet the man who rescued the future thirty-fifth American president." The *Peleliu*'s crew collected $1,500 to help repair Kumana's house.

The following year, Eroni Kumana asked Mark Roche, a visiting American, to place a prized family heirloom "on the grave of his chief," his onetime friend and brother-in-arms John F. Kennedy. It was a white circular piece of "shell money" or "kustom money," fashioned out of a giant clamshell. At a private family ceremony that was held on November 1, 2008, at Arlington National Cemetery and arranged by Kennedy's daughter, Caroline Kennedy, Roche placed the tribute on President Kennedy's grave. In attendance at the ceremony were JFK's sister Eunice Kennedy Shriver, her son Tim Shriver, and Sydney Lawford McKelvy, daughter of JFK's other sister Patricia Kennedy Lawford.

Biuku Gasa died in 2005, and Eroni Kumana passed away at the age of ninety-three on August 2, 2014, the seventy-first anniversary of the sinking of PT 109. Kumana was believed to have had nine children, including a son he named John Fitzgerald Kennedy Kumana.

John F. Kennedy was never able to meet Gasa or Kumana after the rescue. The two men were supposed to travel to the United States to visit Kennedy at the White House, but colonial officials stopped them at the airport and canceled their trip, apparently concerned at their lack of English-language skill and unsophisticated appearance. Instead, they sent the native leader of the second stage of the rescue, Benjamin Kevu, who spoke English with a courtly accent. Kevu appeared on Jack Paar's television show along with Reg Evans, the former Australian Coastwatcher, and met with John F. Kennedy and Barney Ross in the Oval Office.

The previous year, on May 1, 1961, Reg Evans also met with JFK

TOP PT 109 veterans George "Barney" Ross and John F. Kennedy welcome former Solomon Islands Scout Benjamin Kevu to the Oval Office, September 25, 1962. Kevu organized a critical stage of the rescue, smuggling Kennedy over an ocean passage at the bottom of a canoe covered with leaves to meet with Coastwatcher Reginald Evans. (John F. Kennedy Presidential Library)

BOTTOM Kennedy in 1961 with Reginald Evans, the Australian Coastwatcher who helped engineer his rescue in 1943. (John F. Kennedy Presidential Library)

in the Oval Office. Kennedy quipped, "I am sorry I never returned the Japanese rifle you loaned me." Evans replied, "It didn't take me long to get another." Evans died in Australia in 1989.

After World War II, Kennedy's fellow survivors of the PT 109 incident went on to live largely quiet private lives, periodically resurfacing when the PT 109 story made the news.

Lenny Thom survived the war and became an insurance representative with a young child, only to die when his car was hit by a train in 1946.

In 1961, Kennedy rewarded several of his crewmen with federal patronage and political appointments. He named George Ross to a minor position on the staff of the President's Committee on Juvenile Delinquency and Youth Crime; appointed John Maguire United States marshal for the Southern District of Florida; and signed an executive order appointing PT 109 precrash crewman and later PT 59 crewman Maurice Kowal to a National Park Service job. Additionally, he arranged for his PT service friends Paul Fay to be undersecretary of the Navy, William Battle to be U.S. ambassador to Australia, and Byron White to be deputy attorney general to Robert F. Kennedy. JFK appointed White to the U.S. Supreme Court in 1962.

Both Gerard Zinser and Pat McMahon became mail carriers, in Florida and California, respectively.

During the same 1962 episode of the Jack Paar show that Ben Kevu and Reg Evans appeared on, the host asked all the surviving PT 109 survivors to stand up in the audience and be applauded. The camera slowly panned the faces of John Maguire, Gerard Zinser, Barney Ross, Ed Mauer, Raymond Starkey, Pat McMahon, William Johnston, Charles Harris, as well as Ed Drewitch and Maurice Kowal, who left the boat in the weeks before the crash.

They looked to be modest, shy, middle-aged men, eager to rejoin their families and the postwar brotherhood of anonymity shared by millions of other members of the World War II generation.

In the summer of 1963, seven veterans of the PT 109 crew went on a ten-day grand tour of Japan in conjunction with the Japanese premiere of the Hollywood movie *PT 109*. They held three separate reunions with former crew members of the *Amagiri,* toured Tokyo, Osaka, Kobe, and Nikko, and met the mayor and governor of Tokyo. "We were hosted by dignitaries of manufacturing, business and financial Japan," wrote Pat McMahon in an August 16, 1963, letter to President Kennedy. "We received medals, honors and presents galore. The friendships, courtesies and generosities extended us [were] simply overwhelming."

McMahon regaled his beloved commander with a vision of the kind of reunion that Kennedy and his father, Joseph P. Kennedy Sr., had yearned for over the past twelve years, the kind of moment that JFK was hoping to experience himself the following year with the planned first-ever U.S. presidential state visit to Japan. "Had you seen us, with the *Amagiri* crew," wrote McMahon, "and many members of Japanese Navy, and Government officials, in a huge circle, hands joined, singing Auld Lang Syne, at conclusion of [a] garden party in [the Crown] Prince's grounds one midnight in Tokyo, [I] am sure you would have been astounded." According to McMahon, the former chief engineering officer of the *Amagiri* "held onto me like I was a long-lost brother."

None of the survivors ever had an unkind public word to say about John F. Kennedy, and often praised him repeatedly whenever reporters came to call. When Kennedy died, recalled Gerard Zinser in 1998, "I felt that day like I'd lost the best friend of my life. That's what John F. Kennedy meant to me." He insisted on "setting the record straight" about the crash, declaring, "So many people who were not there have criticized him for being at fault in that collision. Well, I was there, and let me tell you, there wasn't a damn thing he could have done to prevent it."

"Lieutenant Kennedy was one hell of a man," PT 109 survivor William Johnston once declared. "I didn't pick him for my skipper, but I kept thanking God that the Navy had picked him for me."

The final survivor of the PT 109, Gerard Zinser, died of Alzheimer's disease in Florida in 2001. He was survived by eight children, twenty-four grandchildren, and ten great-grandchildren. His ashes are buried in Arlington National Cemetery, not far from the grave of his former commander.

The man who is believed to be the last surviving PT boat veteran who served under the command of John F. Kennedy in the South Pacific, ninety-two-year-old John Klee, lives today in California with his wife of sixty-three years, Barbara. Klee served under JFK on the PT 59 for about a week in November 1943.

He still sings the praises of his old skipper. "He got along well with his officers," said Klee, "he was fearless, and he was great with his crew. I only heard plaudits about Kennedy from our crew, many of whom were the remnants of the PT 109, and they were a great bunch. They admired him as a person and as a skipper."

After he led the PT boat operation behind enemy lines to rescue John F. Kennedy and the PT 109 survivors on August 7–8, 1943, U.S. Navy Lieutenant (jg) William "Bud" Liebenow resumed his duties as the skipper of the PT 157. At the end of 1943 he was assigned to the war in Europe to serve under the famous PT commander John Bulkeley to assist the Office of Strategic Services to pick up and drop off agents on the coast of Nazi-held France.

The rescue of John F. Kennedy, it turned out, was not the only remarkable wartime episode in which Bud Liebenow played a part.

"The most notable event of my life and I suppose of the thousands who took part, was the Normandy Beach invasion, D-Day, June sixth, 1944," Liebenow explained. "I was a special officer on board the PT 199 which was assigned patrol duty around the communications vessel controlling the landings near Cherbourg. Our first assignment was to escort the rocket launcher boats into the beach. This was at H-minus four hours. These were LCVP's [Landing Craft, Vehicle, Personnel] modified to hold bank on bank of rockets. They were driven right into the beach and the rockets released. This added up to a lot of explosive power from a very small vessel. You got only one shot—all rockets were released at once—and then you had to get out. The shore battery fire was intense, many of these boats were destroyed. As daylight arrived you could grasp the vastness of the allied armada. There were ships and boats everywhere!" On D-Day, when the USS *Corry* was sinking from a German mine and shore fire, Liebenow and his men on the PT 199 pulled sixty American sailors aboard.

Liebenow received the Silver Star for his actions of the nights of July 2–3, and August 14–15, 1943, when he attacked Japanese destroyers and used the PT 157 as a decoy to divert Japanese planes from attacking a slow-moving U.S. convoy carrying U.S. Marines. Liebenow also received the Bronze Star for missions aboard allied PT boats in dropping off and picking up U.S and Allied spies, soldiers, and airmen along the French coast prior to D-Day.

After the war, Liebenow went on to become an environmental engineer in the railroad industry. "As Jack Kennedy's political star rose, every incident in his life became news," recalled Liebenow. "People became interested in everything he did or said, from the way he combed his hair to what he thought of the pope. When my connection with Kennedy became known through news accounts during the 1960 campaign I began to get 'fan mail' and phone calls. Ninety-nine percent were from people expressing good wishes and sending compliments. The other one percent, which of course you felt the most, were expressions of hate. These expressions came mostly from anti-Catholics. They were worried about having a president under control of the pope. The amazing thing was they somehow blamed me!"

In the 1960 presidential campaign, JFK asked Liebenow to join him on an old-fashioned railroad "whistle-stop" campaign trip across Michigan, where Liebenow was then living. Liebenow was delighted to accept the invitation. According to Liebenow, "Almost everywhere we went, someone would jump out and say "Hey, Jack I was on that boat that picked you up!"

Kennedy would nicely say "thank you," turn to Liebenow, and quietly ask, "Did you ever see this guy?"

"Never saw him before in my life," was his inevitable reply.

"Lieb," Kennedy would say, "if I get all the votes from the people who claim to have been on your boat that night of the pickup, I'll win easily!"

When Kennedy spotted Liebenow and his wife in the audience at one of his inaugural balls in January 1961, he beckoned them to join him on the ballroom stage. A team of Secret Service agents summoned the couple from the audience, and created such a grand path through the huge crowd that to Liebenow, "It felt like the parting of the Red Sea."

"Lieb, I'd like to meet the girl you married," said Kennedy.

Introducing himself to Lucy Liebenow, Kennedy said, "I just want to thank you for what your husband did during the war."

Then Kennedy introduced Bud Liebenow to his Vice President-elect Lyndon B. Johnson, saying, "I owe this guy a lot."

When Kennedy told Johnson about Liebenow's rescue of the PT 109 survivors, remembered Liebenow, the tall Texan "slapped me so hard on the back that I was practically knocked off the stage."

Today, Bud Liebenow lives in a retirement community in North Carolina with Lucy, his wife of seventy-two years. They met in a science lab in college and got married in 1942, days before he shipped off to the South Pacific. His son served as a U.S. Marine Corps captain in Vietnam, and his granddaughter served as U.S. Army captain.

These days, Liebenow works out every day. Four days a week, he presses weights in his gym. On the other three days, he catches a ride to the community pool, where he swims laps.

He just turned ninety-five years old.

On November 19, 2013, John F. Kennedy's daughter, Caroline, was carried in a horse-drawn carriage through the streets of central Tokyo onto the private Imperial Palace grounds of Emperor Akihito of Japan, the son of Japan's wartime emperor, Hirohito.

Entering the imperial reception room, she bowed to Emperor Akihito and presented her credentials as the U.S. ambassador to Japan, a country that still held fond memories of her father. "I think that my story in a way is a great metaphor for the U.S.-Japan alliance," she later told a reporter. "Countries that were once adversaries and enemies in war are now the best of friends and allies."

In her first year and a half in the highly visible post, Caroline Kennedy proved to be a popular, capable, and occasionally outspoken ambassador, who forged a strong working partnership with Prime Minister Shinzo Abe and charmed Japanese audiences with her warm, humble personality.

On March 5, 2015, Prime Minister Abe and Ambassador Kennedy attended the opening ceremony for an exhibition titled "JFK: His Life and Legacy" at the National Archives of Japan in Tokyo. One of the guests was an elderly wheelchair-bound woman in a gold kimono. She was the widow of Kohei Hanami, commanding

Caroline Kennedy, U.S. Ambassador to Japan, meets the widow of Captain Kohei Hanami in Tokyo, March 5, 2015. (U.S. Embassy, Tokyo)

officer of the Imperial Japanese Navy destroyer *Amagiri*. Ambassador Kennedy leaned down, held her hand, and said, "I've been hoping to meet you ever since I became ambassador."

One day early in his presidency, John F. Kennedy sent a televised greeting to the people of the nation he once was at war with, a country he briefly glimpsed as it rose from the ashes of destruction, and a nation he yearned to visit again someday.

"I am a great admirer of Japan," he said. "We are about to have in Washington the annual flowering of your cherry trees which were a gift of your people to us which make our city so beautiful."

"Whenever I look out the window, I'll be reminded of Japan."

ACKNOWLEDGMENTS

I thank my wife, Naomi Moriyama, for translating a wide variety of Japanese documents I consulted in the research for this book; my father, William Doyle, for a lifetime of conversations about what it was like to be at war in the South Pacific in World War II; my mother, Marie Louise Doyle, for her memories of the Kennedys in New York in 1960; and my seven-year-old son, Brendan, for his constant encouragement and enthusiasm.

I also thank:

My editor, Peter Hubbard (whose idea this book was), publicist Sharyn Rosenblum, and their colleagues at HarperCollins; and my agent, Mel Berger of William Morris Endeavor.

The people I interviewed for this book, especially William Liebenow, Welford West, and their fellow veterans of PT boat service in World War II, and Ethel Kennedy and Maxwell Taylor Kennedy for sharing their memories of Japan and the Solomon Islands for this book. Mr. Liebenow was a tremendous help to me in my research and I am very grateful to him for his enthusiasm, encouragement, and the many hours he spent answering my questions about arcane PT boat details and events and dialogue that occurred over seventy years ago.

John K. Castle, Nicholas Meyer, Charles Rockefeller, Lucy Liebenow, Fumiko Miyamoto, Frank J. Andruss, Sr., Bridgeman Carney, Jay Barksdale, Harold E. "Ted" Walther Jr., Tim Connelly, Terrence Finneran, Charlie Jones, (President of PT Boats, Inc.), John Flynn, Shane Kennedy, Danny Kennedy, Dennis E. Harkins, Francis I. Piorek, Eric Klee, John Fairfax, Jan-Losa Naru Butler, and Tom Putnam and the superb staff at the John F. Kennedy Presidential Library, including Stephen Plotkin, Michael Desmond, Stacey Chandler, Laurie Austin, and Corbin Apkin. The JFK Library is a "gold standard" model of what a research archive should be.

Ambassador Caroline Kennedy for making available to me the portrait of her father as a U.S. Navy ensign in 1942 from the closed Jacqueline Kennedy Onassis papers at the JFK Library.

Alyce Guthrie of PT Boats Inc. for helping me track down a number of PT boat veterans; and Nancy Hogan Dutton for helping me track down veterans of the JFK White House.

Ken Kotani, Senior Fellow, International Conflict Division, Japanese Center for Military History and Lecturer of the Japanese National Defense Academy; and Anna Annie Kwai, historian and scholar based in the Solomon Islands.

I am especially gratefull to PT boat experts Bridgeman Carney, Charlie Jones, and Harold E. "Ted" Walther, Jr., for reviewing the book and making a number of useful corrections and suggestions.

NOTES AND SOURCES

This book is based on an examination of a wide range of declassified documents and other materials in the research collections of the John F. Kennedy Presidential Library (JFKL) and a variety of archives in Japan, Australia, and the Solomon Islands.

It is based on author interviews with sixteen surviving contemporaries of John F. Kennedy in the PT boat service, and an extensive series of author interviews with William "Bud" Liebenow, the PT boat commander who bravely and expertly navigated his own PT 157 forty miles into enemy waters in the dark of night to rescue Kennedy and his men, several of whom were wounded. It is also based on author interviews with the very rarely interviewed Ethel Kennedy and her son Max Kennedy, both of whom have intimate family connections with events in this book.

This book is also influenced by the impressive insights of three independent PT boat historians: Frank J. Andruss Jr., Bridgeman Carney, and Harold E. "Ted" Walther Jr.; and by rare or never-before-publicized private letters, photos, and other materials given to the author by them and by friends and relatives of key players in the events.

And finally, this book is influenced by the work of other writers and historians who have examined the PT 109 incident, including John Hersey, author of "Survival," a seminal June 17, 1944, *New Yorker* article on the event; journalist Robert J. Donovan, author of the 1961 book *PT 109: John F. Kennedy in World War II* (McGraw-Hill), which was written with the cooperation of JFK and was the basis of a 1963 movie produced under the direct supervision of JFK and his father; naval historians Clay Blair Jr. and Joan Blair, authors of the 1976 book *The Search for JFK* (Berkley), which included an authoritative exploration of the PT 109 incident and was based in part on a wide range of original interviews conducted by the authors; and historian Nigel Hamilton, author of *JFK: Reckless Youth* (Random House, 1992), an essential biography of the early years of JFK, including his wartime experiences.

AUTHOR INTERVIEWS

William "Bud" Liebenow (skipper of PT 157, tent mate of John F. Kennedy at Rendova base prior to PT 109 sinking, participant in Blackett Strait action on August 1–2, 1943, commander of lead boat in rescue of JFK and PT 109 survivors on August 7–8, 1943), Welford West (PT 157, participant in Blackett Strait action, August 1–2, 1943, participant in rescue of JFK and PT 109 survivors on August 7–8, 1943), John Sullivan (PT 107, participant in Blackett Strait action, August 1–2, 1943), Chester Williams (PT 106, participant in Blackett Strait action, August 1–2, 1943), John Klee (then named Jack Bernard Kahn, served on PT 59 under JFK in November 1943), Edwin Foster Ockerman (instructed by JFK at Melville PT training base, later skipper of PT 103), Howard Aronson (PT 103), Jerome Francis "Pat" Crowley (PT 104), Vernon Byrd (PT 106), Donald Frost (PT 161), Jack Duncan (PT 103), Vincent Conti (PT 171), Bob Kirkpatrick (PT 169), Jack Marshall (PT 171), Joseph Brannan (PT 59), Joseph Derrough (PT 59).

Ethel Kennedy (Mrs. Robert F. Kennedy), Maxwell Taylor Kennedy (son of Robert F. Kennedy), Dan Fenn (JFK White House assistant), Charles Daly (JFK White House assistant), Richard Donahue (JFK White House assistant), Harris Wofford (JFK presidential campaign aide and White House assistant), Jerry Blaine (Secret Service agent on Kennedy White House detail), Clint Hill (Secret Service agent on Kennedy White House detail), Frank J. Andruss Sr. (PT boat historian), Donald Shannon (PT boat historian), Harold E. "Ted" Walther Jr. (PT boat historian), Bridgeman Carney (PT 157 historian and author), Connie Martinson (wife of Leslie Martinson, director of *PT 109* movie), Dunstone Aleziru (grandson of Benjamin Kevu, by email), Mark Zinser (son of PT 109 crewman Gerard Zinser), Jack Kirksey (son of Andrew Jackson Kirksey, crewman on PT 109), Hoyt Grant (stepson of Andrew Jackson Kirksey, crewman on PT 109, by email), Fred Ratchford, Jr. (son of Fred Ratchford, on PT 157 mission to rescue PT 109 crew), Julie Nash and Clint Nash (children of Coastwatcher Benjamin Franklin Nash), Melody Miller (served on U.S. Senate staff of Edward M. Kennedy, met with President John F. Kennedy in White House, by email), Haruko Hosono (daughter of Gunji Hosono, interviewed by her daughter Fumiko Miyamoto), Leo Racine (longtime aide to Joseph P. Kennedy Sr., interviewed by John K. Castle), Tom Cluster (son of JFK's squadron commander, Al Cluster), James MacGregor Burns (JFK historian and author), Susie Wilson (journalist who accompanied Robert and Ethel Kennedy on 1962 Japan trip), John Seigenthaler (Justice Department official who accompanied Robert and Ethel Kennedy on 1962 Japan trip), Brandon Grove (State Department official who accompanied Robert and Ethel Kennedy on 1962 Japan trip). Interviews on JFK as president for author's books *Inside the Oval Office* and *An American Insurrection:* Theodore Sorensen, C. Douglas Dillon, Ralph Dungan, Myer Feldman, Edwin Martin, Pedro Sanjuan, Robert Bouck, Burke Marshall, Nicholas Katzenbach, David Bell.

CHAPTER NOTES

Foreword

"Without the PT 109": *Providence Journal,* November 22, 1993.

"Everything": *Los Angeles Times,* September 20, 1962.

"I firmly believe": Edward J. Renehan Jr., *The Kennedys at War: 1937–1945* (Doubleday, 2002), p. 2.

Prologue: Samurai in the Mist

Kohei Hanami's memories of the collision with the PT 109 are from: translated Japanese newspaper clippings from August 1943 [including an article apparently written by an unnamed Japanese news correspondent or military press officer and filed in Rabaul that was based on interviews with *Amagiri* officers and crew, and another article that includes an extended statement by Hanami, who is not named, presumably for censorship purposes] in Charles O. Daly Papers, PT 109 file, JFKL; Kohei Hanami, "The Man I Might Have Killed Was Kennedy," *Yomiuri* (English-language edition), November 2, 1960; Associated Press article by Kohei Hanami that appeared in various U.S. newspapers on January 17, 1961; Bill Hosokawa, "John F. Kennedy's Friendly Enemy," *American Legion Magazine,* June 1965.

"We are more a freighter convoy": Francis Pike, *Hirohito's War: The Pacific War, 1941-1945* (Bloomsbury, 2015) p. 555.

Yamashiro's account: Yamashiro wrote JFK on several occasions from 1958 to 1962, attempting to explain in detail how he ordered the *Amagiri* to steer away from the PT 109. On August 2, 1962, Yamashiro wrote to author Robert Donovan, demanding apologies and a correction for Donovan's publishing Hanami's version of an intentional ramming. At one point, he declared flatly, "Hanami is telling a lie." Yamashiro also told his story in an article titled "Collision with American PT-109 Boat" in the September 1960 issue of *Sukio* magazine. This material is in President's Office Files, Box 132, Personal Secretary Files: PT 109 — Correspondence—Japanese, JFKL. Donovan maintained that Hanami's version was more credible. Based on the evidence, including Donovan's interviews of Japanese witnesses, the current author agrees, while entertaining the possibility that Yamashiro might have uttered a contradictory order, perhaps mumbled, garbled, or not clearly heard.

These *Nippon News* newsreel reports (in Japanese), archived on the Japanese network NHK website (http://www.nhk.or.jp/shogenarchives/) offer fascinating details on the Japanese side of battles in the Solomon Islands: Rabaul landing, *Nippon News* No. 87, February 3, 1942; Battlefield New Guinea-Solomons, *Nippon News* No. 194, February 16, 1944; Japanese floatplanes, *Nippon News* No. 182, November 29, 1943; Attack on Rabaul Base, *Nippon News* No. 192, February 2, 1944.

"Tokyo Express" convoy shipments: "Detailed engagement report and wartime log book from June 1, 1943 to January 31, 1944, Kure 6th Special Naval Landing Force" (in Japanese), National Institute for Defense Studies, Ministry of Defense Navy Records, Japan Center for Asian Historical Records, National Archives of Japan, contains detailed engagement reports for actions on Kolombangara, North Munda, and other islands, including supplies delivered to the garrison at Kolombangara by the "Tokyo Express."

A key source for detail on the Solomon Islands campaigns is the U.S. Navy Office of Naval Intelligence Combat Narratives series published in 1944 and available on the Japanese National Diet Digital Collection Library *http://dl.ndl.go.jp*, which contains a wide assortment of other Japanese and Allied documents on the Pacific War. Another valuable source is the Japan Center for Asian Historical Records, National Archives of Japan: *http://www.jacar.go.jp*.

An essential Japanese source on the Pacific War from 1937 to 1945 is the 102-volume Senshi Sosho (in Japanese), assembled by the War History Office of Japan's Ministry of Defense in Tokyo in the 1960s and 1970s and based on military records and personal papers and diaries by participants.

Japanese military veteran memories of Solomon Islands campaign: "Air Operations by Japanese Naval Air Force Based at Rabaul, Including

Solomons and New Guinea, Serial No. 446, Records of the U.S. Strategic Bombing Survey, Entry 43, USSBS Transcripts of Interrogations and Interrogation Reports of Japanese Industrial, Military, and Political Leaders, 1945-46," Japanese National Diet Library.

"Why didn't your radio report say": Nigel Hamilton, *JFK: Reckless Youth*, p. 572.

Chapter 1: Give Me a Fast Ship

"I wish to have no connection": Willis Abbot, *The Naval History of the United States* (Peter Fenelon Collier, 1890), p. 82.

"I have been interested in the sea": JFKL News Release, "New Exhibit to Celebrate JFK's Love of the Sea," March 27, 2000.

"I really don't know why": Remarks in Newport at the Australian Ambassador's Dinner for the America's Cup Crews, September 14, 1962, *Public Papers of the Presidents: John F. Kennedy, 1962*.

"an easy, prosperous life": James MacGregor Burns, *John F. Kennedy: A Political Profile* (Harcourt Brace, 1960), p. 23.

"the sound of Joe banging Jack's head": Evan Thomas, *Robert Kennedy: His Life* (Simon & Schuster, 2013), p. 39.

"It is said that famous men": Winston Churchill, *Marlborough* (University of Chicago Press, 2002), p. 33.

"My mother never hugged me": Michael O'Brien, *John F. Kennedy: A Biography* (Macmillan, 2006), p. 55.

"They really didn't have a real home": Robert Dallek, *An Unfinished Life: John F. Kennedy, 1917–1963* (Little, Brown, 2003), p. 32.

"Which room do I have this time?": ibid.

Kennedy boyhood reading: Doris Kearns Goodwin, *The Fitzgeralds and the Kennedys: An American Saga* (Macmillan, 1991), p. 354.

"so surrounded by books": Cari Beauchamp, "Two Sons, One Destiny," *Vanity Fair*, December 2004.

"History made him what he was": Theodore White, "For President Kennedy: An Epilogue," *Life*, December 6, 1963.

"He'd read in the strangest way": In Her Voice: Jacqueline Kennedy, The White House Years, A Shared Love of Words, JFKL online exhibit, http://www.jfklibrary.org/Exhibits/Special-Exhibits/In-Her-Voice-Jacqueline-Kennedy-The-White-House-Years.aspx?p=4.

"He had read almost every book on the American presidents": Nigel Hamilton, *JFK: Reckless Youth*, p. 544.

"The War which found the measure of so many": Arthur M. Schlesinger,

A Thousand Days: John F. Kennedy in the White House (Houghton Mifflin, 2002), p. 87.

"Whether Jack realized it or not": John Hellmann, *The Kennedy Obsession: The American Myth of JFK* (Columbia University Press, 2013), p. 33.

JFK marked copy of *Pilgrim's Way:* Hamilton, *JFK: Reckless Youth*, p. 549.

"didn't have to lift a finger to attract women": Robert Dallek, *An Unfinished Life: John F. Kennedy, 1917–1963* (Little, Brown, 2003), p. 48.

"Dad told all the boys": Lance Morrow, *The Best Year of Their Lives: Kennedy, Johnson, and Nixon in 1948* (Basic Books, 2006), p. 184.

"Still can't get use to the co-eds": Dallek, *An Unfinished Life,* p. 48.

"I've known many of the great Hollywood stars": Lawrence Quirk, *The Kennedys in Hollywood* (Cooper Square Press, 2004), p. 146.

"I can't help it": Nigel Hamilton, *JFK: Reckless Youth*, p. 114.

"It was a great opportunity": JFK biographical film on exhibition in JFKL theater, November 2014.

"I saw the rock where our Lord ascended": Nigel Hamilton, *JFK: Reckless Youth,* p. 114.

"She is still pretty young": John F. Kennedy to Claiborne Pell, undated letter, circa early 1939, Claiborne Pell Papers, Special Collections, University of Rhode Island Library.

"nearly as big as Versailles," "I have seen much, traveled far": Will Swift, *The Kennedys Amidst the Gathering Storm: A Thousand Days in London, 1938–1940* (HarperCollins, 2008), p. 174.

"when he inspected her he had an urge": Donovan, *PT 109*, p. 17.

"Small though they were, the PT boats": Robert Bulkley, *At Close Quarters: PT Boats in the United States Navy* (Naval Historical Division, 1962), p. iii.

Chapter 2: Summit Meeting on Fifth Avenue

"Bulkeley, you've taken me": William Breuer, *Sea Wolf: The Daring Exploits of Navy Legend John D. Bulkeley* (Presidio, 1989), p. 64.

"ruthless businessman and investor": Jacob Heilbrunn, "The Patriarch: Joseph Kennedy Sr.'s Outsized Life," *The Daily Beast*, November 21, 2012.

"From the beginning, Joe knew": Profile of Joseph P. Kennedy by Richard Whelan, *Fortune*, January 1963.

"his quick smile radiated confidence," "down to his underwear": Cari Beauchamp, "The Mogul in Mr. Kennedy," *Vanity Fair*, April 2002.

"operated just like Joe Stalin": Cari Beauchamp, *Joseph P. Kennedy Presents: His Hollywood Years* (Vintage, 2010), p. 307.

"He's a charmer": Cari Beauchamp, *Without Lying Down: Frances Marion and the Powerful Women of Early Hollywood* (University of California Press, 1998), p. 156.

"Kennedy was the first and only outsider": Beauchamp, *Joseph P. Kennedy Presents*, p. 403.

"A smart, rough competitor," "a passion for facts": Profile of Joseph P. Kennedy by Richard Whelan, *Fortune*, January 1963.

"Joe led people into camp": John Fred Weston, *Financial Management in the 1960's: New Challenges and Responsibilities, Readings from Fortune* (Holt, Rinehart & Winston, 1966), p. 26.

"those who had worked with him in the past marveled": David Nasaw, *The Patriarch: The Remarkable Life and Turbulent Times of Joseph P. Kennedy* (Penguin, 2012), p. 120-121.

"It takes a thief to catch a thief!": Beauchamp, *Joseph P. Kennedy Presents*, p. 328.

"Joe Kennedy had been fired": Breuer, *Sea Wolf*, p. 108.

"Things don't happen": Amanda Smith, ed., *Hostage to Fortune: The Letters of Joseph P. Kennedy* (Viking, 2001), p. 670.

"Joe wanted to know": Breuer, *Sea Wolf*, p. 108.

"The PT boat is a great weapon": Hamilton, *JFK: Reckless Youth*, p. 501.

PT boat historian Frank Andruss Jr. offered this additional background on Kennedy's PT boat chronology and his path to the South Pacific: "Kennedy was selected for PT Training in 1942, while attending indoctrination class at Northwestern University in the summer of 1942. He reported for duty at the Motor Torpedo Boat Squadrons Training Center on October 1, 1942. He was an Ensign at the time and was a student in the seventh class, assigned to hut 41. Kennedy was promoted to Lieutenant (junior grade) on October 10th. After training Kennedy was assigned to the training squadron, Squadron 4. He reported for duty aboard PT-101, a Huckins PT, on December 3 1942, and relieved Lt. (jg) Stuart Hamilton, USNR, as commanding officer on December 7. On January 8, 1943, he was ordered to take three Huckins PT Boats, numbered 98, 99, and 101 to Jacksonville, Florida to become part of Squadron 14. During the journey, Kennedy fell ill and reported to the base hospital in Morehead City, North Carolina. The boats continued to Florida and Kennedy would make his way there on his own, reporting back to PT-101 on January 25. He remained with the boat until he was relived of command by Ensign J. T. Thompson on February 23. From there he would receive orders to report to Squadron 2, already in the Pacific." Email to the author.

Chapter 3: Into the Labyrinth

Background on April 7, 1943, attack, "I happened to be looking back": "NOAA CORPS History of the Wartime Experiences of the USS PATH-FINDER," National Oceanic and Atmospheric Administration website, http://www.history.noaa.gov/stories_tales/pathfinder12.html.

"A gallant sight at that hour": Samuel Eliot Morison, *History of United States Naval Operations in World War II: Breaking the Bismarks Barrier* (University of Illinois Press, 2001), p. 182.

"Now we are approaching": Edwin Hoyt, *Yamamoto: The Man Who Planned the Attack on Pearl Harbor* (Lyons Press, 2001), p. 242.

"I was only sixteen years old": *The Kennedy Reader* (Bobbs-Merrill, 1967), p. 27.

"We went to pick him up": David Pitts, *Jack and Lem: John F. Kennedy and Lem Billings, The Untold Story of an Extraordinary Friendship* (Da Capo, 2008), p. 97.

"Welcome to the South Pacific": Donovan, *PT 109*, p. 4.

Chapter 4: The Front Line

Background on history of PT 109: "History of USS PT-109," January 5, 1961, Navy Department, Office of the Chief of Naval Operations, Division of Naval History; in President's Office Files, Box 132, Personal Secretary Files, PT 109: History JFKL. Also, http://www.ptboatforum.com is an excellent forum for historical discussions on PT boats, including the 109. An invaluable collection of wartime reports on PT boat actions is available at: http://www.ptboatforum.com/PT_Boat_Documents.html.

"Dead in the water": Bulkley, *At Close Quarters*, p. 29.

"We eat entirely out of cans": Chandler Whipple, *Lt. John F. Kennedy—Expendable!* (Universal, 1962), p. 88.

"PT sailors thought of themselves as having rugged duty," Bulkley, *At Close Quarters*, p. 153.

"Even before one ripe corpse": Charles W. Koburge, *Pacific Turning Point: The Solomons Campaign, 1942–1943* (Greenwood, 1995), p. 10.

"catatonic trance": Dick Keresey, "Farthest Forward," *American Heritage*, July 1998.

"KILL JAPS": William Manchester, *The Glory and the Dream: A Narrative History of the United States, 1932–1972* (Little, Brown, 1974), p. 329.

"Geez, I don't know if I want to go out with this guy": Nigel Hamilton, *JFK: Reckless Youth*, p. 587.

"Have my own boat now": Smith, *Hostage to Fortune*, p. 550.

"He was a very strong and nice guy": Interview with Hoyt Grant.

"the best type of college kid": Donovan, *PT 109*, p. 75.

"He was terrific": "A Conversation with PT Boat Veterans," forum at John F. Kennedy Presidential Library, June 27, 2005, C-SPAN broadcast.

"He was amiable": Richard Keresey, *PT 105* (Naval Institute Press, 1995), p. 136.

Battle on Kennedy: William C. Battle Oral History, JFKL; and "A Conversation with PT Boat Veterans," forum at JFKL.

"JFK was respected and liked by his crew": William Liebenow, "The Incident," article in *Knights of the Sea* by PT Boats Inc. (1982), courtesy of William Liebenow.

"The biggest shit in the Pacific": Hamilton, *JFK: Reckless Youth*, p. 551.

"Things are still about the same," "I have an entirely new crew": Martin Sandler, *The Letters of John F. Kennedy* (Bloomsbury, 2013), p. 25.

"Have a lot of natives around": Annette Tapert, *Lines of Battle: Letters from American Servicemen, 1941–1945* (Pocket Books, 1989), p. 91.

"What actually happened," "No one out here has the slightest interest": Sandler, *The Letters of John F. Kennedy*, p. 26.

"As far as the length of the war": Blair and Blair, *The Search for JFK*, p. 186.

"Feeling O.K.," "I figure should be back within a year": Sandler, *The Letters of John F. Kennedy*, p. 28.

"As to conditions, they are not bad," "We go out on patrol every other night": Smith, *Hostage to Fortune*, p. 550.

"That bubble I had about lying," "I read in *Life* magazine": John F. Kennedy to Kathleen Kennedy, June 3, 1943, John F. Kennedy Personal Papers, Box 5, JFKL.

"There was an old Catholic missionary": Interview with Joseph Brannan.

"Crash Kennedy": Blair and Blair, *The Search for JFK*, p. 193.

"a long, shining arrow": Gene Kirkland, "The Unknown History of PT 109, July 1942–April 1943," http://pt-king.gdinc.com/PT109-3.html.

"We always ran with all three engines": Interview with William "Bud" Liebenow.

"Most of the torpedoes we had": Hamilton, *JFK: Reckless Youth*, p. 612.

"super-human ability": Ted Sorensen, *Kennedy* (HarperCollins, 2010), p. 18.

"The use of PT boats as barge destroyers": Bulkley, *At Close Quarters*, p. 131.

Attack on *McCawley*, actions of July 17–18, "I got confused": Bulkley, *At Close Quarters*, pp. 118–20.

"My shoes were soaked": Maurice Kowal interview by Frank J. Andruss, Sr., courtesy of Frank Andruss Sr.

"He had been somewhat shocked": Arthur Schlesinger, *Robert Kennedy and his Times* (Houghton Mifflin, 2012), p. 25.

Chapter 5: The Raid
"All twenty PT boats": Keresey, *PT 105*, p. 71.
"that I had seen one pilot's": Ibid., p. 74.
"We'd been playing poker": Hamilton, *JFK: Reckless Youth*, p. 555.
"He was a friendly, capable PT boat officer": Interview with William "Bud" Liebenow.
"Most of us had been out": Keresey, *PT 105*, p. 76.
"I was down on the dock": Hamilton, *JFK: Reckless Youth*, p. 556.
Kirksey's premonition and dialogue, PT 109 casting off: Donovan, *PT 109*, pp. 89–90.
"It was as dark": Hamilton, *JFK: Reckless Youth*, p. 557.
"things were going along": Ibid., p. 571.

Chapter 6: The Battle of Blackett Strait
Unless otherwise noted, details and dialogue of "the Battle of Blackett Straight," the sinking of the PT 109, the stranding of the crew and their rescue, in this book, are from: John Hersey's *New Yorker* article "Survival"; *PT 109* by Robert J. Donovan (pp. 88-165); *The Search for JFK* by Clay and Joan Blair (pp. 209-270); *JFK: Reckless Youth* by Nigel Hamilton (pp. 556-602); *Lonely Vigil* by Walter Lord (pp. 255-275); interviews with William Liebenow (PT 157), Welford West (PT 157), John Sullivan (PT 107), Chester Williams (PT 106); William Liebenow, "The Incident," in *Knights of the Sea* by PT Boats, Inc. (1982); "Sinking of PT 109 and subsequent rescue of survivors," an after-action overview report favorable to Kennedy and probably based in part on extensive interviews with Kennedy, Ross, and Thom, written in the days after the rescue by Navy intelligence officers Lieutenant Byron R. White and J. G. McClure; and Commander Thomas Warfield's (somewhat defensive) after-action report dated August 21, 1943, "PT Operations 1–2 August 1943 (revised)", both in JFKL, John F. Kennedy Personal Papers, Box 6, Folder: Souvenirs— Narrative on Sinking of PT 109 and rescue, August 22, 1943. The Blairs donated their extensive collection of oral histories for *The Search for JFK* to the University of Wyoming archives, where they are open to researchers. Unless otherwise noted, quotes in this book from George Wright, Thomas Warfield, Johnny Iles, Bryant Larson, Al Cluster, Philip Potter, Paul Fay, Richard Keresey, John Hersey, Leonard Nickoloric, Hank Brantingham, Dusty Rhodes, Glen Christiansen, Homer Facto and Barney Ross are from the Blair Oral Histories at the University of Wyoming.

"PT 109" is an undated narrative by David Powers, in the Powers Papers "PT 109" file, JFKL. Based on its contents, this seven-page document may have been based in part on conversations Powers had with Kennedy over the years about PT 109.

Three other essential accounts of the incident are: Associated Press, "Kennedy's Son Is Hero in Pacific as Destroyer Splits His PT Boat," in *New York Times,* August 20, 1943; Leif Erickson, "11 on Rammed PT Boat Saved from Jap Isle," *Chicago Tribune,* August 18, 1943; and Stephen Plotkin, "Sixty Years Later, the Story of PT-109 Still Captivates," *Prologue* magazine, National Archives, Summer 2003.

In 2014, author John J. Domagalski published a valuable history of the PT 109 and its commanders: *Into the Dark Water: The Story of the Officers of PT 109* (Casemate).

Kennedy's medical records are in JFKL, John F. Kennedy Personal Papers, Series 8, Navy Records, Officer Misc. Correspondence.

In November 2014, the author came across a six-page document at the JFKL, in Kennedy's Pre-presidential Papers, House Files, Box 96, Patrick McMahon File, "Folder: Boston Office Files—Speech Files '46-'52" (with an additional copy marked "Department of Special Collections, Stanford University Archives" in the Paul B. Fay Personal Papers, Box 1, Folder PT 109, JFKL) that contained previously unpublished passages of Kennedy's memories of the crash. The document appears to be a template of a speech draft that Kennedy adapted for different audiences in his 1946 campaign for Congress. Small passages from the document were quoted by Kenneth P. O'Donnell and David F. Powers with Joe McCarthy in *Johnny, We Hardly Knew Ye* (Pocket Books, 1973), and author Michael O'Brien in *John F. Kennedy: A Biography* (St. Martin's Press, 2005). The passages that are quoted in this book as "JFK narrative," which the author believes are previously unpublished, are significant: Kennedy settles a historical controversy by confirming that he did receive a specific radio report of Japanese destroyers in the area; he refers to "mist" on the water, an otherwise little-reported condition; and he fixes the time of the crash at exactly 2:27 A.M.

If Kennedy's back was injured as a direct result of the collision, he made no complaint of it, either at the time or in subsequent weeks. In years to come, much was made in the Kennedy literature of a supposed back injury Kennedy suffered at this moment, and a supposed previous college football injury, but neither supposed injury appears in Kennedy's highly detailed naval medical records. According to Kennedy's own private testimony to his doctors captured in the documents at the John F. Kennedy Presidential Library, two significantly acute events occurred in 1938, when he suffered intense back pain while on a motor trip on rough roads in Europe; and in August 1940, while making a

tennis serve, when he felt "something had slipped" in his back, which was followed by periodic episodes of severe, sometimes immobilizing pain that required hospitalization. In 1955, one of Kennedy's physicians, Dr. Janet Travell,
concluded that Kennedy was born with his left side slightly smaller than his
right, and this minor congenital deformity may have contributed to his back
troubles as an adult.

Speculation differs on what parts of the PT 109 sank at what times. Clay
and Joan Blair interviewed four survivors and concluded that the boat was not
immediately split in two by the crash, as most earlier accounts had reported,
but that the sections remained connected below the water for an unknown
time: "the rear section, containing the three heavy engines, was badly mangled
and sank below the water and the bow lifted to an angle of perhaps 30 to 40
degrees. All four survivors we consulted remember the steep angle of the bow,
which would indicate that Ross and Zinser are probably right [that the pieces
remained connected]." Whether or not the rear starboard section of the boat
was initially severed and separated from the forward port section, the testimony
of survivors suggests that at least some piece of the starboard aft section of the
boat was separated from the boat at the time of the crash.

Additional key material consulted on Kennedy's naval career, PT 109, the
crash and its aftermath, and the book and movie on the incident are in these
files at the JFKL (thanks to archivist Stephen Plotkin for helping identify and
assemble many of these resources): JFK Personal Papers, Box 4a, Folder: Kennedy, Joseph P., Letters to JFK, 1940-45; JFK Personal Papers, Box 5, Folders:
1943-Family and 1943-1944, Clippings; JFK Personal Papers, Box 6, Folders:
Souvenirs—Narrative on Sinking of PT 109 and rescue, August 22, 1943 (this
file includes a number of JFK letters from the period); JFK Personal Papers,
Boxes 11 (three folders of various Official Navy Records of JFK) and Box 11a: 14
folders of various Official Navy Records of JFK, listed as Record Group 313,
South Pacific Force, Miscellaneous Records 1942–43, Bureau of Medicine and
Surgery, Naval Hospital Charleston, S.C., Naval Hospital Chelsea, MA, Office
of Naval Intelligence; Officer Fitness Reports Jacket; Officer Miscellaneous
Correspondence and Orders Jacket; Officer Selection Board Jacket; Officer Service Record #1, Officer Service Record #2; Requests for Records; Medical File
of Dr. William Herbst, 1961–64; Pre-Presidential Papers, Box 481, General
Files, Folder: Japan: P.T. 109; Box 549, Folder: PT boat; Box 1049, Speeches and
the Press, Folder: P.T. 109; Box 1100, Folder: PT 109; President's Office Files,
Box 132, Personal Secretary Files: Folders pertaining to PT 109 incident, history, book by Donovan and movie, listed as PT 109—Correspondence—General;
PT 109—Correspondence—Japanese; PT 109—Correspondence—Robert
Donovan; PT 109—Correspondence—Solomon Islanders; PT 109—History;

PT 109—Movie; PT 109—Peter Tare Inc.; Dave Powers Personal Papers, Box 14, Folder JFK Issues: PT 109; Oral Histories: William Sutton, Robert Donovan, William Battle, William Liebenow, Paul Fay, Biuku Gasa; Vertical File: P.T. Boats/PT 109; JFK Scrapbook of wartime items, audiovisual archive; George Ross interview, audiovisual archive.

"more fucked-up than Cuba": Robert Donovan, Oral History, JFKL.

"the shrill voice of a man gripped by fear": Keresey, *PT 105,* pp. 83, 84.

"This stupidity meant": Ibid., p. 87.

"There was more confusion in that battle": *The Search for Kennedy's PT 109,* National Geographic television program, 2002.

"This was perhaps the most confused": Bulkley, *At Close Quarters,* p. 123.

"Ship at two o'clock!": Gerard Zinser obituary, *New York Times,* August 29, 2001.

"As soon as I decided": Leo Damore, *The Cape Cod Years of John Fitzgerald Kennedy* (Prentice-Hall, 1967), p. 67.

"He goofed off": Interview with PT 103 veteran Jack Duncan. Duncan reported that Brantingham, whom he worked for later in the war, told him this in a conversation years later.

"Since roaming enemy bombers": Keresey, *PT 105,* p. 45.

"We were patrolling at low speed," "I can best compare it": Inga Arvad, "Kennedy Lauds Men, Disdains Hero Stuff," *Boston Globe,* January 11, 1944.

"The destroyer then turned": Damore, *The Cape Cod Years of John Fitzgerald Kennedy,* p. 67.

Was the PT 109 cut in two at the time of the crash? In the end, accounts by survivors and researchers differ widely on this point. In the days after the collision, Coastwatcher Reg Evans visually tracked debris that is widely believed to be part of the PT 109. John Kennedy later referred to the boat being "cut in two" in the crash, as do many accounts, but the exact shapes and sizes of the PT 109 wreckage created by the collision, and precisely which pieces sank when, has never been clearly established.

For an interesting discussion of this topic, see: http://www.ptboatforum .com/cgi-bin/MB2/netboardr.cgi?st=0&nd=10&fid=102&cid=101&tid=2470& pg=33&sc=20

Of 531 PTs that entered U.S. Navy service, 69 were lost, including the PT 109, which was the only PT to be sunk by ramming from an enemy vessel.

Was the crash Kennedy's fault? Over the years, some have criticized Kennedy's performance in the PT 109 incident, including some veterans of the PT boat service. The criticism usually focused on Kennedy's decision to patrol with two of his three engines disengaged, and on claims that he did not have his crew alert.

To William Liebenow, Kennedy's decision to muffle two of his engines in combat was a reasonable one, though one that was forbidden in Liebenow's own squadron. "The night of August 1 was his [Kennedy's] first major operation with Squadron 9," Liebenow explained. "Our practice was, when in danger of attack or in enemy waters, keep all three engines engaged. There was, however, some logic in operating with one engine engaged—mainly, one engine exhaust created less wake and therefore the boat was harder to spot. By using one engine you might be able to sneak in closer to the enemy and fire your torpedoes without being seen. As far as we were concerned, the ability to maneuver and get away fast far outweighed the fact of not being spotted. Anyhow, that's what we were trained to do and that's the way we did it." Liebenow added, "In later questioning Kennedy implied that the PT 109 had only one engine engaged and that he would not recommend patrolling this way. This does not satisfy some people, they argue that even with one engine the 109 should have been able to avoid being rammed. I would say that those people have never been in close operations in a PT boat against the enemy. One engine operation was probably a mistake but the same thing could have happened with all three engines engaged. I believe Kennedy when he said he didn't know how it happened."

To defend themselves, some PT skippers improvised such procedures to minimize their telltale wakes, such as patrolling at very low speed, running with their engines muffled, or running with two of the three engines in neutral and only the center one engaged, which best minimized the wake but maximized the time it would take to reach high speed for evasive action. This last technique was thought dangerous by many skippers as it slowed a boat's response time, and in the case of Squadron Ten, which Kennedy was now temporarily working with, it was not allowed, but Kennedy may not have known this. The tactic was also forbidden in Squadron Nine, where Lieutenant William "Bud" Liebenow recalled, "We always ran with all three engines in gear. We never took them out of gear. [Commander Robert] Kelly [a legendary figure from Bulkeley's original squadron in the Philippines] and [Lieutenant Hank] Brantingham [who also served with Bulkeley] were experienced in combat. They knew all the tricks. If Kelly or Brantingham came on your boat and saw you didn't have three engines in gear, they would kill you."

It is true that Kennedy did not have all his men in an alert condition; four men, Thom, Kirksey, Johnston and Harris, were all lying down relaxing on the deck at the time the *Amagiri* approached the PT 109, and the latter three are believed to be dozing or fast asleep. It was not unheard of for PT skippers to allow men to take a nap when they were off their duty shift, but it wasn't the way things were done, for example, in Liebenow's Squadron Nine, which was previously run by the tough, exacting and highly respected commander Robert Kelley. "In our squadron," remembered Liebenow, "when we were on patrol, nobody slept."

At the time of the crash, the PT 109 crewmen were exhausted from days of constant night patrols and lack of sleep, and it's understandable why some were trying to catch up on sleep, but an interesting question is whether the boat could have escaped the collision if Kennedy had all his men up, and alert, serving as lookouts.

In Kennedy's 1946 narrative of the incident, he writes that the Japanese destroyer "broke out of the mist", which was a weather condition that few if any other accounts describe. Mist combined with near-total darkness would of course have reduced his visibility even more. The *Amagiri* would have been churning up some phosphorescence at its bow, but the most visible phosphorescence would have been in its wake, most visible to an observer perpendicular to or behind the *Amagiri,* not viewing it head-on as Kennedy was.

A related and somewhat mystifying question is, if Kennedy had already received a timely, clear warning of Japanese destroyers in the area (as he admitted in his 1946 narrative), why he didn't have his whole crew on alert and all three engines engaged, ready for fast maneuvering. Kennedy's probable fear of attack by Japanese floatplanes may explain why he was patrolling on only one engine.

In the September 15, 1943 edition of PT boat newsletter *Mosquito Bites,* Kennedy candidly blamed the collision on his decision to patrol on one engine: "Lt. (jg) Jack Kennedy believes that the reason that he was unable to get out of the way of the Jap destroyer which rammed him was because only one of his engines I was in gear. He strongly advises that, whenever enemy destroyers are known to be in a patrol area, all engines should be in gear."

There were sporadic rumors that General Douglas MacArthur wanted to court-martial Kennedy for his performance in the PT 109 incident, but MacArthur publicly denied this and no evidence to support the charge has been found.

In the end, the collision that sunk the PT 109 was probably a one-in-a-million, fluke event that Kennedy had no way to defend against in time, even if he had all three engines engaged and his crew fully alert, given the darkness, the lack of accurate radio communications, the speed of the *Amagiri,* and the clear intention of its captain to turn into and ram the American boat. A different PT boat skipper with more combat experience might have operated that night in a way that avoided the collision.

In the PT 157, around the time Kennedy's boat was hit, Liebenow saw a distant flash of light on the horizon, and figured a PT boat had scored a torpedo hit on a Japanese target. "We headed that way for maybe a half an hour and didn't see anything," he recalled, "so we went back to our patrol area and stayed there until daylight and went home. We were the last boat that came in to Rendova. It might not have been the 109, it might have been a [Japanese] shore battery firing. But we had no idea that the 109 had been hit. If anybody should have been looking for him [Kennedy] it would have been J. R. Lowrey's boat [the PT 162], which was with the 109 when it got sunk. But when all that happened, they got out of there and went back to the base and reported that everybody was lost."

Ross memories of crash: Renehan, *The Kennedys at War*, p. 263.

"I was hurled into the air": Gerard Zinser obituary, *New York Times*, August 29, 2001.

"Fifteen PT boats ventured out": Keresey, "Farthest Forward," *American Heritage*, July 1998.

Details of events on board the *Amagiri* from Haruyoshi Kimmatsu's point of view: Haruyoshi Kimmatsu and Joachim Heinrich Woos, "The Night We Rammed J.F.K.," *Argosy*, December 1970.

"This was perhaps the most confused": Bulkley, *At Close Quarters*, p. 123.

Chapter 7: Lost at Sea

"McMahon and I": Damore, *The Cape Cod Years of John Fitzgerald Kennedy*, p. 67.

"We seemed to be drifting": Ibid., p. 68.

"As dawn came up": Renehan, *The Kennedys at War*, p. 264.

"What do you want to do": Hersey, "Survival."

Kennedy swimming the backstroke: Hellmann, *The Kennedy Obsession*, p. 54.

Chapter 8: Land of the Dead

Benjamin Franklin Nash thoughts and biography: Interviews with Nash's children, Clint Nash and Julie Nash.

Background on Coastwatchers: Walter Lord, *Lonely Vigil: Coastwatchers of the Solomons* (Viking Press, 1977); Eric A. Feldt, *The Coast Watchers* (Lloyd O'Neil, 1975). Also, "Reports from Coastwatchers in the Solomon Islands Area, 1942–1944," National Archives of Australia, Melbourne, is an extraordinary document containing scores of highly detailed real-time intelligence reports from coastwatching stations across the Solomons theater of battle. Messages between Coastwatcher Reginald Evans and PT boat staff at Rendova were relayed through Coastwatching stations at Munda (code name "PWD") and/or Guadalcanal (code name "KEN"). For simplicity these messages are referred to as between Evans and Rendova.

"The coastwatchers' working conditions": "I never heard one of them say anything": Keresey, *PT 105*, p. 173.

"quiet, good-humored farming man," "so long in the legs," "The barges would come in on the dark side": Undated paper on Benjamin Nash, courtesy of the Nash family.

"the Coastwatchers saved Guadalcanal": Alan Powell, *War by Stealth: Australians and the Allied Intelligence Bureau 1942–1945* (Melbourne University Publishing, 1996), p. 48.

"I could get down on my knees": *Semaphore,* Royal Australian Navy publication, May 2014.

"If it wasn't for local help," "really went inside the local people": Anna Annie Kwai, "Islanders in the Second World War: A Solomon Islander Perspective," subthesis submitted in partial satisfaction of master of arts, history, Australian National University, November 2013.

"generous, egalitarian, wealthy": Geoffrey Mills White, *Remembering the Pacific War* (Center for Pacific Studies, 1991), p. 33.

Details and dialogue of Warfield boat captains meeting: Interview with William "Bud" Liebenow; also comments by Dick Keresey in "The Search for Kennedy's PT 109," National Geographic program, 2002.

PT boat historian and former naval officer Ted Walther pointed out that the PT 109 survivors were not "written off for dead" in the technical sense as they were not listed as MIA or KIA in the seven day period they were lost. In an email to the author, he noted that Commander Warfield "probably should have sent boats to search, but starting on August 3 the PTs at Rendova started interdicting and attacking Japanese barge traffic that was resupplying Japanese troops ashore on the northwestern end of New Georgia and Kolombangara (Blackett Strait, Diamond Narrows area, Northern Sound, and Kula Gulf, not to Ferguson Passage). They set up a new Op area which was east of Makuti Island, (7 miles away to south east) and off Gatere, Kolombangara (7 miles away to east) away from Kennedy's crew. Fact of the matter is, in one day, the war moved on and the PT 109 crew was passed by, because of the operational commitments." But while Warfield never authorized a full-scale, proper attempt at search-and-rescue, he did keep tracking Evans's reports of wreckage, encouraged him to check for survivors, and apparently authorized at least one aerial attempt to spot for wreckage or survivors.

Presented with PT 169 skipper Philip Potter's claim of having conducted a short search, William Liebenow told the author, "No, I don't think anybody searched for survivors." Warfield ordered no immediate search of the scene, despite Potter's claimed report to Warfield that the PT 109 was hit. The timing and details of any air search missions for the PT 109 initiated by Warfield are unclear and are not mentioned in Warfield's after-action report of the events.

On August 2, Warfield had indeed cancelled any hope of a waterborne search, but he declared years later to Clay and Joan Blair, "I'm sure we had an air search, some kind of reconnaissance looking for them. I couldn't tell the fliers what to do. I couldn't even get them to send night fighters up against the float planes, but I'm sure I told [Admiral] Wilkinson's staff to get some kind of reconnaissance up there after them." Warfield's communications officer Lieutenant James Woods agreed, remembering, "That very morning we had them send up some air search. They looked around up there but they didn't see anything. Then, in the ensuing days, we got dispatches from Halsey and, well, everybody but the president, telling us to find Kennedy. And we sent more aircraft the next day and the day after. We were in daily contact with the coast watcher, Evans."

"The tragedy was": Keresey, *PT 105,* p. 93.

"stupid, useless, and frightening," "All this adds up": Dick Keresey, "Farthest Forward," *American Heritage,* July 1998.

"That was a subject that wasn't discussed": "The Search for Kennedy's PT 109," National Geographic program, 2002.

"I never thought of them": Dick Keresey, *PT 105,* p. 92.

"universal experience of passage": John Hellmann, *The Kennedy Obsession,* p. 43.

"What I would give for a can of grapefruit juice!" Michael O'Brien, *John F. Kennedy: A Biography,* p. 149.

"never allowed us to sit around and mope," "Pappy lay in the water": Renehan, *The Kennedys at War,* p. 267.

Chapter 9: The Hand of Fate

Biuku Gasa, Eroni Kumana and John Kari detail in this and following chapter: Biuku Gasa Oral History, Oral History Collection, JFKL; The PT-109 Rescue: The Scouts Stories, MS 84-57, JFKL; Hugh Laracy and Geoffrey White, eds., "Taem Blong Faet: World War II in Melanesia," A Journal of Solomon Islands Studies, No. 4, 1988, pp. 85-97.

"Awed PT sailors in Kula Gulf": Samuel Eliot Morison, *History of United States Naval Operations in World War II: Breaking the Bismarks Barrier,* p. 219.

"I have a letter for you, sir," "You've got to hand it to the British," "To

Senior Officer, Naru Is.": The text of this message was first reported by Hersey in "Survival" as authored by Lieutenant Wincote of the New Zealand infantry, a disguised name required by wartime censors. Subsequent accounts corrected this to Reginald Evans, the Australian Coastwatcher.

"I recall the day very, very clearly": "PT 109 Story," Jack Paar Show, October 1962, Film TNN:4, JFKL.

Kumana and Gasa landing at Roviana Island, encounter with George Hill: George Hill letter to John F. Kennedy, October 21, 1957, David Powers Papers, PT 109, JFKL.

Chapter 10: The Rescue

Some accounts have described a "funeral service" or "simple funeral" being conducted at the Rendova base after the PT 109's disappearance, but this author had not found a clear record of one occurring at either Rendova or Tulagi. A Catholic Mass "being said" for someone, as Johnny Iles described occurred at Tulagi, is a traditional mass that includes a usually brief mention of the person's name as a dedication. When asked about it in 2015, William Liebenow did not remember any such a service being held at Rendova, and if one were held for his fellow officer and tentmate, surely he would have been invited.

"did service above and beyond": John F. Kennedy to Clare Boothe Luce, October 20, 1943, Clare Boothe Luce Papers, Manuscript Division, Library of Congress.

"Dear Folks; This is just a short note": Thomas Maier, *The Kennedys: America's Emerald Kings* (Basic Books, 2004), p. 147.

"I never heard one of them say anything": Keresey, *PT 105*, p. 92.

Chapter 11: Life and Death at the Warrior River

"if your boat was sunk": Hamilton, *JFK: Reckless Youth,* p. 607.

"I think all these things came together": Ibid, p. 608.

"Kennedy did a fine job": Hamilton, Ibid., p. 611.

PT 59 armament, Bofors cannon retrofitted with Japanese motorcycle handlebars: Interview with John Klee.

"It had so many guns": Hamilton, *JFK: Reckless Youth,* p. 611.

"I did all I could to prevent the attack": Ibid, p. 608.

"What are you doing here?," "Have a picked crew": Renehan, *The Kennedys at War,* pp. 277, 278.

Jack Bernard Kahn/John Klee on JFK: Interview with John Klee.

"If people asked me later, when did I first think Kennedy would ever be president," "He always had that sense of leadership": Hamilton, *JFK: Reckless Youth*, p. 630.

"fine, upstanding lad": Maier, *The Kennedys: America's Emerald Kings*, p. 166.

"On the bright side": Sandler, *The Letters of John F. Kennedy*, p. 29.

"It would certainly be nice," "We have been having a difficult time": Pitts, *Jack and Lem*, p. 99.

"The war goes slowly here": James W. Graham, *Victura: The Kennedys, a Sailboat, and the Sea* (ForeEdge, 2014), p. 74.

"The Japs have this advantage": Sheldon Stern, *The Week the World Stood Still: Inside the Secret Cuban Missile Crisis*, (Stanford University Press), pp. 25–28

"Not much news to report": Blair and Blair, *The Search for JFK*, p. 291.

"They will not send anyone back," "Feeling fine": Blair and Blair, Ibid, p. 294.

"When I read that we will fight the Japs": Schlesinger, *Robert Kennedy and his Times*, p. 50.

Details and dialogue of PT 59 rescue of Marines: Donovan, *PT 109*, pp. 174-184; Blair and Bair, The Search for JFK, pp. 296-297; Greg Bradsher, "Operation Blissful: How the Marines Lured the Japanese Away from a Key Target—and How 'The Brute' Got Some Help from JFK", *Prologue* magazine, National Archives, Fall 2010.

"What the hell are *you* doing here?," "Never mind that": Keresey, *PT 105*, p. 153.

"There were Japs on the shore and the Marines were in the water": Maurice Kowal interview by Frank J. Andruss Sr., courtesy of Frank Andruss Sr.

"What would you think of this?" "Jesus Christ, Mr. Kennedy, there's no way. We don't know what's up there!," "I hope he doesn't go through with this": Hamilton, *JFK: Reckless Youth*, p. 622.

Note: Mysteriously, two different versions of Kennedy's medal citation were published: one in Robert Donovan's 1961 book *PT-109*, which was written with Kennedy's cooperation; and another that appeared in Kennedy's Navy biography and is signed by the highest authority.

The Donovan version, which may have been the draft language that Kennedy's squadron commander Al Cluster composed for a proposed Silver Star, was undated, and signed by South Pacific Commander Admiral William Halsey. It read: "For heroism in the rescue of three men following the ramming and sinking of his motor torpedo boat while attempting a torpedo attack on a Japanese destroyer in the Solomons Islands area on the night of August 1-2, 1943. Lieutenant Kennedy, Captain of the boat directed the rescue of the crew and personally rescued three men, one of whom was seriously injured. During the following six days, he succeeded in getting his crew ashore, and after swimming many hours attempting to secure aid and food, finally effected the rescue of his men."

The second citation, signed by Secretary of the Navy James V. Forrestal and dated May 19, 1944, was the final version: "For extremely heroic conduct as Commanding Officer of Motor Torpedo Boat 109 following the collision and sinking of that vessel in the Pacific War Theater on August 1-2, 1943. Unmindful of personal danger, Lieutenant (then Lieutenant, Junior Grade) Kennedy unhesitatingly braved the difficulties and hazards of darkness to direct rescue operations, swimming many hours to secure aid and food after he had succeeded in getting his crew ashore. His outstanding courage, endurance and leadership contributed to the saving of several lives and were in keeping with the highest traditions of the United States Naval Service."

The second version clearly reflects a fuller investigation of the facts of the incident. The reference to Kennedy attempting a torpedo attack is deleted. Despite Kennedy's claims that he was in the process of doing this when the *Amagiri* hit, the awards board must have correctly concluded that he simply had no time for it. The reference to "personally" saving three men is correctly deleted, as Kennedy personally saved only Patrick McMahon, and is replaced with "contributed" to the "saving of several lives." Also, the reference that Kennedy "finally effected the rescue of his men" is deleted, perhaps because someone in the review process recognized the critical impact of Coastwatcher Reginald Evans and his scout network. But the citation clearly states that it is for "extremely heroic conduct" by Kennedy. In the eyes of the U.S. government, he was a legitimate hero.

The main mystery is why John F. Kennedy would have made the incorrect, more favorable version available to author Donovan to be presented to the world as the official citation. It was possibly either an oversight on Kennedy's part—or a deception. If it was the latter, it would not be out of character for Kennedy, who, for example, as a presidential candidate, allowed his medically-diagnosed Addison's Disease to referred to publicly, and inaccurately, as a "slight adrenal deficiency."

On June 12, 1944, six days after D-Day in Europe, in a small presentation at the Chelsea Naval Hospital in Chelsea, Massachusetts, Kennedy was formally awarded the Navy and Marine Corps Medal for his actions after the sinking of the PT 109, a medal that Joseph Kennedy Sr. had lobbied his friend the Secretary of War James Forrestal to arrange. The commanding officer of the hospital, a doctor named Captain Frederick L. Conklin pinned the medal on Kennedy in a small ceremony that took place against a stark brick wall. Apparently no one in his family was able to attend the ceremony, but a few photographs were taken.

Thomas Warfield retired as a Rear Admiral and died in 1988. In January 1944 he was awarded a Silver Star "for conspicuous gallantry and intrepidity in action as Commander of Motor Torpedo Boat Squadron TEN (MTB-10), operating against enemy Japanese forces in the Solomon Islands Area in 1943." In extreme contrast to the memories of naval personnel who remembered Warfield as a commander who led from the rear rather than the front, the citation language described Warfield in exalted, heroic terms: "During the New Georgia Campaign, Commander Warfield personally led his boats on many daring patrols and, with extreme skill and fearless devotion to duty, attacked enemy barges and aircraft. On one occasion, he made a land reconnaissance trip to Kolombangara in order to obtain information concerning hostile installations and barge routes and later, boldly passed outside our own lines on Vella Lavella and penetrated deep into Japanese territory, remaining for a week to search for suitable base sites. Without thought of the great hardships or the ever-present danger, he gained information of the utmost importance and timeliness, thereby contributing to the success of our forces in that vital area. His inspiring leadership and cool courage in the face of grave peril were in keeping with the highest traditions of the United States Naval Service."

Chapter 12: The Winged Chariot

"But at my back I always hear": Handwritten notation made by JFK on page 150 of 1951 travel journal, book 2, October–November, John F. Kennedy Personal Papers, Boston Office, 1940-1956, Personal File, JFKL.

"None of that hero stuff": Inga Arvad. "Kennedy Lauds Men, Disdains Hero Stuff," *Boston Globe*, January 11, 1944.

"What joy to see him": Beauchamp, "Two Sons, One Destiny," *Vanity Fair*, December 2004.

According to Kennedy's Navy biography, his 1944 postings were: "Motor Torpedo Boat Squadron Training, Center, Melville, Rhode Island 15 Feb. 1944–Mar. 1944"; "Submarine Chaser Training Center, Miami, Florida Mar. 1944–30 Oct. 1944"; "Naval Hospital, Chelsea, Massachussetts, May 1944–Dec. 1944". For some six months, Kennedy was shuttling between Florida and the Chelsea Naval Hospital. Research by Clay and Joan Blair for *The Search for JFK* found that Kennedy had unsuccessful spinal surgery that summer at New England Baptist Hospital, after which he was diagnosed with colitis, which explained his eating problems in the South Pacific and confirmed the colitis diagnosis that triggered his separation from the PT 59. Doctors recommended he be retired from the Navy on account of chronic colitis, not for a back injury as was often reported. He was placed on the retirement list on March 1, 1945.

Background on the Stork Club and JFK's experiences there: Ralph Blumenthal, *Stork Club: America's Most Famous Nightspot and the Lost World of Café Society* (Little, Brown, 2), pp 1, 2, 15, 212, 213, 259.

"From the late 1930's to the mid-1950's": Pete Hamill, "The In Crowd," *New York Times,* May 7, 2.

"If you were at the Stork": Luis Quintanilla, Elliot Paul, Jay Allen, *All the Brave* (Modern Age Books 1939), p. 10.

"What appealed to me about the Kennedy story": Hellmann, *The Kennedy Obsession,* p. 42.

"He drew me a map of the area": Hamilton, *JFK: Reckless Youth,* p. 644.

"I realize, of course, that his fate": Herbert Parmet, *Jack: The Struggles of John F. Kennedy* (Dial Press, 1980), p. 119.

"Hersey's 'Survival' produces John F. Kennedy": Hellmann, *The Kennedy Obsession,* p. 61.

Campbell on myth: Joseph Campbell, *The Hero with a Thousand Faces* (New World Library, 2008), p. 23.

"What I really want to know": Sandler, *The Letters of John F. Kennedy,* p. 37.

"he had completed probably more combat missions": "Joseph P. Kennedy, Jr.," http://www.jfklibrary.org/JFK/The-Kennedy-Family/Joseph-P-Kennedy-Jr.aspx.

"I'm now shadowboxing": Goodwin, *The Fitzgeralds and the Kennedys,* p. 698.

"I can feel Pappy's eyes," "I'll be back here with Dad": David Koskoff, *Joseph P. Kennedy: A Life and Times,* p. 405.

"It was like being drafted": Beauchamp, "Two Sons, One Destiny."

"My brother Joe was the logical one": John Davis, *The Kennedys: Dynasty and Disaster,* p. 135.

"I got Jack into politics. I was the one": Koskoff, *Joseph P. Kennedy,* p. 405.

On April 22, 1946 press release: David Powers Papers, JFKL.

"There's our man, son": Parmet, *Jack,* p. 160.

"No one was ever unaware": Hamilton, *Reckless Youth,* p. 755.

"He wasn't much of a braggart": Interview with Dan Fenn.

"I remember the New England Hardware Banquet": William J. Sutton Oral History, JFKL.

JFK traced his confidence to these speeches: James Cannon audiotape of dinner party conversation, January 5, 1960, audiovisual archives, JFKL.
"My story about the collision": Goodwin, *The Fitzgeralds and the Kennedys,* p. 714.
"Christ!" "We had millions of them!": Hamilton, *Reckless Youth,* p. 755.
"Blanketing the district with copies": O'Donnell and Powers, *Johnny, We Hardly Knew Ye,* p. 66.

Chapter 13: Mission to Tokyo

Details of the JFK-RFK trip to Japan in 1951 are from interview with Gunji Hosono's daughter Haruko Hosono (interviewed by her daughter Fumiko Miyamoto; among other details, the elder Ms. Hosono recalled her father's first impressions upon meeting JFK in 1951, which he shared with her the same night in 1951); Robert F. Kennedy, *Just Friends and Brave Enemies* (Harper & Row, 1962), pp. 1–4; Robert F. Kennedy's Pre-Administration papers, 1951, Mid-East & Asia, Patricia Kennedy Immunization Record, Robert F. Kennedy Passport, Travel Diary, 10/5/51–11/2/51, JFKL; Charles O. Daly Papers: Japan-related correspondence (including correspondence with John Gardiner) JFKL; Tokuji Hosono, "The Achievements of Activities and Scholarship of Gunji Hosono the Uncrowned Internationalist" (in Japanese), Takushoku University paper, January 31, 2001; John F. Kennedy Personal Papers, Boston Office Files, Personal, Box 11, Political Miscellany 1945–1956, Asian trip 1951; John F. Kennedy Personal Papers, Boston Office, 1940–1956, Personal File, 1951 travel journal, book 2, 1951, October–November.

One of the exceedingly few documents at the JFKL referring to JFK's sudden evacuation from Tokyo is a handwritten undated note in John F. Kennedy Personal Papers, Boston Office Files: Personal Box 11, Political Miscellany 1945–1956, Asian trip 1951; on Pan American Airways letterhead from "Ridgeway" that reads: "Am sorry to learn that illness has interrupted your trip. I extend to you my best wishes for a speedy recovery and a pleasant and profitable continuance of your journey." General Matthew Ridgway was the head of the occupation authority at the time and may have met with Kennedy before Kennedy fell ill. Some accounts have added Korea to Kennedy's Asia trip itinerary, and Kennedy mentioned Korean affairs in his post-trip broadcast, but the author has not come across documentation that places John, Robert, or Patricia Kennedy as having touched down in Korea during this trip. I have estimated the dates of the Kennedy's stay in Tokyo in November 1951 from passport and visa forms and hotel records in the JFKL files above.

"they didn't think he would live": *John Fitzgerald Kennedy—As We Remember Him* (Courage Books, 1965), p. vi.

"by the standards of modern civilization": John W. Dower, *Embracing Defeat: Japan in the Wake of World War II* (Norton, 2), p. 550.

Hosono-Hanami-JFK postwar contacts, "flabbergasted," "It had been years," "a ghostly visitor from the past," Hanami career, JFK meeting Fujio Onozeki: Bill Hosokawa, "John F. Kennedy's Friendly Enemy," *American Legion Magazine,* June 1965.

Chapter 14: The Greatest Actor of Our Time

In Senate office Kennedy kept PT 109 model and rescue coconut: "The U.S. Senator John F. Kennedy Story," 1958 campaign promotional film, JFKL.

Richard Donahue and Charles Peters on 1960 West Virginia primary: "50th Anniversary of 1960 West Virginia Democratic Primary," Kennedy Forum event, C-SPAN broadcast, May 12, 2010.

Broder on Kennedy's reaction: David S. Broder, "How the 1960 West Virginia Election Made History," *Washington Post,* May 16, 2010.

FDR, Jr's attack on Humphrey, "Of course, Jack knew," "I always regretted my role," "RFK was already a full-blown tyrant": David Pietrusza, *1960: LBJ vs. JFK vs. Nixon: The Epic Campaign That Forged Three Presidencies* (Sterling, 2008), pp. 122-124.

"pain in the ass:" interview with Richard Donahue.

Kirksey family interactions with JFK: Interviews with Jack Kirksey and Hoyt Grant.

Details of PT 109 movie production: Nicholas J. Cull, "Anatomy of a Shipwreck: Warner Bros., the White House, and the Celluloid Sinking of PT 109," in E. Smyth, ed., *Hollywood and the American Historical Film* (Palgrave Macmillan, 2012), pp. 138-164; Lawrence Suid, *Sailing on the Silver Screen: Hollywood and the U.S. Navy* (Naval Institute Press, 1996), pp. 151-158; Ted Johnson, "Making of John F. Kennedy Biopic 'PT 109' Was Hardly Smooth Sailing," *Variety,* August 13, 2013.

"just this side of the Bobbsey Twins:" Thomas Reeves, *A Question of Character: A Life of John F. Kennedy* (Free Press, 1991), p. 311.

Details of Robert F. Kennedy and Ethel Kennedy trip to Japan, 1962: Interviews with Ethel Kennedy, Susie Wilson, John Seigenthaler Sr., Brandon Grove. Also: Robert F. Kennedy, *Just Friends and Brave Enemies* (Harper & Row, 1962), pp. 57–68; Jennifer Lind, "When Camelot Went to Japan," *National Interest,* July 1, 2013; Megan Dick, "The Kennedy Heritage and U.S.-Japan Relations," in "The United States and Japan in Global Context:

2014," Edwin O. Reischauer Center for East Asian Studies, Paul H. Nitze School of Advanced International Studies, Johns Hopkins University; Brandon Grove, *Behind Embassy Walls: The Life and Times of an American Diplomat* (University of Missouri Press, 2005), pp. 90–92; Edwin O. Reischauer, *My Life Between Japan and America* (Harper & Row, 1986), pp. 254–55; *Pacific Stars and Stripes,* February 7, 1962; *The Man Who Shook Hands With 10, Japanese,* United States Information Agency film, 1962, JFKL; "Ethel Skakel Kennedy gets hit in the stomach by accident in Japan," newsreel clip posted on https://www.youtube.com/watch?v=36SLwEBMY7M as of March, 7, 2015; "Travels with Bobby and Ethel Kennedy," manuscript by Susie Wilson, courtesy of Susie Wilson; Robert F. Kennedy Attorney General Papers—Box 40: Dr. Gunji Hosono Correspondence, 1962–1964, Box 44: Japan, 1958–1964, Boxes 263–64, 267–68: Goodwill Trip, Japan, February 1–28, 1962: Correspondence and News Clippings.

"I cannot overemphasize": "Letter From the Ambassador to Japan (Reischauer) to the Under Secretary of State (Ball) Tokyo, February 12, 1962," Foreign Relations of the United States, 1961–1963, Volume XXII, Northeast Asia, Document 351.

RFK meets Kohei Hanami: Interview with John Seigenthaler Sr.

"Kennedy's most characteristic quality": Norman Mailer, "Superman Comes to the Supermarket," *Esquire,* November 1960.

Kennedy's first moments in the Oval Office, "What the hell do I do now?,"

"There were the marks of a navy vet:": Hugh Sidey, *Time,* December 1, 1980.

Oval Office JFK mementoes: Kenneth P. O'Donnell and David F. Powers with Joe McCarthy, *Johnny, We Hardly Knew Ye* (Pocket Books, 1973), pp. 250–51; Theodore C. Sorensen, *Kennedy* (Harper & Row, 1965), p. 375; JFKL Oval Office exhibit dated 1998.

"He was an incendiary man": Gerard S. Strober and Deborah H. Strober, *Let Us Begin Anew: An Oral History of the Kennedy Presidency* (HarperCollins, 1993), p. 156.

"Kennedy was a magnificent natural leader: Interview with Myer Feldman for *Inside the Oval Office.*

"When he came into the room": Interview with Pedro Sanjuan for *Inside the Oval Office.*

"He treated us more as colleagues": Sorensen, *Kennedy,* p. 374.

"I can't imagine a better boss": Interview with Myer Feldman for *Inside the Oval Office.*

"Everybody on the staff": Interview with Ralph Dungan for *Inside the Oval Office.*

Kennedy and Secret Service agent: James N. Giglio, *The Presidency of John F. Kennedy* (University Press of Kansas, 1991), p. 257; Ralph G. Martin, *Hero for Our Time: An Intimate Story of the Kennedy Years* (Macmillan, 1983) p. 245.

"They always give you their bullshit": Richard Reeves, *President Kennedy: Portrait of Power* (Simon & Schuster, 2011), p. 363.

Clint Hill on JFK: Interview with Clint Hill.

In 2015, Kennedy aide Melody Miller recalled in an email to the author, "I know from my long time on Sen. Edward Kennedy's staff and dealing with his interviews about his brothers, that the war impacted John Kennedy as it did the others of his generation. They may have been young, but they grew up faster and were more seasoned and mature for their age when they came home, especially when they'd been in combat. It made a huge difference during the Cuban Missile Crisis as President Kennedy knew the horrors of war first hand. Men had died in front of him, and he'd saved others from death. He lost his older brother. He knew the grief of family loss, as well as that of buddies lost. He also now had children of his own that he wanted to be safe and to inherit a peaceful word. I've been fortunate to have a ringside seat to a lot of people who made history during my forty years on the RFK and EMK Senate staffs, and I feel strongly about the legacy of President Kennedy. He was not perfect, but he was wise beyond his years. I had the memorable experience of personally meeting him in the Cabinet Room of the White House where he signed my copy of *Profiles in Courage*. He was even more than wise. He was incandescent."

From 1995 to 2015, the former Palm Beach estate of Joseph P. Kennedy was owned by John K. Castle, a New York-based private equity CEO who purchased the property from the Kennedy family for $5,000,000 in 1993 and meticulously restored the estate to its original condition when it served as JFK's Winter White House. "I think this home was incredibly important to President Kennedy," Castle explained to the author. "It was from here that he went off to war, and it was here that he recovered from the war. As president-elect, he chose his cabinet here, and as president he spent many happy days here with his family, including the last weekend before he died." Castle even sees a connection between his Palm Beach property and Kennedy's PT 109 saga. He noted, "As a young man Kennedy spent many days here learning to swim and pilot small boats in a tropical environment, experiences that prepared him for life in the wartime South Pacific." There's something else that would have struck a chord with Kennedy—the Palm Beach estate is surrounded by coconut trees, which regularly dropped coconuts on Castle's lawn. In 2015, Castle and his wife Marianne sold the 11 bedroom, 12 bathroom, 15,000-square-foot oceanfront property for a reported $31 million.

"It really made an impression on himself": *The Search for Kennedy's PT 109*, National Geographic program, 2002.

RFK briefed on multiple assassination attempts against Castro: "Minutes of Meeting of the Special Group (Augmented), October 4, 1962," declassified White House document, National Archives, National Security Archive. The memo includes the passage, "another attempt will be made against the major target which has been the object of three unsuccessful missions, and that approximately six new ones are in the planning stage," a clear reference to Castro.

"He's always said that it was a major mistake": Arthur M. Schlesinger, Jr., *Robert F. Kennedy and His Times* (Houghton Mifflin Harcourt, 2012), p. 713.

"like God, fucking anybody": Richard Reeves, *President Kennedy*, p. 291.

"half his time thinking about adultery": Michael Beschloss, *The Crisis Years, Kennedy and Khrushchev*, 1960–1963 (HarperCollins, 1991), p. 227.

Congress blocked domestic program, popularity plunged from 83 to 57 percent: Thomas A. Bailey, *New York Times Magazine*, November 6, 1966.

Epilogue: The Rising Sun

"He died in time to be remembered": John Galloway, ed., *The Kennedys & Vietnam* (Facts on File, 1971), p. 49.

"He always seemed to be striding": James Reston, *New York Times Magazine*, November 15, 1964.

John Hellman on Kennedy's imagery: John Hellmann, *The Kennedy Obsession: The American Myth of JFK* (Columbia University Press, 1997), passim.

"He was the greatest actor of our time": Hugh Sidey, *Time*, November 14, 1983.

"The Japanese response to the assassination": Reischauer, *My Life Between Japan and America*, p. 258.

Kohei Hanami thoughts and statements on JFK's death: Bill Hosokawa, "The Man Who Sank John F. Kennedy's Boat," *American Legion Magazine*, June 1965. Eight months after the PT 109 was sunk, the *Amagiri* was blown up and sunk by a magnetic mine off Borneo.

Max Kennedy on PT 109, Solomon Islands trip, JFK Jr., Dick Keresey, Eroni Kumana and Biuku Gasa: Interview with Max Kennedy. Additional detail from National Geographic 2002 program on Robert Ballard expedition, *The Search for Kennedy's PT 109*. Ballard wrote of the expedition in Robert Ballard and Michael Hamilton Morgan, *Collision with History: The Search for John F. Kennedy's PT 109* (National Geographic, 2002). The first island that the survivors reached, which they called Bird Island and went by the names of Plum Pudding Island and Kasolo, is now called Kennedy Island.

Kevu, Evans and crew on Jack Paar show: "PT 109 Story," *The Jack Paar Show*, October 1962, Film TNN:4, JFKL.

McMahon's August 16, 1963 letter to JFK: President's Office Files General Correspondance, 1963: McE-McK JFKL.

Klee on Kennedy: Interview with John Klee.

"The most notable event of my life," "As Jack Kennedy's political star rose": Liebenow, "The Incident," *Knights of the Sea*.

1960 campaign exchanges of JFK and Liebenow, Liebenow biographical details: Interview with William "Bud" Liebenow.

"I am a great admirer of Japan": JFK interview with NHK Japan network, early 1961, film FON: 14B, JFKL.

Postscript on PT Boats: the author asked PT boat historian and former Naval Special Warfare Combatant craft crewman Harold E. "Ted" Walther, Jr. for his opinion on what the highlights and impact of PT boats were in World War II. He wrote:

PT BOATS FINEST HOURS

1. Squadron 1 GM's DeJong and Huffman shooting down first Kate at Pearl Harbor, Dec 7, 1941.

2. Squadron 3 conducting first offensive operations in Philippines (Dec 8, 1941-April 1942) and Rescuing Gen MacArthur.

3. Squadron 1 burying dead at sea after Midway, including two Japanese pilots.

3a. Later rescue by Squadron 1 boats of Capt Eddie Rickenbacker MOH, and 7 crewmembers of B-17D Ser No. 40-3089, 11th BS/ 5BG/ 13AF on October 21, 1942.

4. Squadron 3(2) and Squadron 2, combating the Tokyo Express almost every night at Guadalcanal from 12 October 1942-1 February 1943, as the campaign progressed up the Solomons chain later in 1943-44, joined by Squadrons 5, 6, 9, and 10, 11, 19, 20. Barge hunting.

4a. 0200 14 Oct 1942 PT 38, 46, 48, 60, got underway from Tulagi and attacked Tokyo Express as it retired from shelling Henderson Field. PT 38 fired 4 torpedoes at a Destroyer and observed 1 hit, PT 60 fired 2 torpedoes and observed 2 hits on another Destroyer, PT 48 slowly closed a Destroyer and at 200 yards was caught in its searchlight beam, PT 48 turned (so close the crew could see the hull plates and rivets) and sped down the length of the Destroyer pouring .50 caliber rounds into the superstructure.

4b. 9 Dec 1942: LT. John M. "Jack" Searles in PT 59 while on patrol with PT 44 (LT. Frank Freeland), sinking Japanese submarine I-3, recovering Japanese documents, code books etc. and discovering how Japanese were resupplying forces ashore via Sub and Barge.

4c. 12 Dec 1942: LT. Lester Gamble in PT 45 sinking IJN *Teruzuki* ("Shining Moon") joining him on this patrol was LT Henry "Stilly" Taylor in PT 40 and LT jg. William E."Bill" Kriener lll in PT 37.

4d. Recovery of Squadron 10 boats from Stanvac Manila sinking.

4e. Incident and following rescue of PT 109 crew.

4f. Daylight Cove raids.

4g. PT 167 being attacked by 12 Japanese torpedo planes and being torpedoed (torpedo skipped through crews quarters forward, one plane hit the boats antenna and crashed in the sea and the boat returned to base.

5. Squadron 6 Div 17, RON 7.8.12. New Guinea campaign attacking Japanese shipping, barge hunting, and attacking shore installations, working with NCDU, 7th Amphibious Scouts, Alamo Scouts and Australian Commandos.

5a. PT 190 and PT 191 "Ordeal In Vitiaz Strait", Dec 27, 1943, being attacked by 28 Japanese aircraft.

6. Squadrons 15, 22, and 29 in action in Mediterranean. These 3 Squadrons did a lot, Torpedo and Gun attacks against German destroyers but also worked with British Commando, USN Scouts and Raiders, and USN Beach Jumper units.

7. Squadron 2(2), 30, 34, 35, operations on Mason Dixon line at Normandy, also attack on Cherbourg.

7a. Squadron 2(2) was a 3 boat Squadron (71, 72, and 199) specifically tasked with supporting O.S.S. operations in France, Holland, and Denmark.

8. Squadrons 7, 12, 21, 33, and 36 (45 Boats) heading N/NW from Mios Woendi, New Guinea to Leyte Gulf (1100+ miles) and being the vanguard for the Battle of *Surigao Strait,* working with Alamo Scouts and Philippine Guerillas *and rescuing paratroopers of 503 Airborne Combat Team and returning* Gen MacArthur to Corregidor.

8a. PT 489 Squadron 33 and PT 363 Squadron 18 in the successful rescue of a downed Navy pilot in Wasile Bay, Halmahera Island in Indonesia, despite intense fire from Japanese forces

As an additional mention: MTBSTC, MTBRTU, and Squadron 4, at Melville, also follow on training sites at Miami Shakedown and PT base Toboga, Republic de Panama, during the course of the war 15,000 volunteer officers and enlisted men passed through the schools and follow on training, and were sent on to 42 Squadrons. Medals and Heroics aside, To stand up a training program and train all these men from a small piece of land in Rhode Island, is truly the finest hour of PT Boats.

Their impact on the war?

They filled a void, a stop gap measure to buy time for larger ships to be built, and they took the fight to the enemy, and went in were larger ships couldn't because of uncharted reefs, shallow water etc. When they could not attack capital ships, they found new employment, hunting barges and interdiction. Barges were used by the Japanese to reinforce island garrisons with men, weapons, equipment, and supplies. These were also used by the Germans in the Mediterranean, called Flak Lighters, they were considerably larger and more heavily armed.

While everyone has visons of PT Boats roaring in and letting loose torpedoes at larger ships, it was soon discovered at Tulagi that stealth was the best tactic and weapon the PT's could use. They would approach the Tokyo Express routes in groups of two or three boats at low speeds as to not create and illuminate a phosphorescent wake (which also attracted Japanese Jake float planes, which would fly up the wake and drop a bomb on the boat) when the Express was sighted, the boats would either maneuver into an intercept position or lie in wait and ambush the ships. When torpedoes were launched, the boat(s) would turn and high speed it out of the area, sometimes using a smoke screen to help mask their exit wake. Later in the war when hunting barges, when a enemy was encountered, extreme violence of action and superior firepower was brought to bear on the enemy, resulting in a short action usually not lasting more than minutes. Then using speed to exit the area.

In the Battle of *Surigao Strait*, which was the last true torpedo boat action, 39 PT boats (from Squadrons 7, 12, 21, 33, and 36) were used as a scouting force, they were to report Japanese movements through the Strait to Adm. Oldendorf's 7th Fleet battle force. They're secondary mission was attack the Japanese force, of the 39 boats, 15 boats in the force launched 35 torpedoes. The results as per ACQ pg 389: 14 missed, 1 ran erratically (PT 146), 1 ran hot on deck (PT 493), 11 were unobserved, and 7 were claimed as hits, with PT 137 claiming hits on the light cruiser *Abukuma*, which was later sunk by USAAF bombers on 10/26/44 off Mindanao. PT's also claimed hits on destroyer *Asagumo*.

Thanks to the PT's warning and reports to the 7th Fleet Battle Force, only one destroyer, *Shigure*, from the first force survived, and the second force which the *Abukuma* was part of, turned tail and in doing so the heavy cruiser *Nachi*(second force flagship) collided with the burning and damaged heavy cruiser *Mogami* (from first force)and the destroyer *Shiranuhi* was sunk in retreat, by US planes.

APPENDIX A:
JFK'S LOST 1946 NARRATIVE OF THE SINKING OF PT 109: UNPUBLISHED EXCERPTS

On the third day of August in the second year of the war, the PT 109 with two other PT boats were patrolling near the island of Kolombangara in the northern Solomons.

The three PT boats were patrolling at a slow speed to prevent their wake in the brilliantly phosphorescent water giving away their position to the enemy planes that had been circling over their heads since early evening. About midnight a report was picked up that Japanese destroyers were in the area, proceeding at slow speed to relieve the Japanese garrison at Kolombangara.

At 2:27 in the morning a forward lookout on the torpedo boat reported an object off the starboard bow. The visibility at that time was poor—the sky was cloudy—and there was a heavy mist over the water.

The reported object was a Japanese destroyer but it was going at extremely high speed—estimated later to be over 40 knots. It broke out of the mist on top of the PT 109—and smashed into it—splitting it from bow to stern.

Only one man—Patrick McMahon, was in the engine room on the PT 109 at the time of the collision. His first knowledge of his impending ordeal came when the Destroyer broke through the engine room. McMahon was thrown against the starboard bulkhead. A tremendous burst of flame from the exploding gas tanks covered him. He pulled his knees up close to his chest and waited to die.

Patrick McMahon was a native of California. He was forty-one years old with a wife and son and before the war he taught at a small public school near Pasadena. At the time of Pearl Harbor his son joined the Navy and volunteered for submarine service. McMahon continued to teach for a few restless months and then one day told his wife that he was going to join the Navy, too. He enlisted in the Navy, was assigned to boot camp, and in one of those queer inexplicable acts, the United States Navy assigned him to a motor torpedo boat school at Melville, Rhode Island, for PT boat duty, although he was well over the age limit for these hard-riding boats.

After completing his course, he was assigned to an engineering staff for shore duty and some months later proceeded to the Solomon Islands to work around the base. His age prevented him, it was thought, from sea duty. However, as the casualties mounted during the long Solomon Island campaign, the need for trained engineers became greater.

And that is how he eventually found himself—with his legs curled under him on that early August morning waiting to die. Patrick McMahon, however, did not die. He was carried by the momentum of the Japanese Destroyer down under the Destroyer's propellers which turned and twisted him until he came to the surface, nearly five hundred yards from the wreckage of the motor torpedo boat. He came up to the surface in a sea of flame but with his hands he managed to clear a small area of water around him.

The survivors of the crash of the PT 109 were not picked up for eight days. During that time McMahon's burns, which covered his face, body, and arms, festered, grew hard, and cracked in the salt water, and his skin peeled off. McMahon, however, did not utter a word of complaint. His only answer to questions about how he felt was a weak, but courageous smile. When the survivors were finally picked up, McMahon was sent to a hospital at Guadalcanal. He remained at the hospital over four months and on his release, he was ordered back to the United States for release from the service. . . . McMahon, however, requested that he be permitted to remain at Tulagi and help in the repair of old engines.

He worked every day—explaining to the new engineers the intricacies of 1800 horse power Packard engines, and, frequently, disregarded the doctor's advice and worked on the engines himself.

I saw him often with the thin skin of his hands cut and bleeding at the end of a day's work. But he still had that smile. McMahon's courage was an inspiration to us all.

APPENDIX B:
1952 LETTERS BETWEEN JFK AND
KOHEI HAMAMI, FORMER CAPTAIN
OF THE *AMAGIRI*

166 Kofune, Ubado-mura
Yamagun, Fukushima-ken
Japan

September 15, 1952

Dear Mr. Kennedy,

I am informed from Dr. Gunji Hosono that a warship sunk by destroyer of the Japanese navy during the Solomon Islands Battle in August 1943 was under your command. This is a big surprise to me as I happened to be the Commander of the destroyer which sank your ship. When I read the Time magazine of August 18, 1952 which mentioned the battle in question, my memory being refreshed, I can vividly recall what happened at that time.

I regret very much that I missed the opportunity of meeting you during your last visit to Japan. As I was living in the Fukushima Prefecture, northern part of Japan, I could not make contact with you during your brief stay in Tokyo although Dr. Hosono succeeded in locating me after great difficulty. I am looking forward to seeing you on your next visit to Japan.

Now allow me to take this opportunity to tell about myself. I had been the destroyer commander since October 1940. In view of the international crisis at that time the Imperial Japanese Navy was prepared for the worst while attaching the last hope in the eventual success of the America-Japanese diplomatic talk. As even we young officers were quite aware of the risk of fighting the combined force of the U.S. and British navies with our inferior naval strength, the attack of Pearl Harbor which was entirely secret to us, therefore, seriously disturbed us.

While most of our naval officers except the war like minority were naturally pessimistic about the outcome of the war, the unexpected victory at the commencement of the war and the skillful propaganda of the General Tojo's cabinet led us to entertain a wishful thinking for the chance of victory. Following our defeat at the Midway Islands, however, the whole situation changed against Japan and became favorable to the United States which displayed tremendously the strength of war political and the fighting spirit.

I was engaged in the Battle of the Solomon Islands following the seizure of Laboul [Rabaul] (New Britain Islands). I was very much concerned with the situation which then was further aggravated by the successive defeat in the Battle of Guadalcanar [Guadalcanal].

From November 1942 to May 1943 I was assigned to the duty in the Track [Truk] Islands water. It was early June 1943 I was transferred to Laboul [Rabaul] again as the commander of the destroyer Amagiri. From that time the counter-attack of the American force became increasingly offensive. As Americans controlled the air, we were in no more position to attack in daytime and we had to operate in night, attempting in vain to prevent, by destroyer force, the transportation of the American men and munitions.

We met the disastrous defeat in Kure in early June when our flag ship was instantly sunk at the first encounter by your fleet, equipped with radar (which we were not aware) and this was followed by the subsequent defeat with the result that we were forced to retreat to Laboul [Rabaul] after the series of the unsuccessful battle.

In one of the night battle in early August 1943, I sighted a bold enemy boat of small size was heading directly toward my destroyer of a larger type. Having no time to exchange gunfires as ships came so close to each other, my destroyer had to directly hit the enemy boat, slicing in two. To my great surprise this boat happened to be the P.T. boat which was under your command. I take this opportunity to pay my profound respect to your daring and courageous action in this battle and also to congratulate you upon your miraculous escape under such circumstances.

I come to know from *Time* magazine that you are going to run for the next election of Senators.

I am firmly convinced that a person who practice tolerance to the former enemy like you, if elected to the high office in your country, would no doubt contribute not early to the promotion of genuine friendship between Japan and the United States but also to the establishment of the universal peace.

In my country the election is being held at present for the Diet members. I do wish the best of your success in the coming election in your country.

> With personal regards,
> Sincerely yours,
> (signed)
> Kohei Hanami
> Former Commander of the Destroyer "AMAGIRI"

Kohei Hanami
166 Kofune, Ubado-mura
Yamagun, Fukushima-ken
Japan

Dear Commander:

I hope you will excuse my delay in replying to your very kind and generous letter of September 15. I was involved at the time in a most intensive political campaign and I have recently been attempting to get settled in my new task.

Your letter was most helpful and we released it to the press with very beneficial results and I think it helped build good will between our two countries. I am taking the liberty of forwarding to you an autographed picture and an article which appeared in the *Reader's Digest,* August 1944, written by John Hersey describing the incidents that occurred after the *Amagiri* sunk us, which you might find of interest. It is my great hope to have an opportunity to visit Japan again and if so, I will look forward to having a chance to talk with you. I think it most important that the relations between Japan and the United States remain firm and strong for our own mutual security, I intend to work as Senator toward that end. I would be very glad to hear from you on any occasion when you might have thoughts that might be of interest.

With many thanks again for your courtesies and best wishes for your future success.

> Cordially,
> John F. Kennedy

APPENDIX C:
JFK'S 1957 NARRATIVE ON PT 109

One day in 1957, Kennedy's thoughts went back to the Solomon Islands, and to the native men who saved his life.

He jotted down his memories of the rescue, as best as he could remember, on sheaves of yellow lined paper now on file at the John F. Kennedy Presidential Library. In the notes, one of the exceedingly few written accounts of the defining event of his life, the PT 109 incident, in Kennedy's own voice, he simplifies events somewhat and condenses Eroni Kumana and Biuku Gasa into a single figure:

> I do not remember his name.
>
> I never knew it, but I will always remember him.
>
> In August 1943 the P.T. boat I commanded had been rammed and cut in two while attacking [sic] a Japanese destroyer. A week later, the survivors, and some were badly hurt, were living on the thin edge of existence on a narrow reef drinking rain water—eating a few odd coconuts—freezing at night—and wondering how it would all end.
>
> About the 7th day we saw a native off the shore in a small canoe. He came in somewhat fearfully to the beach. He spoke no English. We carved out a message about our approximate position on a green coconut and repeated the name of our base—Rendova—Rendova—and pointed east. We watched him disappear with all of our hopes overload-

ing his small canoe. A day later a large canoe arrived with several natives who built a shelter—made a fire—gave us food. I rode with them between some islands to where a New Zealander "coast watcher" [Kennedy did not learn Reg Evans's name until 1961, and still considered him a New Zealander, based on the Hersey article] who was living in the jungle had his camp. He told me that our friend had come by and told him of our troubles, and then had left the same evening to row many miles to our home base.

He arrived there at Kolombangara a day later and a P.T. boat came to pick us up. He came with them and rode back with us. He shook hands with each of us when we got off the boat and then disappeared—back in to the jungles and islands of the Solomons.

We came from powerful United States. He came from a jungle home in the islands. We had had all the advantages of modern civilization. In our eyes he was strange and backward. Yet in our hour of need he alone saved us. He never had seen us before, he has never seen us since. Indeed perhaps he has forgotten about us, but we remember him. Yes, we will always remember him.

INDEX

Note: Page numbers in *italics* indicate photos

About the Author

WILLIAM DOYLE served as director of original programming and executive producer during his seven years at HBO. He is the author, with former U.S. Navy SEAL Chris Kyle, of the *New York Times* bestseller *American Gun: A History of the U.S. in Ten Firearms*. His other books include *A Soldier's Dream: Captain Travis Patriquin and the Awakening of Iraq, An American Insurrection* (winner of the American Bar Association's Silver Gavel Award and the American Library Association's Alex Award; and a Robert F. Kennedy Book Award finalist), *Inside the Oval Office* (a *New York Times* Notable Book), and *A Mission from God* (with James Meredith). He was co-producer of the PBS special *Navy SEALs: Their Untold Story*, for which he co-wrote the companion book. He lives in New York City.